Wrox's ASP.NET 2.0 Visual Web Developer™ 2005 Express Edition Starter Kit

David Sussman and Alex Homer

WILEY

Wiley Publishing, Inc.

Wrox's ASP.NET 2.0 Visual Web Developer™ 2005 Express Edition Starter Kit

Published by
Wiley Publishing, Inc.
10475 Crosspoint Boulevard
Indianapolis, IN 46256
www.wiley.com

Copyright © 2006 by Wiley Publishing, Inc., Indianapolis, Indiana

ISBN-13: 978-0-7645-8807-5
ISBN-10: 0-7645-8807-9

Manufactured in the United States of America

10 9 8 7 6 5 4 3 2

1MA/SR/RS/QV/IN

Library of Congress Control Number is available from the publisher.

Credits

Senior Acquisitions Editor
Jim Minatel

Development Editor
Kevin Shafer

Technical Editors
Dan Maharry
Richard Purchas

Production Editor
Pamela Hanley

Copy Editor
Foxxe Editorial Services

Editorial Manager
Mary Beth Wakefield

Production Manager
Tim Tate

Vice President & Executive Group Publisher
Richard Swadley

Vice President and Publisher
Joseph B. Wikert

Project Coordinator
Michael Kruzil

Graphics and Production Specialists
Lauren Goddard
Denny Hager
Barbara Moore
Alicia B. South

Quality Control Technicians
Laura Albert
Leeann Harney
Jessica Kramer

Proofreading and Indexing
TECHBOOKS Production Services

About the Authors

David Sussman is a hacker in the traditional sense of the word. That's someone who likes playing with code and working out how things work, which is why he spends much of his life working with beta software. Luckily, this coincides with writing about new technologies, giving him an output for his poor English and grammar. He lives in a small village in the Oxfordshire countryside. Like many programmers everywhere, he has an expensive hi-fi, a big TV, and no life. You can contact Dave through his own company, ipona Limited: davids@ipona.co.uk.

Alex Homer is a computer geek and Web developer with a passion for ASP.NET. Although he has to spend some time doing real work (a bit of consultancy and training, and the occasional conference session), most of his days are absorbed in playing with the latest Microsoft Web technology and then writing about it. Living in the picturesque wilderness of the Derbyshire Dales in England, he is well away from the demands of the real world—with only an Internet connection to maintain some distant representation of normality. But, hey, what else could you want from life? You can contact Alex through his own software company, Stonebroom Limited: alex@stonebroom.com.

Contents

Contents

Contents

Acknowledgments

Producing a book like this is a huge development effort that involves a lot of people—many of whom work behind the scenes and never get the public recognition they deserve. In an attempt to recognize this, we would like to thank everyone at the publishers, John Wiley & Sons, who worked so hard to turn our manuscripts into a book.

However, none of this would have been possible without the help of the ASP.NET team at Microsoft. In particular, Scott Guthrie—who's unique vision for ASP.NET as a development environment, and willingness to share his visions and provide support for the community as a whole—made our task so much easier. Thanks guys, and keep on building great Web programming tools!

Introduction

This book shows you just how powerful, and yet easy to use, the new Web development environment from Microsoft really is. *Visual Web Developer 2005 Express Edition*, along with the relational database *SQL Server 2005 Express Edition*, allows you to build great Web sites using drag-and-drop techniques, wizards, and a huge range of developer-friendly tools and controls. The book demonstrates this by leading you through the creation of a fully featured and highly interactive e-commerce Web application, like those you are used to seeing on the Internet today.

Visual Web Developer is an environment based on the latest release of the Microsoft .NET Framework, version 2.0, which includes the Web programming and runtime features that make up ASP.NET 2.0. ASP.NET has evolved over the previous several years from the original Microsoft Active Server pages (ASP) scripting platform that pioneered many of the current techniques in Web programming.

However, ASP.NET leaves the scripting world behind. It offers a development environment that generates compiled code, includes a full range of tools that enable implementation of even the most complex feature quickly and easily, and provides plenty of resource-based help and code creation assistance. On top of all this, the execution efficiency of the .NET platform means that your Web sites and applications run more quickly and reliably than ever before.

This is not a reference book. You will not find listings of the objects, classes, properties, and methods of each feature in ASP.NET. Instead, this book is task-focused to provide you with the experience of working in Visual Web Developer, quickly getting to grips with the environment and ASP.NET, and learning how to achieve the kinds of requirements you will meet every day as you build your applications. For example, after a brief section on installing Visual Web Developer and an introduction to the development environment, Chapter 1 gets you building pages that display and allow you to edit the data in a database.

As you progress through the book, you will learn about the following:

- ❑ Designing the structure of your Web site
- ❑ Implementing the database
- ❑ Displaying and editing data
- ❑ Building a shopping cart
- ❑ Publishing your finished site

All of the tools and examples you need are on the CD-ROM provided with this book, and you can run the finished example on your own machine—or even on our Web site at `www.daveandal.net/books/8079`.

So, what are you waiting for? Power up your machine, install Visual Web Developer, and get started building your next great Web site!

Conventions

To help you get the most from the text and keep track of what's happening, we've used a number of conventions throughout the book.

Try It Out

The Try It Out is an exercise you should work through, following the text in the book.

1. They usually consist of a set of steps.
2. Each step has a number.
3. Follow the steps through with your copy of the database.

How It Works

After each Try It Out, the code you've typed will be explained in detail.

> **Boxes like this one hold important, not-to-be forgotten information that is directly relevant to the surrounding text.**

Tips, hints, tricks, and asides to the current discussion are offset and placed in italics like this.

As for styles in the text:

❑ We *highlight* important words when we introduce them.

❑ We show keyboard strokes like this: Ctrl-A.

❑ We show filenames, URLs, and code within the text like this: `persistence.properties`.

❑ We present code in two different ways:

```
In code examples we highlight new and important code with a gray background.
```

```
The gray highlighting is not used for code that's less important in the present
context, or has been shown before.
```

Source Code

As you work through the examples in this book, you may choose either to type in all the code manually or to use the source code files that accompany the book. All of the source code used in this book is available for download at `www.wrox.com`. Once at the site, simply locate the book's title (either by using the Search box or by using one of the title lists), and click the Download Code link on the book's detail page to obtain all the source code for the book.

Once you download the code, just decompress it with your favorite compression tool. Alternately, you can go to the main Wrox code download page at `www.wrox.com/dynamic/books/download.aspx` to see the code available for this book and all other Wrox books.

Errata

We make every effort to ensure that there are no errors in the text or in the code. However, no one is perfect, and mistakes do occur. If you find an error in one of our books, like a spelling mistake or faulty piece of code, we would be very grateful for your feedback. By sending in errata you may save another reader hours of frustration, and at the same time you will be helping us provide even higher-quality information.

To find the errata page for this book, go to www.wrox.com, and locate the title using the Search box or one of the title lists. Then, on the book's details page, click the Book Errata link. On this page, you can view all errata that has been submitted for this book and posted by Wrox editors. A complete book list including links to each book's errata is also available at www.wrox.com/misc-pages/booklist.shtml.

If you don't spot "your" error on the Book Errata page, go to www.wrox.com/contact/techsupport .shtml and complete the form there to send us the error you have found. We'll check the information and, if appropriate, post a message to the book's errata page and fix the problem in subsequent editions of the book.

p2p.wrox.com

For author and peer discussion, join the P2P forums at p2p.wrox.com. The forums are a Web-based system for you to post messages relating to Wrox books and related technologies and interact with other readers and technology users. The forums offer a subscription feature to e-mail you topics of interest of your choosing when new posts are made to the forums. Wrox authors, editors, other industry experts, and your fellow readers are present on these forums.

At http://p2p.wrox.com you will find a number of different forums that will help you not only as you read this book but also as you develop your own applications. To join the forums, just follow these steps:

1. Go to p2p.wrox.com and click the Register link.
2. Read the terms of use and click Agree.
3. Complete the required information to join as well as any optional information you wish to provide and click Submit.
4. You will receive an e-mail with information describing how to verify your account and complete the joining process.

   You can read messages in the forums without joining P2P but in order to post your own messages, you must join.

Once you join, you can post new messages and respond to messages other users post. You can read messages at any time on the Web. If you would like to have new messages from a particular forum e-mailed to you, click the Subscribe to this Forum icon by the forum name in the forum listing.

For more information about how to use the Wrox P2P, be sure to read the P2P FAQs for answers to questions about how the forum software works as well as many common questions specific to P2P and Wrox books. To read the FAQs, click the FAQ link on any P2P page.

Getting Started

Developing sites and applications for the Web finally comes of age with the release of Microsoft Visual Web Developer (VWD 2005 Express Edition) and version 2.0 of the .NET Framework. VWD is one of the "Express" products that Microsoft provides as an expansion of the Visual Studio product line. These are lightweight, easy-to-use, and easy-to-learn tools aimed at hobbyists, students, and novice developers.

VWD is a lightweight tool for building dynamic Web sites and Web services. While there have been other tools and technologies around for a long time, the great new features in VWD and .NET 2.0 make it even easier to build, test, deploy, manage, and extend your Web sites and Web applications. This chapter starts the process of demonstrating the capabilities of VWD, and showing you how easy it is to build attractive, high-performance Web sites with ASP.NET 2.0.

In this chapter, you will:

❑   See the completed example application

❑   Install and set up Visual Web Developer 2005 and SQL Server 2005 Express Editions

❑   Install the example application files for this book

❑   View the example database and execute a test query

❑   Generate a simple page that uses the example database

The last two items in this list perform two tasks. They confirm that the database is properly installed and accessible, thus avoiding any problems that may arise later on. They also let you see just how powerful (and yet easy to use) VWD and ASP.NET 2.0 actually are. You will be amazed at how quickly and easily you can create a page that includes many features that previously would have required a great deal of code and development work.

About the Example Application

In this book, you will be building a Web site that displays and sells products — a common scenario for many Web developers today. It is not a complicated site in comparison to many "out there" but is extensive enough to demonstrate most of the features of ASP.NET 2.0 and VWD, as well as showing you the prime techniques and approaches that are used as the foundations for almost all Web sites built using version 2.0 of .NET. The product you will see in the demonstration site is not complicated either. The site is a fictional online pizza parlor that sells and delivers pizzas and drinks to customers.

Figure 1-1 shows the page in the example application that lists the items available from "Pizza Pretty Quick," or as you will see it described throughout the book, "PPQ." The page header and the menu you see at the left are part of a master page. This makes is easy to achieve a consistent look and feel for the whole site, and saves a lot of work both when creating new pages and when updating the site design. Data for the list of available items comes from a database table stored in a local copy of SQL Server 2005 Express Edition running on the same machine as VWD.

Figure 1-1: The completed site, showing the list of items you can order

The installation routine for VWD allows you to install SQL Server Express as part of the main program installation. Alternatively, if required, you can access data stored in SQL Server 2000 or SQL Server 2005 on another machine. The set of examples you can download for this book contains the SQL Server database.

Installing Visual Web Developer

Visual Web Developer 2005 Express Edition is available along with SQL Server 2005 Express Edition on the CD-ROM included with this book. Both are also available for download (along with other "Express" products) from Microsoft at http://msdn.microsoft.com/express. You can install it on Windows 98, Windows 2000 Professional or Server, Windows XP with Service Pack 2, or Windows Server 2003. In this book, you will see it running on both Windows XP and Windows Server 2003. Installation is easy, as you will see in the following step-by-step guide, and there is no other configuration required after installation.

Step by Step — Using the Setup Wizard

Follow these steps to use the Setup Wizard:

1. If you are installing from the book's CD-ROM and the installer doesn't automatically begin when you insert the CD, double click on setup.exe to start the Setup Wizard. If you downloaded the software, double-click on the downloaded program file to start the Setup Wizard. In the Setup Wizard, step through the screens that concern providing feedback and accepting the license agreement. You may also have to install other updates, such as XP Service Pack 2 or the latest Windows Installer, during this process, and these may require a reboot during the installation.

2. Continue to click Next until you reach the Installation Options page that shows the list of products for installation (Figure 1-2). Make sure that SQL Server 2005 Express Edition is included, and it is also a good idea to install the MSDN Express Library as well. You will see references to help topics in these pages in various places within this book.

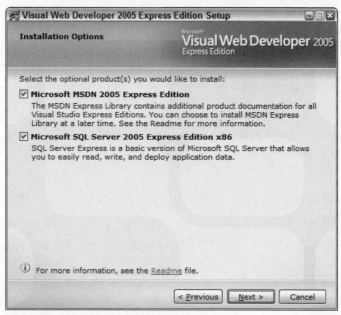

Figure 1-2: Installation Options page

If you would like to read more about the installation and any issues it may have, then you can click the Readme link on the installation options screen (Figure 1-2).

3.   Click Next. In the Destination Folder page (see Figure 1-3), confirm the path where VWD will be installed. It is recommended that you leave it set to the default. This page shows a summary of the products for installation, and the disk space requirements.

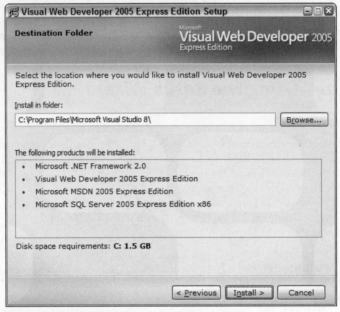

Figure 1-3: Destination Folder page

4.   Click Install to start the installation. After it completes, you will find entries in the Programs section of your Start menu for Visual Web Developer and SQL Server. The SQL Server section includes a tool that you can use to set the configuration options for SQL Server if you want to change the services or protocols it uses. This may be necessary if you want to be able to access SQL Server from another machine, but no changes are required when accessing it from the local machine (as you will see in this book).

5.   Start up VWD to confirm that it has been successfully installed. You will see the Start Page and some empty docked windows, as shown in Figure 1-4.

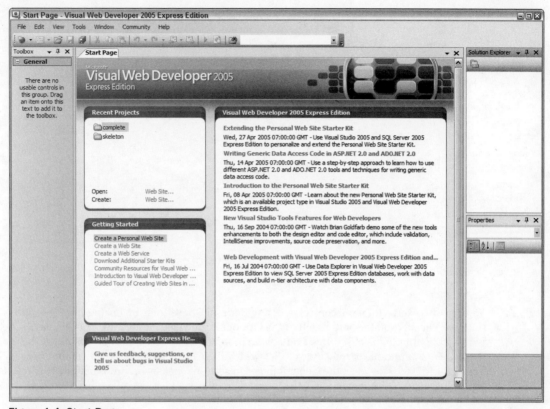

Figure 1-4: Start Page

6. VWD is extremely configurable, so you can change many features to suit your preferences. Click Options on the Tools menu to open the Options dialog (see Figure 1-5). Here you see a simplified view of the options you can set. These include general options, the fonts and colors used in the various windows within the IDE, the formatting options for the text and code you type, and the target browser or HyperText Markup Language (HTML) standard that you want to be used for validating your page content.

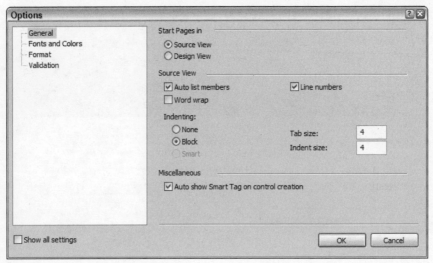

Figure 1-5: Options dialog box

7. You can also exert a lot more control over a wider range of settings by ticking the "Show all settings" checkbox at the bottom left of the Options dialog (see Figure 1-6). This displays a tree with literally hundreds of settings available in more than 75 pages of options. Some of these of these are not applicable to the kinds of files you will create in VWD, or when writing code using Visual Basic 2005. However, the General pages in sections such as Environment, Help, Projects and Solutions, Text Editor, and HTML Designer are worth a visit as you get used to using the tool (and you now know where to look for these settings!).

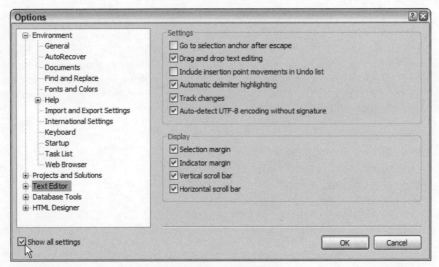

Figure 1-6: Selecting the "Show all settings" checkbox

After installing the Visual Web Developer tool, you should install the example files for the Pizza Pretty Quick application described in the book. To download the examples (or to see the application running online), go to www.daveandal.net/books/8079. You can also download the examples from the Wrox Books Web site at http://eu.wiley.com/WileyCDA/WileyTitle/productCd-0764588079.html.

The examples download file contains two versions of the PPQ application. One is a skeleton site containing the database, the images, and other resources used in the application, but without the ASP.NET pages that you will create by working through the chapters in this book. The other is a completed version of the application that you can run to see what it looks like, how it works, and modify or experiment with as you wish—without having to build the pages yourself first.

The next section describes the process for installing the samples, setting up the file permissions that are required, and testing the application to make sure that it is working properly on your machine.

Step by Step — Installing the PPQ Example Files

Follow these steps for installing the PPQ example files:

1. Download the example files from one of the locations detailed earlier. The download file is a ZIP file, and you must extract the files from it into a folder on your machine, making sure that you retain the folder structure within the examples ZIP file. Extract the examples into a new folder named C:/Websites/PPQ/, or into a folder of the same name on another drive. You will see the two subfolders named skeleton and complete within the PPQ folder (see Figure 1-7).

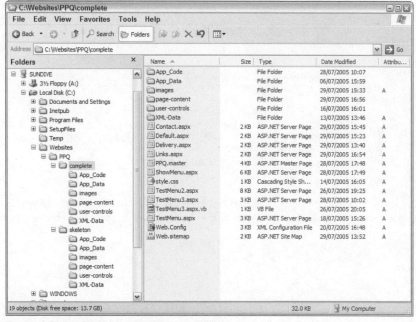

Figure 1-7: Subfolders inside the PPQ folder

2. If you are running Windows XP and you have Internet Information Services (IIS) installed, you must now grant the accounts named ASPNET and NETWORK SERVICE (under which ASP.NET executes, depending on whether you installed SP2) the required permissions to access the database provided with the example files. (This and the remaining steps are not required in Windows Server 2003, or if you do not have IIS installed.) In Windows Explorer, right-click on the subfolder named `App_Data` within the `skeleton` folder and select Properties. In the App_Data Properties dialog, select the Security tab and click the Add button to open the "Select Users or Groups" dialog, as shown in Figure 1-8. Click the Locations button, and select the name of your machine (not the domain it is part of) and click OK; then enter the account name **ASPNET** in the text box and click the Check Names button. The full account name, including the machine name, is underlined to indicate that is was located.

Figure 1-8: Select Users or Groups dialog

3. Click OK to return to the Select Users or Groups dialog, ensure the new entry ASPNET is selected in the upper list, and select the Write option in the lower list box (see Figure 1-9); then click OK.

Figure 1-9: Selecting the Write option

If you cannot see a Security tab in the App_Data Properties dialog, you have Simple File Sharing enabled. Select Folder Options from the Tools menu, and select the View tab. At the bottom of the list, uncheck the option named Use Simple File Sharing. This option does not appear in Windows Server 2003 because this operating system does not support simple file sharing.

However, the Use Simple File Sharing option does not appear in Windows XP Home Edition either, because this operating system uses only simple file sharing. In this case, you must restart your machine and hold down the F8 key as it starts, and then select Safe Mode. Log in as Administrator after Windows starts up in safe mode, and navigate to the C:\WebSites\PPQ folder in Windows Explorer. When you right-click on the App_Data folder and select Properties, you will see that the Security tab has now appeared.

4.   Now, repeat the process from step 2 to give Write permission to the NETWORK SERVICE account for the App_Data folder within the skeleton folder of the examples.

If you have not yet installed Service Pack 2 for Windows XP, you will not have an account named NETWORK SERVICE, and so you can skip step 3.

5.   Repeat the process again from step 2 to give Write permission to the ASPNET and NETWORK SERVICE accounts for the App_Data folder within the completed folder of the examples.

The application, including the database, is now installed and ready to use.

Viewing the PPQ Example Database

With Visual Web Developer up and running, you can now look at the example database used for the PPQ application. This demonstrates the database access features that VWD provides and will give you a feeling for the way that the sample data is organized and used within the application.

Step by Step — Viewing the PPQ Database

Follow these steps to view the PPQ database:

1. In VWD, select Open Web Site from the File menu and ensure that the File System option is selected in the left-hand side of the dialog (see Figure 1-10). Select the folder named `complete` within the examples, and click Open.

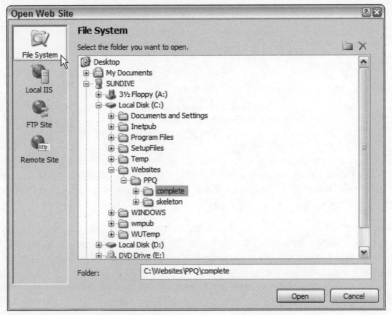

Figure 1-10: File System option

2. The Web site is loaded into VWD, and the files that make up the application can be seen in the Solution Explorer window. (If the Solution Explorer window is not visible, open it by selecting Solution Explorer from the View menu.) As shown in Figure 1-11, notice that the database in the App_Data folder is also visible.

Figure 1-11: Solution Explorer window

3. In fact, VWD has automatically attached the database to SQL Server Express. Select Database Explorer from the View menu to open the Database Explorer window (see Figure 1-12). If you are prompted to give yourself "dbo" permission at his point, select "yes." The Database Explorer window shows the data connections set up for VWD to use. You will see the database shown there as well, and you can expand the tree-view list to see the categories of objects for the database. (If, when you select the Database Diagrams entry, you are prompted to create the items necessary to support diagramming click Yes.) As you select each item in the list, you see details of this item appear in the Properties window, such as the connection string and provider details that VWD is using to connect to SQL Server Express.

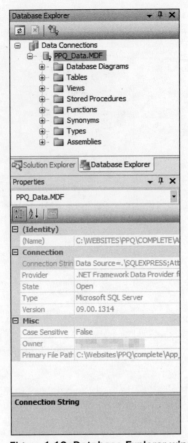

Figure 1-12: Database Explorer window

The Solution Explorer and Database Explorer windows dock at the right-hand side of the main VWD window by default, but you can drag any of the windows to a docked or floating position using their title bars. As you drag, small arrow indicators become visible allowing you drop the window into another one, or dock it at the side of the main VWD window. Use the drop-down menu (the "down-arrow" icon) in the title bar or the Auto-Hide feature (the pin-shaped icon) to set up the window positions you require. If you cannot reorganize windows in the way you want to, you can go back to the original window layout using the Reset Window Layout command on the main Window menu.

4. Now that the database is available in VWD, you can test that it is working properly, and see the kinds of data it contains. Right-click on the data connection name and select New Query from the pop-up menu that appears (see Figure 1-13).

Figure 1-13: Selecting New Query

5. This opens the Query Editor in the main central section of the VWD window. (You can close or auto-hide the Toolbar window to make more room as shown in the screenshot.) The Add Table dialog also appears automatically, showing a list of tables in the database that you can use in your new query, as shown Figure 1-14.

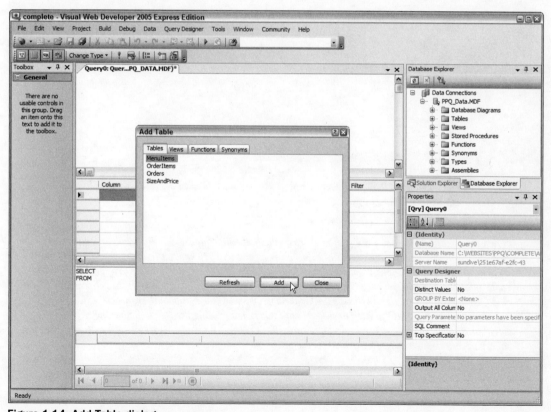

Figure 1-14: Add Table dialog

6. Select the table named MenuItems, and click Add to add this table to the Diagram pane at the top of the Query Editor window. Then click Close. In the list of columns that appears in the Diagram pane, select the columns named `MenuItemType`, `ItemName`, `PizzaToppings`, and `GraphicFileName`. You can either tick the checkboxes to add them to the grid, or drag and drop them there. Notice how VWD creates the equivalent SQL statement in the section below the grid, as shown in Figure 1-15.

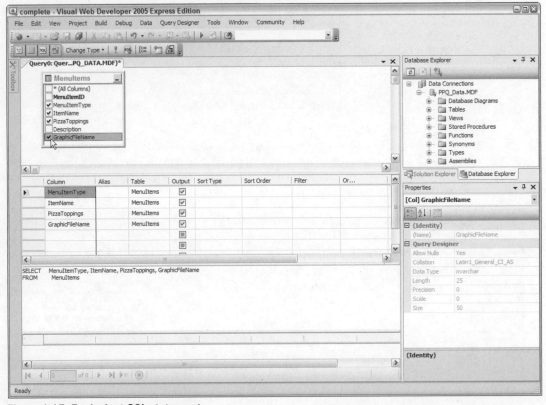

Figure 1-15: Equivalent SQL statement

The Query Editor provides a range of ways to create and edit a database query. You can add tables to the top section of the window, and then drag the columns you want to show into the Criteria grid in the center of the window — where you also specify any filtering or sorting you want to apply to the rows. Alternatively, you can, type (or copy and paste) a SQL statement directly into the lower section of the Query Editor. This section, below the Criteria grid, shows the equivalent Transact-SQL (T-SQL) commands used by VWD to fetch or update data when you execute the query. Below the SQL window, right at the bottom of the central window, is another grid that displays the results of executing the query or any error messages generated by the query.

7. The Criteria grid section specifies not only the columns for the query, but also any sorting or filtering you require. As a simple example, use the drop-down lists in the Sort Type column of the grid to set the sort order for the rows as Ascending by `ItemName`, then Descending by `ItemPrice`, as shown in Figure 1-16. Select the columns named `MenuItemType`, `ItemName`, `PizzaToppings`, and `GraphicFileName`. Again, you will see the equivalent SQL statement appear in the SQL pane below the grid.

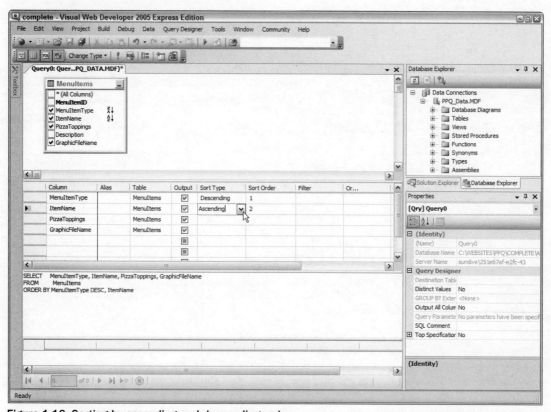

Figure 1-16: Sorting by ascending and descending order

8. Click the Execute button (the button in the toolbar with a red exclamation mark) and the results of executing this query appear in the bottom pane of the Query Editor window (see Figure 1-17).

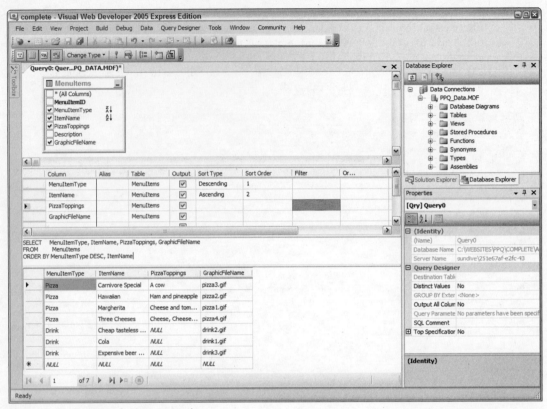

Figure 1-17: Results of query execution

You can also use VWD to work with data that is located in a remote SQL Server or other database, as well as with local data (as we do in this book). Right-click on the root entry named Data Connections at the top of the Database Explorer window, and select Add Connection. . . . This opens the Add Connection dialog where you specify details of the database server to which you want to connect. At the top of this dialog is the Data source (type), and the default is Microsoft SQL Sever (SqlClient). This is the most efficient way to access a SQL Server database, because it uses the built-in high-speed inter-face called Tabular Data Stream (TDS) that is native and exclusive to SQL Server.

However, you can click the Change button (see Figure 1-18) and select a different data source type if required. For example, you can connect to an Access database file, any database system that has an open database connectivity (ODBC) provider available, direct to a persisted SQL Server (MDF) file, or to an Oracle database. You can even specify, using the checkbox at the bottom of the window, if this should be the default data source (type) to use in the future.

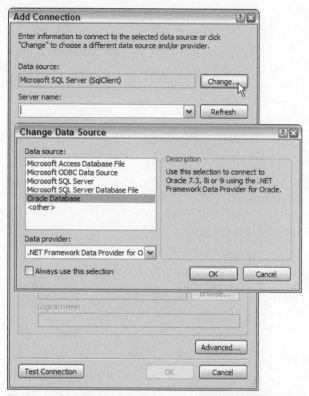

Figure 1-18: Adding a connection to a database server other than SQL Server

After specifying the data source type, you can use the drop-down Server name list to see all the databases of the type you selected that advertise their presence and are available. You can also type an instance name directly. For the default instance, you just need to enter the machine name, or you can access a named instance (such as a remote Microsoft Data Engine (MSDE) or SQL Server Express instance) by appending the instance name to the machine name separated by a backslash. Figure 1-19 shows a connection to the default instance of SQL Server running on a remote machine named DELBOY, and to the Northwind database on that machine.

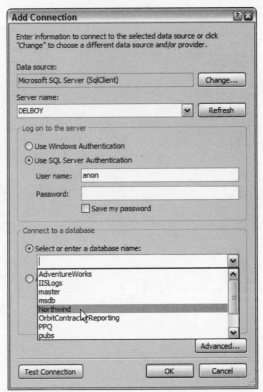

Figure 1-19: Connecting to the Northwind database on a remote machine named DELBOY

Figure 1-19, you must specify details of a suitable account within SQL Server. If, for any reason, you cannot install SQL Server Express or want to experiment with a different database, you can use the process just described to connect to a suitable database. You can confirm that the connection to the target database is working by clicking the Test Connection button before you close the Add Connection dialog.

Figure 1-19 is the option to connect to a SQL Server (MDF) database file. In this case, you specify the file location using the Browse button near the bottom of the Add Connection dialog. As before, you must specify the database server name to which the file will be attached and the authentication type you want to use.

Another feature is the ability to specify the fine details of the connection. Click the Advanced button near the bottom of the Add Connection dialog to open the Advanced Properties dialog. For example, you can turn on or off features such as Multiple Active Results Sets and Asynchronous Processing, which saves resources and increases efficiency, if you do not require these features. Figure 1-20 shows a connection to a database file, and some of the many options available in the Advanced Properties dialog.

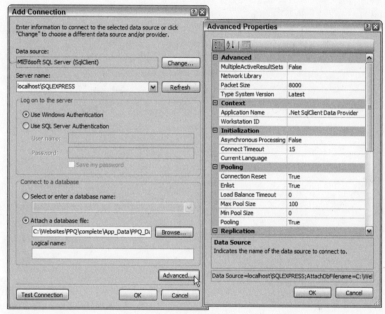

Figure 1-20: Connecting to a database MDF file and setting the Advanced Properties of the connection

Reading and Displaying Data with ASP.NET

Now that you have set up VWD and SQL Server Express, and have seen some of the features that allow you to access data, this chapter concludes by showing you just how quickly and easily you can build an ASP.NET page that uses the values stored in a database. The task is to create a list of the types of pizza and drinks available from Pizza Pretty Quick (PPQ), by extracting and displaying values from the MenuItems table in the database.

1. Start VWD so that the Start Page is displayed (see Figure 1-21), and click the link to Open a Web Site. Alternatively, you can select Open Web Site from the File menu.

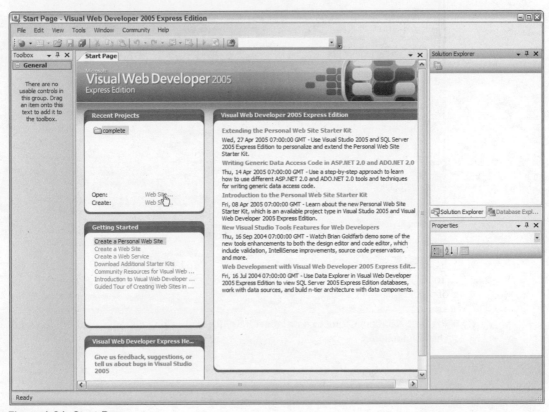

Figure 1-21: Start Page

2. In the Open Web Site dialog, ensure that File System is selected in the top left of the dialog, and navigate to the `skeleton` folder within the `C:\Websites\PPQ` folder where you installed the example files (see Figure 1-22).

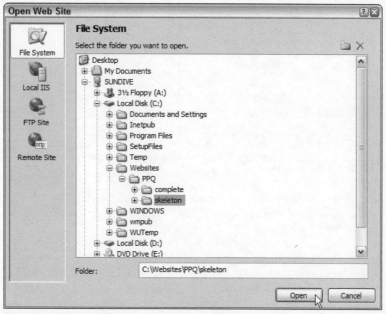

Figure 1-22: Navigating to the `skeleton` **folder**

3. Click OK, and you then see the files that make up the site in the Solution Explorer window. Switch to the Database Explorer window, and you see the database that is in the `App_Data` folder of the site. VWD automatically attaches any MDF file it finds in the folder named `App_Data` when it opens a site, and this is what has happened here. You can expand the tree to see the contents of the database, as shown in Figure 1-23.

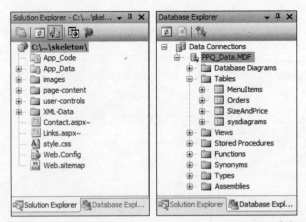

Figure 1-23: Expanding the tree to see the contents of the database

If you cannot see the Solution Explorer or Database Explorer windows, use the options on the View menu to make them visible. Alternatively, select Reset Window Layout from the Window menu. You can also close the Start Page now.

4. Switch back to Solution Explorer and right-click on the top-level entry (C:\...\skeleton\) in the Solution Explorer window and select Add New Item, or select Add New Item from the Website menu, to open the Add New Item dialog (see Figure 1-24). Select Web Form, change the Name to **TestMenu.aspx**, and leave the Language set to Visual Basic. Also leave the other two checkboxes unticked.

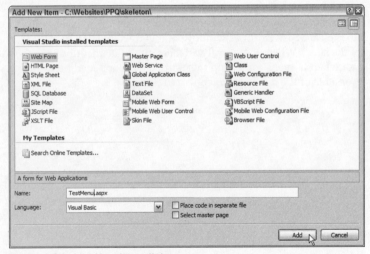

Figure 1-24: Add New Item dialog

5. Click Add and the new page is added to the site (it appears in the Solution Explorer window) and is displayed in the main VWD window. At the same time, the Toolbox is populated with a list of all the available ASP.NET controls. At the moment, you are in Source view (as shown by the indicator just below the main editor window shown in Figure 1-25), so the HTML and an empty code section (delimited by `<script>` tags) is visible.

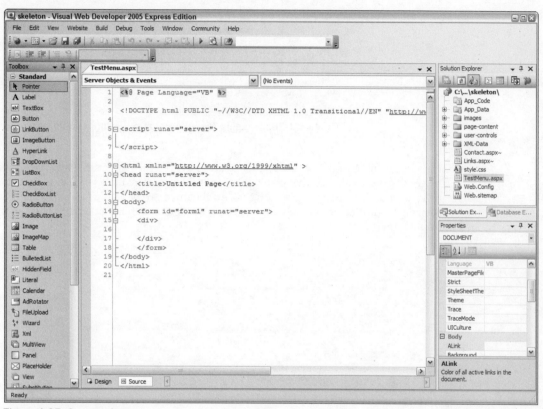

Figure 1-25: Source view

6. Click on the Design button at the bottom of the main window (just below the Editor pane and next to the Source button that is currently highlighted) to switch the Design view. Then go to the Database Explorer window, and make sure that the list of Tables in the PPQ database is displayed. Click on the table named MenuItems and drag it onto the page in the main Editor pane, as shown in Figure 1-26.

Figure 1-26: Dragging MenuItems onto the main editor pane

7. Now the magic begins. You will see that VWD creates a grid in the page using the new ASP.NET `GridView` control, with columns that match those in the source data table (such as `MenuItemID`, `MenuItemType`, and `ItemName`). It also adds a control named `SqlDataSource` to the page, just below the grid. In addition, to the right of the grid, a Task pane with the title GridView Tasks appears (see Figure 1-27).

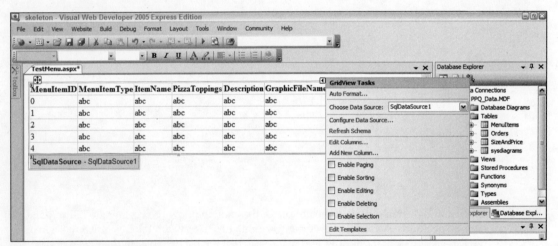

Figure 1-27: GridView Tasks pane

Note: If you previously experimented with the free tool named WebMatrix for versions 1.0 and 1.1 of ASP.NET, you will probably be feeling a strange sense of familiarity creep over you looking at the results shown here. WebMatrix was, in many ways, a test platform for the ASP.NET 2.0 concept of using data source controls and intelligent grid controls to display data. The Web Matrix `MXDataGrid` control was the forerunner to the new ASP.NET 2.0 `GridView` control, and the Web Matrix `MXSqlDataSource` control was the forerunner to the `SqlDataSource` (and other data source) controls in ASP.NET 2.0.

8. The list of checkboxes on the GridView Tasks pop-up is just too tempting to ignore, so go ahead and tick them all to enable paging, sorting, editing, deleting, and selection. At each stage, you'll see the grid in the page change to reflect the features you specify — such as adding the paging controls below the grid, turning the header text for each column into a hyperlink, and adding the Edit, Delete, and Select links to each row (as shown in Figure 1-28). Then click the Auto Format link at the top of the GridView Tasks pop-up.

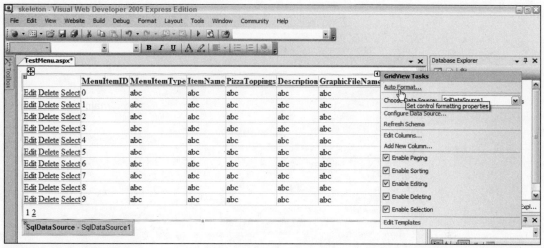

Figure 1-28: Adding links

The pop-up task panes like the GridView Tasks pane shown in Figure 1-28 can be displayed and hidden by clicking on the small square icon that contains a left- or right-facing arrow. This icon appears at the top right of any control that provides a task pane when you move the mouse over that control.

9. The Auto Format dialog that opens from the Auto Format link shows a list of preconfigured styles that you can apply to the GridView control. Select one (see Figure 1-29), and click OK.

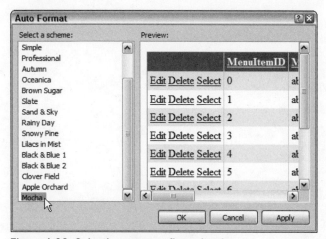

Figure 1-29: Selecting a preconfigured style

10. You will see the grid change to reflect the new style. However, before you run the page, there are a few other changes you can make to produce a nicer result. Two of the columns in the grid display information that is not really relevant in this page. The first column, named `MenuItemID`, contains the ID value for each menu item, while the column named `GraphicFileName` contains the file name of an image for each item. So, in the GridView Tasks pane, click the Edit Columns link to open the Fields dialog (see Figure 1-30). In the Fields dialog, locate the `MenuItemID` column in the Selected fields list, and remove it by clicking the button marked with a cross next to the list. Then repeat this process to remove the `GraphicFileName` column from the grid.

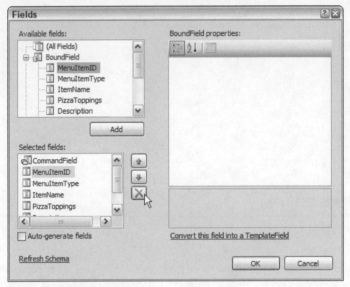

Figure 1-30: Fields dialog

11. Click OK to close the dialog, and you will see the updated `GridView` control in the page. You can see that it now only contains four columns from the source data table (see Figure 1-31).

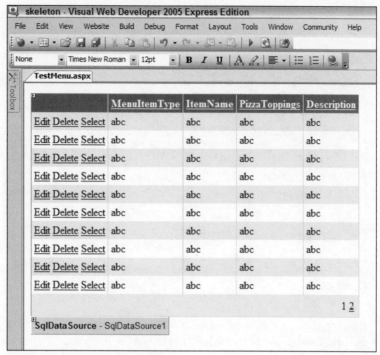

Figure 1-31: Updated GridView

12. Now you can run the page to see the results. Click the Start Debugging button in the Toolbar above the main editing window, or just press the F5 key. Alternatively, you can select Start Debugging from the Debug menu. At this point, the Debugging Not Enabled dialog appears (see Figure 1-32) because there is no `web.config` file in the application folders. VWD needs a `web.config` to be able to "turn on" debugging (by setting a value in this file). The best course of action is to select the first option, whereupon VWD will create a default `web.config` file and set the appropriate values. This also means that you will not see this dialog every time you run a page, and VWD will be able to provide more information on any errors that it encounters.

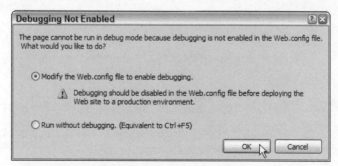

Figure 1-32: Debugging Not Enabled dialog

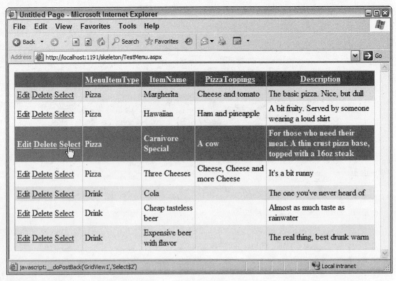

Figure 1-32

13. Now a browser window opens, and you will see your new ASP.NET page appear. You can select a row simply by clicking the link in the left-hand column, and that row is highlighted automatically (see Figure 1-33).

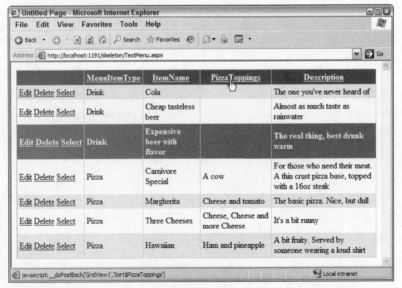

Figure 1-33: Automatically highlighting a row

14. You can also sort the rows in a different order by clicking on the links in the title bar, and if there were more than 10 rows in the table you would be able to change to a different page of results. In this case, paging controls would appear at the bottom of the grid, as you'll see in later examples (see Figure 1-34).

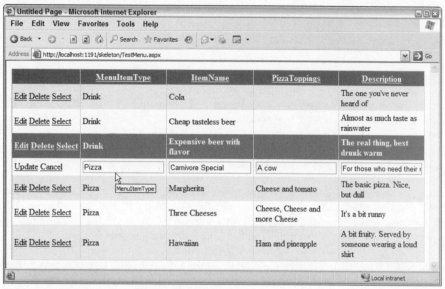

Figure 1-34: Selecting a different page of results

15. You can even edit the values in the rows (see Figure 1-35), and save these values back to the database by clicking the Update link that appears when a row is in "edit mode." And all of this without writing any code at all!

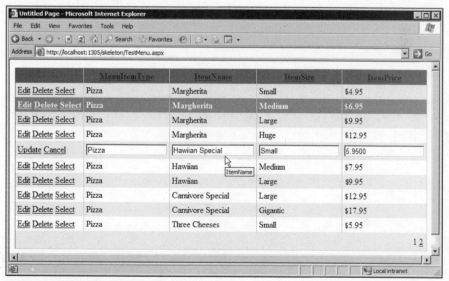

Figure 1-35: Editing row values

Notice that the URL in the address bar, and the icon for VWD's built-in Web server that appears in the notification area of the Windows taskbar, indicate that the page is running on your local machine (localhost), but using a nonstandard port number (usually port 80 is used for a Web server). You will see a different port number because VWD chooses one at run time. This means that you can run VWD on a machine without a Web server installed to develop your site. And you can also run it on a machine that does have a Web server such as Internet Information Server (IIS) installed without interfering with the operation of that Web server.

Summary

In this first chapter, you have seen how easy Visual Web Developer (VWD) 2005 Express Edition is to install, configure, and use to create powerful and attractive Web pages — quickly and with very little effort. Because the standard installation also includes SQL Server 2005 Express Edition, you don't even have to have a database server available to be able to build data-driven pages (although, as you saw, you can use any database server or file-based database such as Microsoft Access if you prefer).

VWD is a remarkable tool for building a whole range of Web sites, Web applications, and Web Services, as you will discover throughout the remainder of this book. You will also see and learn about the amazing new features and capabilities of ASP.NET version 2.0, which make building high-performance Web applications and Web sites so much quicker and easier than ever before.

In this chapter, you installed VWD and used it to access a database through SQL Server Express. You also saw some of the features of the VWD interface and its capabilities. The discussion skipped over much of the detailed working of these features so that you could quickly get a feel for how it works and what it can do. You will, of course, see a lot more detail in later chapters of this book.

In summary, this chapter covered:

❑ A preview of the completed example application

❑ Installation and set up of Visual Web Developer 2005 and SQL Server 2005 Express Editions

❑ Installation of the example application files for this book

❑ Viewing the example database and executing a test query

❑ Generating a simple page that uses the example database

In Chapter 2, you will begin a more detailed journey through the features of VWD and ASP.NET 2.0 by looking at the design of the PPQ Web site, how master pages can make things so much easier, and how you can plan and implement navigation between the pages of your site.

Designing a Web Site

In Chapter 1, you saw how easy Visual Web Developer (VWD) 2005 Express Edition is to install and use. You also saw how it includes the SQL Server 2005 Express Edition database server, which you can use to power your Web sites and Web applications. In this chapter, you will move on to start designing and building a simple (but effective) Web site that demonstrates the power of both VWD and ASP.NET 2.0.

The site, Pizza Pretty Quick (PPQ), sells pizzas and drinks online, taking the data about the menu items from a database and storing orders placed by customers in the same database. The design and implementation of the site shows the way that VWD makes working with ASP.NET 2.0 easy and highly productive, without getting too involved in complex issues regarding application architecture.

The topics you will see in this chapter are:

❑   Designing a Web site

❑   Building and using a Master Page and Content Page

❑   Converting an existing page to a Content Page

❑   Checking for accessibility

This chapter begins with an overview of the issues you must consider when you start to design and build a Web site like PPQ.

Designing a Web Site

If you are blessed with artistic and graphical-design capabilities, you will probably be able to design your Web site so that it looks good — and perhaps even stands out from the crowd. For the rest of us, the process of designing the appearance and "look and feel" for a professional result usually involves consulting a qualified graphical designer. However, for this example, the site follows a tried-and-trusted layout that mimics the great majority of sites already out on the Web, with no pretense of being anything more than a demonstration of the development techniques.

However, that does not mean you can just throw the pages together with no thought about the layout. You should consider several issues before you start to build any pages. Increasingly, legislation requires Web sites be accessible to all users, including those with sight and movement impairments. You should also think about whether one language is sufficient, or if you may have to translate the site into other languages now or in the future. Moreover, you must decide how data will be stored and accessed in your application.

Making Web Sites Accessible

It is very easy to build a Web site, test it in your favorite browser, and then deploy it without considering how other users might perceive the site. In most countries of the world, governments are implementing legislation that requires commercial and state-sponsored Web sites to provide acceptable access to all users, irrespective of their special requirements. Blind, partially sighted, and color-blind users must be able to access and understand the content, and navigate around the site. Users with movement difficulties (for example those that cannot use a mouse or even a conventional keyboard) should be able to do likewise.

Special browsers (or "user agents," to give them the correct name) are available that look or work in a completely different way from normal Web browsers such as Internet Explorer, Netscape, or Firefox. They may be page readers that provide only an audible rendering of the page content. Alternatively, the user agents may be character-based, displaying only text and with no images or "active" content. They may even generate Braille or other output through a special console.

To support all these kinds of user agents is not easy, but several things can be done to make it much easier for users, without requiring huge extra development effort. For example, you can implement a standard page structure across the site that makes it easier for unsighted users to appreciate the layout of each page. You can include special links that ease navigation and save time when viewing the page. Moreover, you can provide alternative content and links that make it easier for all nongraphical user agents to impart useful information to the user. You will see many of these techniques used in the example application.

> *Microsoft provides a series of guides and tutorials for building accessible applications at* www.microsoft .com/enable. *The World Wide Web Consortium (W3C) publishes guidelines and recommendations of the Web Accessibility Initiative (WAI) at* www.w3.org/WAI/about.html.

Multilingual Web Sites and Globalization

Many Web sites are available in only one language, which is fine if you can be sure that all your prospective visitors can understand that language. However, if you are building a Web site or application that provides a public service, especially if connected with a government-sponsored or regulated activity, you may have to provide the content in more than one language. This involves not only direct translation of the content, but also issues such as the text direction (right to left rather than left to right). You may also need alternative images to meet the requirements of the demographic target group, or just to fit in with the text direction. In addition, there are, of course, things such as date, number, and currency formats to consider.

ASP.NET 2.0 contains several features designed to assist the development of multilingual sites and applications. A set of classes in the System.Globalization namespace assists you when working with dates and other types of culture-specific information, and a set of classes in the System.Resources namespace allows manipulation of text strings and other types of resources. For simplicity, however, the PPQ example site implements only one language (U.S. English) and uses U.S. date, currency, and number formats.

For more details of globalization and multilingual support within the .NET Framework, search the SDK index for "globalization," "localization," and "culture." Also check out the examples at http://beta
.asp.net/QUICKSTARTV20/aspnet/doc/localization/localization.aspx.

Designing the Appearance of the Site

The PPQ example Web site follows a conventional design (see Figure 2-1). It contains a banner image at the top, a navigation bar to the left, and the content of the page to the right. At the bottom of every page is a set of text links to other pages, and there is a "bread-crumb trail" displayed in each page that allows users to see where they are in the site's hierarchy, and navigate back to a specific section.

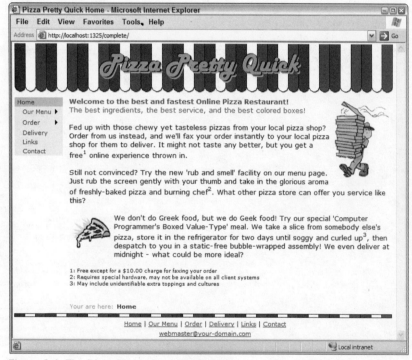

Figure 2-1: The Pizza Pretty Quick Web site

Providing a list of text links to the other main pages at the bottom of every page is an accepted way to assist blind or partially sighted users. Specialist user agents usually "read out" the page contents from top to bottom, and so placing links at the bottom of the page makes it easier for such users to navigate through the site.

All of the pages follow this simple design, with only the right-hand "content" section differing. This allows the use of a template or "Master Page" to ensure that each page follows the correct structure and contains the required standard content. It also means that updates to the overall structure or appearance of the site are possible simply by changing the Master Page.

Templates and Master Pages

Web developers have found various ways to implement standard sections of content that are common across multiple pages in a site. However, many of these approaches (such as separate text files and user controls in ASP.NET 1.*x*) cannot really be classed as Master Pages. They are just ways of inserting standard content into multiple pages. Other techniques involve creating a special code class based on the ASP.NET Page class, and then using this to implement a template-style solution.

ASP.NET 2.0 supports a new feature called Master Pages, which automatically provides all the features you need to create multiple pages based on the same underlying template. VWD also supports the Master Pages approach, and provides a great environment for building such pages and their content.

Figure 2-2 shows how you can see exactly what the result will be, even though the final page is created from two sections (the Master Page and a Content Page).

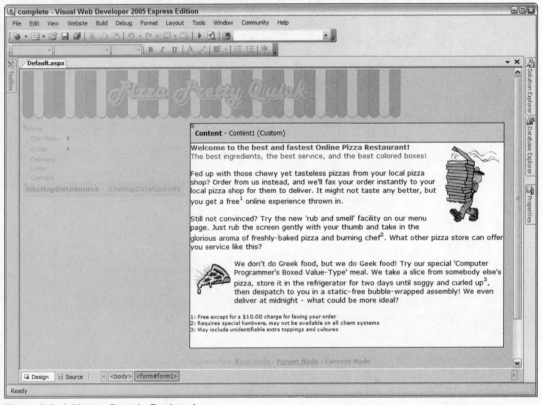

Figure 2-2: A Master Page in Design view

Navigation and Menus

The left-hand navigation bar or "menu" is ubiquitous in Web sites today, simply because it is the obvious place to locate links to other pages. Irrespective of the browser window size, the links are visible when the page first displays and provide a useful conceptual map of the whole site — which users often glance over before moving to the page content.

> *The use of the word "menu" on a site that sells fast food is somewhat confusing but difficult to avoid. In this book, the term navigation bar means the left-hand "menu" of page links, while the display of items available for sale is the "pizza menu" page. However, as you will see, Microsoft refers to the main ASP.NET navigation control as a* Menu *control!*

ASP.NET 2.0 provides a series of controls that generate both the navigation bar links and the "bread-crumb" links. They use either an XML-formatted text file or a collection of items that lists the pages on the site. However, the text links at the bottom of the page are not generated automatically in this way. Instead, you will use a custom user control to generate these links from an XML file, demonstrating an alternative technique (see Figure 2-3).

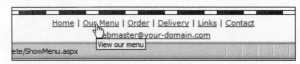

Figure 2-3: The text links at the bottom of the pages

Text Styles and Style Sheets

The PPQ site uses the common sans-serif face for the display, as is the case in many Web sites. Microsoft designed certain fonts for use on the Web in a browser, optimized to give an easy-to-read display of small text. Examples are Verdana and Tahoma, as used in the PPQ site. However, for headings and large bold text, Arial provides a better appearance. The example site uses a Cascading Style Sheet (CSS) to specify these styles for all pages, meaning users only download it once — and subsequently reload it from their browser cache. If the user agent does not provide graphical output, it can ignore and not download the style sheet.

However, not all visitors will be using Windows, and so they may not have the specified fonts installed. Therefore, the style sheet must also specify other suitable fonts, and the common technique is to use the standard CSS face style names, such as "sans-serif". In addition, to allow users to resize the text displayed in their browser window, the font sizes are specified using the standard size names, such as "x-small," "small," and "large" (see Figure 2-4).

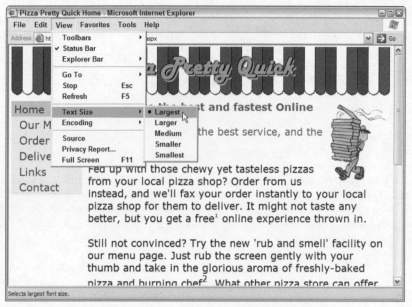

Figure 2-4: Changing the displayed text size in the browser

Designing the Underlying Workings of the Site

So far, the topics discussed have concentrated on what the site will look like. However, now it is time to consider the underlying "working parts." Web site and application design, despite much vocal complaint from bodies such as the U.S. Architecture Guilds and the U.K. Royal Institute of British Architects, is generally now referred to as "software architecture." The software architect takes into account all the requirements of the application, balances it against factors such as the technologies available and the cost, and comes up with a design for the working parts of that application. The primary "working parts" in most applications involve data access.

Data Access

It may seem strange to leave the topic of data access to last, when it is probably the most important aspect of getting the site working. This means that it is also likely to be the place you start your development. While there is nothing wrong with this, it is easy to get involved in data retrieval, storage, and display issues without considering the other design issues mentioned earlier. This is why data-access considerations reside here.

Today, the move in software is toward distributed, multitier, and service-oriented architectures. All these place features such as data access in separate "layers" or "tiers," so that the code can be reused and the physical layout of the application (such as the number and distribution of servers) can be changed without requiring rewriting of the code. At the extreme, the service-oriented architecture (SOA) model makes each component of the process a separate service, which exposes interfaces that other components and services can use irrespective of location, platform, and operating system.

The SOA model is beyond the requirements of the simple PPQ site, and the coverage of this book. However, to demonstrate the possibilities, the example site uses several different data-access approaches. To extract and display data in the pizza menu pages, the controls on the page talk directly to the database. This may be with a parameterized SQL statement or through a stored procedure in the database.

However, to store the data entered by the user when placing an order, the site uses a separate data-access layer that exposes and handles the data as a series of objects. This means that adapting the application to work with other databases (or to integrate with other applications) requires only that the data-access layer be adapted as required. Moreover, the separate data-access layer can be located on separate, and even multiple servers, to provide increased availability and throughput as PPQ becomes a worldwide supplier of high-quality fast food to the public.

Building a Master Page and Content Page

It is now time to start creating some pages, and the obvious place to start is with the Master Page that defines the structure of all the other pages in the site. You will see in this section how you can create a Master Page using VWD, and in it define the common layout structure for the pages of your site. Then, after the Master Page is complete, you will see how to build Content Pages that "plug into" the Master Page to create the final rendered output.

Creating the Page Structure as a Master Page

This section demonstrates how you can create the Master Page for the PPQ site, laying out the content sections and including features that make it easier for all users to access and navigate through the pages and the site.

1. Start VWD and select the `skeleton` project from the Start Page (see Figure 2-5), or select Open Web Site from the File menu and navigate to and select the `C:\Websites\PPQ\` folder.

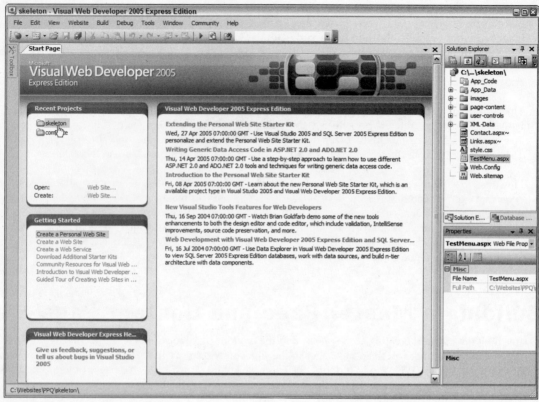

Figure 2-5: Start page

2. You will see the folders and files in the `skeleton` solution appear in the Solution Explorer
window. Close the Start Page, then either right-click on the top entry in the Solution Explorer
window (`C:\...\skeleton\`) and select Add New Item, or select New File... from the File
menu. Both actions open the Add New Item dialog. Select Master Page, change the name to
PPQ.master, and click Add (see Figure 2-6).

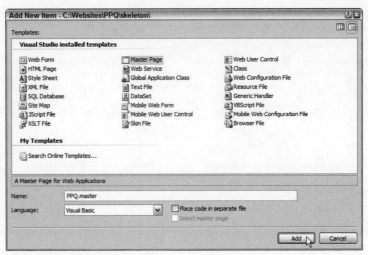

Figure 2-6: Add New Item page

For this example, we are using the "code inline" model, where the page itself contains the HTML content, the ASP.NET server controls, and the server-side code in a `<script runat="server">` *section. You can change to the "code behind" model by setting the checkbox next to the Language drop-down list. In this case, VWD will place the server-side code into a separate file and use the new partial classes feature of .NET version 2.0 to combine the code with the ASP.NET page and its constituent controls when the page is compiled and runs for the first time.*

3. The new Master Page opens in the main window. You can click the "pin" icons in the title bar of the Solution Explorer and Properties windows (and any other windows you have open) to view more of your new Master Page. You can see that it contains the usual `<head>` and `<body>` sections—in fact, it looks just like an ordinary Web page. The one main difference is that it contains an ASP.NET `ContentPlaceHolder` control within the `<div>` element on the `<form>` (see Figure 2-7).

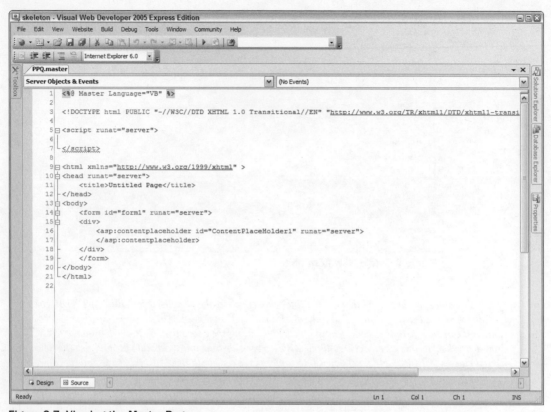

Figure 2-7: Viewing the Master Page

Notice that the first line of the file indicates that this is a Master Page file using the @Master *page directive. Normal ASP.NET pages contain the* @Page *directive. In a Master Page, the* ContentPlaceholder *control defines the areas where the content will come from a separate file (a Content Page). However, before looking at that, the next step is to populate the Master Page with the other controls required for the PPQ site. These include the outline table that will hold the* ContentPlaceHolder *controls, and the images for the top banner and for navigation assistance for nonsighted users.*

4. You are looking at the page in Source view at present, so the HTML and control definitions are visible. This is fine, because there is no visible content in the page. You can edit a page in either Source or Design view, and the changes are visible in both views as you switch between them. However, some things are easier to achieve in Source view, such as setting the properties of the main `<body>` element, as you will do now. Click on the `<body>` element in the code and open or view the Properties window. This allows you to add the attributes you want to the element by setting the properties. To ensure that the banner you will place at the top of the page goes right to the edge of the browser window, set the LeftMargin and TopMargin properties to zero. You will see the corresponding attributes appear in the code in the main window (see Figure 2-8). You can also change the *content* of the `<title>` element from Untitled Page to Pizza Pretty Quick. Notice how this is not a property of the `<title>` element but just a part of the page content.

Figure 2-8: Changing the `<body>` content

In the future, when you see instructions to set the properties of a control or element, you should do so in the same way as here by using the Properties window. You can add or edit the attributes themselves, directly within the Code Editor window. The Properties window then reflects the changes. However, it is generally better to use the Properties window to ensure that you get the correct attribute name and format — for example, if the value you enter contains double quotation marks, VWD automatically wraps the value in single quotation marks to maintain the correct syntax and well formedness.

5. Now it is time to create the layout structure of the Master Page. This example uses an HTML table for laying out the various parts of the content, though you could use CSS if you prefer. HTML tables are generally easier to work with unless you are very familiar with CSS, and they are correctly supported on almost all browsers and specialist user agents. Go to the Toolbox (open it from the View menu or press Ctrl-Alt-X if it is not visible) and scroll down to the HTML section, open it, and click on the `Table` control. Then drag it onto the editor window, placing it at the end of the opening `<form>` tag, as shown in Figure 2-9.

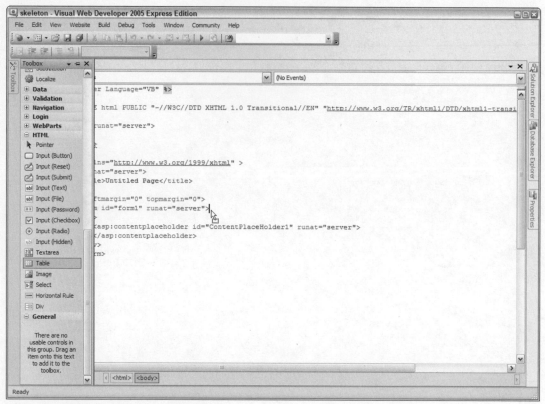

Figure 2-9: Dragging the `Table` control

6. This inserts the HTML to generate a three-row, three-column table. Now you can drag and drop, or cut and paste, the controls in the page to match the layout you need. The code in Listing 2-1 shows what is required — notice that there is a `<div>` control in the second row of the table that will display the navigation links. To add a control to the page, simply drag it from the Toolbox and drop it into the appropriate place in the editor window (in either Source or Design view). VWD automatically generates different values for the ID of each control. Remember to set the `ColSpan` properties of the first and last `<td>` elements. You can also add some "dummy" content to the table so that you can see what it looks like in Design view and can make it easier to drag and drop other controls into the table cells later on.

Listing 2-1: Layout Controls

```
...
<form id="form1" runat="server">
  <table>
    <tr>
      <td colspan="2">
        Header goes here
      </td>
    </tr>
    <tr>
      <td>
```

```
            <div>
              Links<br />Links<br />Links<br />Links<br />Links
            </div>
          </td>
          <td>
            <asp:contentplaceholder id="ContentPlaceHolder1" runat="server">
              Content<br />Content<br />Content<br />Content<br />Content
            </asp:contentplaceholder>
          </td>
        </tr>
        <tr>
          <td colspan="2">
            Footer and text links go here
          </td>       </tr>
      </table>
    </form>
    ...
```

7. Now you can switch VWD to Design view using the button below the main Editor window and see the results so far. Okay, so it does not look like much—but at least the main structural layout of the page is complete (see Figure 2-10).

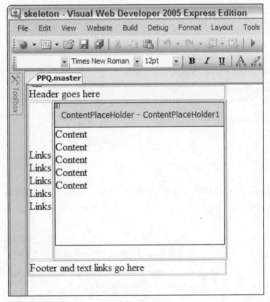

Figure 2-10: Structural layout

8. To complete this section of the chapter, you will populate the top row of the table with the heading banner. In fact, there are three images to go into this section—the first two are "Skip To" links that make it easier for users of page readers and text-based user agents to navigate the site, and the third is the heading banner image. The first two links are images embedded in hyperlink elements, which point to the relevant sections of the page so that users can follow the link and skip directly to that section. So, delete the text from the header row of the table, and drag three Image controls from the HTML section of the Toolbox into it (see Figure 2-11).

Do not use the Image *control in the Standard controls section of the Toolbox.*

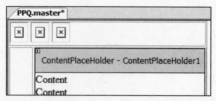

Figure 2-11: Populating the heading banner

The W3C Web Accessibility Initiative guidelines suggest the use of "Skip To" links where pages contain more than just minimal content that is repeated at the top of every page; for example, a series of hyperlinks (such as a list of other branches of your corporation) or multiple images. An alternative approach is to use CSS absolute positioning to place this content later in the flow of the page source but still have it rendered at the top of the page in a normal Web browser. For more details on CSS, see www.w3.org/Style/CSS.

9. Now you can set the properties of these Image controls. The first two will be the "Skip To" links, so in the Properties window for each of these, set the values of the properties shown in Table 2-1. If you have trouble selecting the image controls on the page in Design view after resizing them, try using the left and right arrow keys to move through the controls on the page. Alternatively, you can switch back to Source view and select them there to set the property values.

Table 2-1: "Skip To" Properties

Property	Value
TabIndex	0 for the first Image control, and 1 for the second Image control.
Height	1
Width	1
Alt	Skip to Navigation Links for the first Image control, and Skip to Page Content for the second Image control.
Border	0
HSpace	0
Title	Skip to Navigation Links for the first Image control, and Skip to Page Content for the second Image control.
VSpace	0

10. There are some other properties to be set as well. For the "Skip To" link images, go to the Properties window, select the Src property, and click the "..." button to open the Select Project Item dialog. Select the images subfolder of the example files, select the image named blank.gif (a 1-pixel square, transparent GIF image), and then click OK.

Figure 2-12 shows the dialog for selecting the image file.

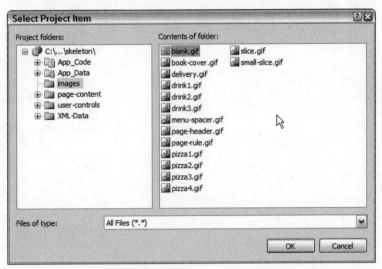

Figure 2-12: Select Project Item dialog

The idea is that the "Skip To" links will not be visible in a graphical Web browser, but other page readers and text-based browsers will read them and allow the user to follow the links. Using small transparent images helps to hide them.

11. There is still not much to show for all the work you have done, so select the remaining Image control, and set the Src property to the file named page-header.gif in the images subfolder. Then set the Alt and Title property values to Pizza Pretty Quick Logo, and the HSpace and VSpace property values to zero. Notice how VWD automatically detects the size of the image (though it does not add these attributes to the <img> element). Figure 2-13 shows the result.

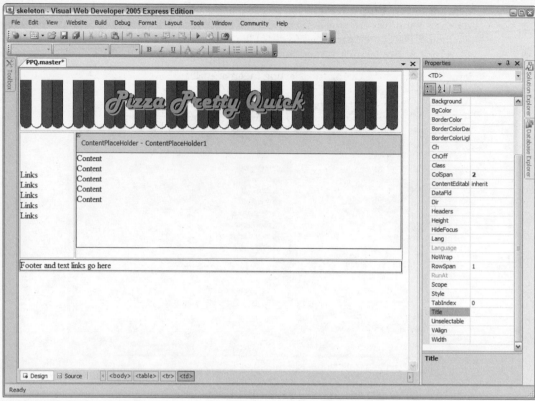

Figure 2-13: Adding the logo

Setting both the Alt *and* Title *properties adds extra attributes to the element rendered into the page at run time. This gives the best chance that nonstandard user agents will read and display or use these attribute values.*

12. So far, you have inserted only image controls into the page. Now you must turn the first two, which implement the "Skip To" links, into hyperlinks that target the correct parts of the page. You cannot use the ASP.NET Hyperlink control for this, because you need to set specific properties of the Image itself — something that is not possible in VWD for a Hyperlink control. So, switch to Source view and type in the HTML that is required to implement the two hyperlinks and their target anchors, as shown highlighted in Listing 2-2.

Listing 2-2: HTML for hyperlinking target anchors

```
...
<table>
  <tr>
    <td colspan="2">
      <a href="#navigation">
        <img src="images/blank.gif" alt="Skip to Navigation Links" border="0"
             height="1" width="1" title="Skip to Navigation Links" tabindex="0" />
      </a>
```

```
    <a href="#content">
      <img src="images/blank.gif" alt="Skip to Page Content" border="0"
          height="1" width="1" title="Skip to Page Content" tabindex="1" />
    </a>
      <img src="images/page-header.gif" alt="Pizza Pretty Quick Logo"
          title="Pizza Pretty Quick Logo" />
    </td>
  </tr>
  <tr>
    <td>
      <a name="navigation" />
      <div>
        Links<br />Links<br />Links<br />Links<br />Links
      </div>
    </td>
    <td>
      <a name="content" />
      <asp:contentplaceholder id="ContentPlaceHolder1" runat="server">
        Content<br />Content<br />Content<br />Content<br />Content
      </asp:contentplaceholder>
    </td>
  </tr>
  ...
```

This just shows how flexible VWD actually is. It can work with existing pages, HTML content, ASP.NET controls, and code, as well as create new pages, HTML content, ASP.NET controls, and code. In addition, as you have just seen, VWD allows you to mix your development approach as you go along to suit the requirements of your site or application.

13. Unfortunately, the neat layout, including line breaks, as shown in Listing 2-2 causes problems with the final display of the page because this extraneous "white space" (content that is not actually part of the output) adds a space between each image element. Therefore, you need to edit it in Source view to remove this extra white space, as shown in Listing 2-3. It makes it harder to see what the content actually is, but placing the end "/>" of each "Skip To" image element on a new line means that you can more easily find where each element ends and the next one starts. You do not need to worry about the white space at the end of the third image control that displays the banner. If you now switch to Design view, you will see that the banner starts much closer to the left-hand edge of the page.

Listing 2-3: Removing White Space

```
...
<tr>
  <td colspan="2"><a href="#navigation"><img src="images/blank.gif"
      alt="Skip to Navigation Links" border="0" tabindex="0"
      height="1" width="1" title="Skip to Navigation Links"
      /></a><a href="#content"><img src="images/blank.gif"
      alt="Skip to Page Content" border="0"
      height="1" width="1" title="Skip to Page Content" tabindex="1"
      /></a><img src="images/page-header.gif"
      alt="Pizza Pretty Quick Logo" title="Pizza Pretty Quick Logo" />
  </td>
</tr>
...
```

It has taken a while to fully describe each step of the process of starting to build a Master Page. However, this example should give you a feel for the way that the editing features of VWD work, how to create new items, and how to work with the Properties and other windows. You have seen how you can edit a page in a range of ways and while in different views (Source view or Design view). In later sections of this book, you will see somewhat less detail for each step of the examples because you are now familiar with the basics of working with VWD.

Choosing the Correct Element and Control Type

One point to notice is that the content of the page is a mixture of item types. It contains "normal" HTML elements, such as the <body> element and the various <table>, <tr>, and <td> elements you added to generate the page layout structure. Because your ASP.NET code will not manipulate or reference any of these elements, there is no reason for them to be anything other than simple HTML.

Elements that ASP.NET code *will* manipulate or reference must be declared as server controls. In other words, they must contain the attribute runat="server" in their declaration—as the ContentPlaceHolder control in the example does. You will use predominantly server controls throughout the pages you build in ASP.NET. However, server controls do exert much more load on the server when generating the page, compared to just declarative HTML and other content. Therefore, where they are not required, they should be avoided and the standard HTML controls used instead. This is what happened when you used the Image control from the HTML section of the Toolbox for the images in the Master Page. The Image control in the Standard section of the Toolbox is a server control, yet server-side access is not a requirement for these images in the page.

The Master Page you are building cannot be viewed directly. If you try to open it in a Web browser, you will see a message stating that "This type of page is not served." Later, you will build a Content Page that uses this Master Page, at which point you will be able to see what it looks like in a browser. Before then, however, you will add the navigation controls to the Master Page.

Adding the Navigation Links

The left-hand section of the Master Page will contain a navigation bar that provides links to other pages in the PPQ site. You will add this navigation bar and other navigation features next. ASP.NET can automatically generate sets of navigation links in a range of visual formats. This section of the chapter shows you how.

1. With the skeleton project open in VWD, locate the Menu control within the Navigation section of the Toolbox and drag and drop it onto the editor window directly after the opening <div> tag, as shown in Figure 2-14.

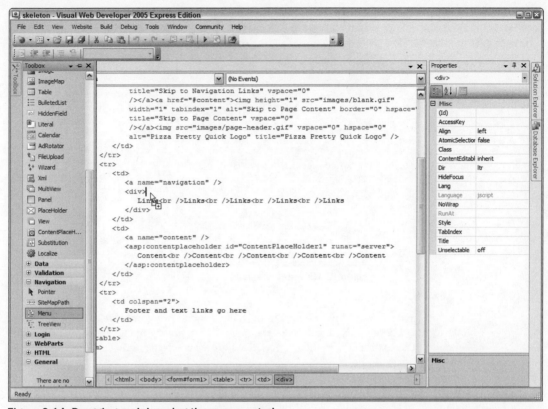

Figure 2-14: Dragging and dropping the Menu control

2. Switch to Design view, and you will see the new Menu control (you can delete the text "Links" from this section of the page now). Click on the small arrow that appears at the top right of the control when you move the mouse pointer over it. This opens the Menu Tasks pane, where you will see the Edit Menu Items. . . option (see Figure 2-15).

Figure 2-15: Menu tasks

This option opens a useful Menu Item Editor dialog that allows you to create a list or collection of links for use when ASP.NET generates the menu at run time. You can also open this dialog by selecting the Items property in the Properties windows when the Menu control is selected within the editor window.

Figure 2-16 shows some of the properties of one of the links in a menu you could create for the PPQ site. However, the problem with using this approach is that the list of page links created this way is only available to the Menu control. Instead, you will use an XML-formatted file that defines the links to the pages within the PPQ site, which other controls can access as well.

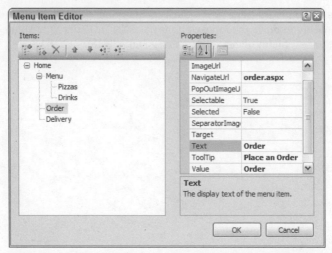

Figure 2-16: An example of a menu created with the Menu Item Editor

3. In the example application, you will be using an XML sitemap file to define the links for the navigation controls in the page. This means that you also need a `SiteMapDataSource` control, which interfaces the `Menu`—and any other navigation controls—to the XML sitemap file. You can drag a `SiteMapDataSource` control from the Data section of the Toolbox onto the editor window, but an easier way to add this control is to use the Menu Tasks pane you saw earlier in step 2. Click on the small arrow that appears at the top right of the `Menu` control when you move the mouse pointer over it to open the Menu Tasks pane. In the Menu Tasks pane, open the drop-down list for Choose Data Source and select the <New Data Source. . .> option (see Figure 2-17).

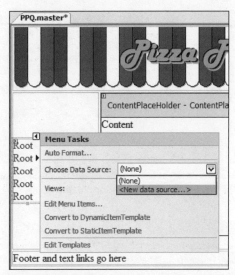

Figure 2-17: Choose Data Source drop-down list

4. This opens the Data Source Configuration Wizard. For a `SiteMapDataSource` control, this Wizard offers two options: Site Map or XML File. In fact, these are very similar options—both are XML files containing a list of links for the site. However, the option you need is the first. As you can see from the text in the dialog, this option assumes that the data for the control will come from a file located in the root folder of the application (see Figure 2-18). The name of this file must be `Web.sitemap`.

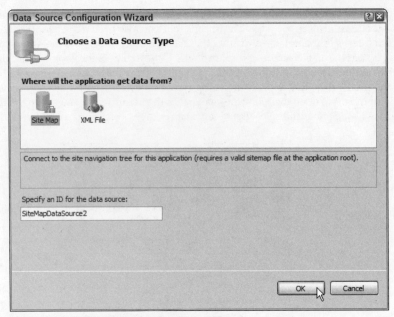

Figure 2-18: Data Source Configuration Wizard

The examples include a Web.sitemap *file containing the links used in the PPQ site. If you want to try creating your own* Web.sitemap *file, select New File from the File menu, and select the Site Map option in the Add New Item dialog that appears. This creates a template XML file that you can extend and populate to match your requirements. Open the* Web.sitemap *file provided with the examples to see the way that it defines the navigation links.*

5. By default, when using a SiteMapDataSource control with a sitemap file, the Menu control only displays a single link — the one defined as the root of the sitemap file. In the examples, this is the "Home" link. Instead, you want the menu to show the next level of links as well, so that the "Our Menu," "Order," "Delivery," "Links," and "Contact" links are always visible. To achieve this, select the menu control in the page and go to the Properties window. Change the value of the StaticDisplayLevels property from the default of 1 to 2 so that the second level of links also becomes static content (see Figure 2-19).

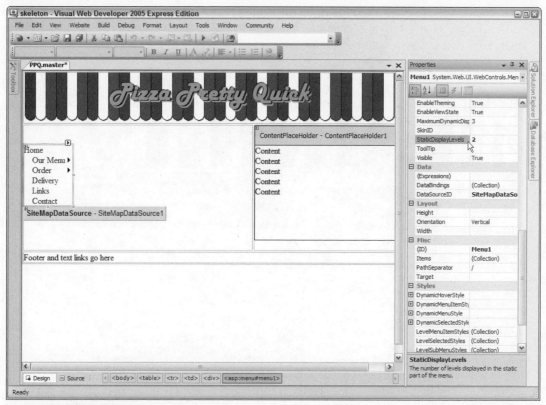

Figure 2-19: Enabling the second level of links

Notice that the `DataSourceID` *property for the* `Menu` *control indicates where the data to populate the control comes from. It is set to* `SiteMapDataSource1`, *which is the ID of the* `SiteMapDataSource` *control that the Data Source Configuration Wizard added to the page. You can switch to Source view any time to see what the various configuration dialogs, Properties windows, and wizards are actually doing—which helps you to understand how ASP.NET works and how common combinations of controls (such as a data source control and a data display control) are interlinked. You saw this interaction in Chapter 1 with the* `GridView` *control and a* `SqlDataSource` *control, and you will see it again many times throughout this book.*

6. Now open the Menu Tasks pane for the Menu control again, and select Auto Format. In the Auto Format dialog, choose a scheme for the menu control formatting, as shown in Figure 2-20.

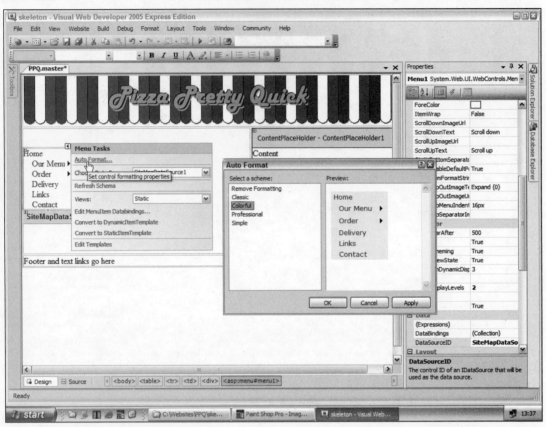

Figure 2-20: Auto Format dialog

7. Finally, go back to the Navigation section of the Toolbox and drag a SiteMapPath control onto the page, dropping it into the table cell at the right-hand side of the page below the ContentPlaceHolder control. Click on the small arrow button to open the SiteMapPath Tasks pane, and select Auto Format. . . (see Figure 2-21). In the Auto Format dialog, select the same scheme as you did for the Menu control. The SiteMapPath control implements the "bread-crumb trail" navigation control, taking its data from the Web.sitemap file in the root folder of the application.

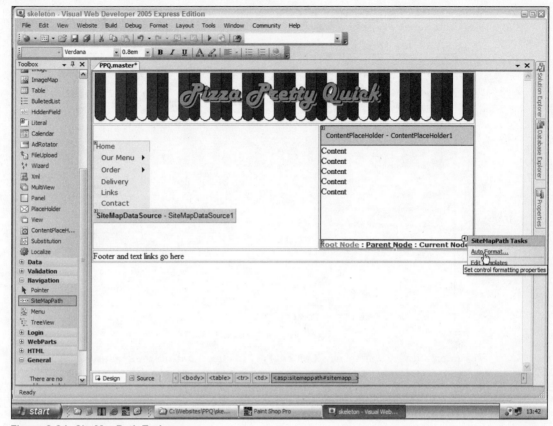

Figure 2-21: SiteMapPath Tasks pane

That wraps up the task of creating the navigation links for now. You will come back to this throughout the book as you build more pages and implement new features. However, the Master Page as it stands now will be sufficient for the tasks of starting to create some Content Pages. Remember that the whole idea of using a Master Page is that you can change it over time to update your site, and all the Content Pages will automatically reflect these changes.

Building Your First Content Page

In this section of the chapter, you will build your first Content Page. This will also allow you to see just what the Master Page you have created looks like at run time. The Content Page you will build is simple, in that it contains only the "welcome" message and details about the Pizza Pretty Quick Corporation. Users see this page when they first open the site, and so it is stored with the filename `default.aspx`.

1. With the Master Page in Design view, right-click on the `ContentPlaceHolder` control and
   select Add Content Page from the shortcut menu (see Figure 2-22).

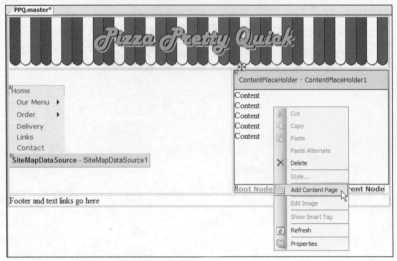

Figure 2-22: Selecting Add Content Page

2. This automatically creates a new Content Page, names it `Default.aspx` (providing that the
   project does not already contain a page with this name), and opens this new Content Page in
   Source view. Listing 2-4 shows the entire contents of the new page.

Listing 2-4: Contents of new page

```
<%@ Page Language="VB" MasterPageFile="~/PPQ.master" Title="Untitled Page" %>
<asp:Content ID="Content1" ContentPlaceHolderID="ContentPlaceHolder1"
          Runat="Server">
</asp:Content>
```

The attribute `MasterPageFile="~/PPQ.master"` *in the* `@Page` *directive shows that this is a
Content Page, which will be embedded as a section of output inside a* `ContentPlaceHolder` *control
in the specified Master Page. The tilde (~) before the path and name of the Master Page is a shortcut
way of saying, "starting from the root folder of the application." All that a Content Page can contain is
one or more* `Content` *controls, as shown in Listing 2-4. Each Content control must include the*
`ContentPlaceHolderID` *attribute that indicates which* `ContentPlaceHolder` *control in the
Master Page it will inhabit. In this case, there is only one and it has the ID value*
"ContentPlaceHolder1."

3. To see the real magic of VWD, however, switch the new Content Page (`Default.aspx`) to
   Design view. Now the content of the Master Page is grayed and cannot be edited, while the
   `Content` control that is actually located in the `Default.aspx` page shows, and can be edited
   and populated with the required HTML, text, controls, and other content (see Figure 2-23).

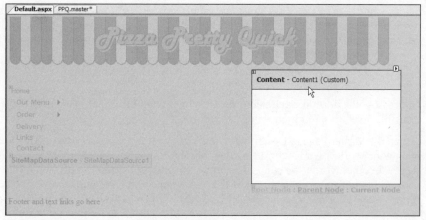

Figure 2-23: Design view of Master Page

4. All you need to do now is create the content for the `Default.aspx` page. However, to save you time, we have provided this in a file named `default.aspx.txt`, stored in the `page-content` folder of the examples. Open this file in VWD, select all the content, and copy and paste it inside the `Content` control in the `Default.aspx` page (see Figure 2-24).

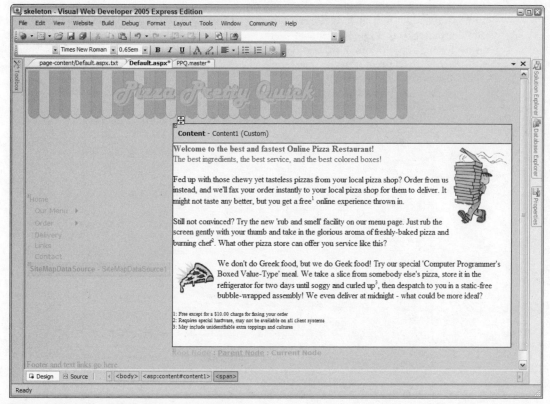

Figure 2-24: Content for page

5. Before you run the page, there are a few other "tidying up" tasks to complete. Right-click outside the Content control, and select Edit Master from the shortcut menu. Add the following reference to the CSS style sheet for the application to the page, inside the <head> element and after the <title> element:

```
<link href="style.css" rel="stylesheet" type="text/css" />
```

Notice how the pop-up IntelliSense features help you to complete the element by suggesting the available attributes and their values as you type.

6. Switch the Master Page to Design view, and click near to the Menu control. The bottom of the main window (below the editing area) shows the hierarchy of elements that are currently "in scope," in other words, the containers of the currently selected element (which is the <div> surrounding the Menu control). Select the <td> element that contains the <div> and Menu control. As you move your mouse over the "<td>, a "drop-down" arrow button appears. (see Figure 2-25).

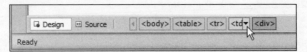

Figure 2-25: Hovering over the <td> to reveal a shortcut menu

7. Click drop-down" arrow button, and then click Select Tag on the shortcut menu that opens. In the Properties window, set the VAlign property to top so that the content will appear at the top of this table cell. Then click the Style property entry and use the (...) button to open the Style Builder dialog. Select Edges in the left-hand section of the dialog, and enter the values 3, 3, 3, and 5 for the Top, Bottom, Left, and Right Padding selectors, as shown in Figure 2-26. Then click OK to close the dialog.

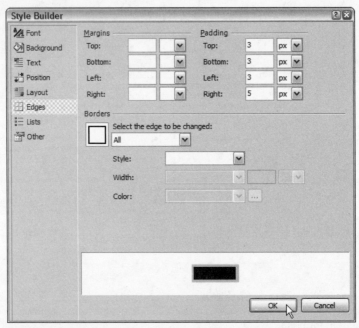

Figure 2-26: Assigning values to the edges

8. Select the Content control in the right-hand side of the Master Page window, and then repeat the process by selecting this <td> tag and setting the VAlign property to top. Set the Style property values in the Edges section of the Style Builder dialog to the values 3, 3, 5 (not 3), and 5 for the Top, Bottom, Left, and Right selectors. This creates some white space between the Menu control and the content in the right-hand side of the page.

9. Finally, go to the Standard section of the Toolbox and drag an Image control onto the page, dropping it at the left-hand end of the last row of the table, just in front of the text "Footer and text links go here." Add a carriage return to the page after the Image control, so that the text wraps to the next line below the Image control. With the Image control selected, go to the Properties window and set the ImageUrl property to the file named page-rule.gif in the images subfolder of the examples, and set the GenerateEmptyAltText property to True (see Figure 2-27).

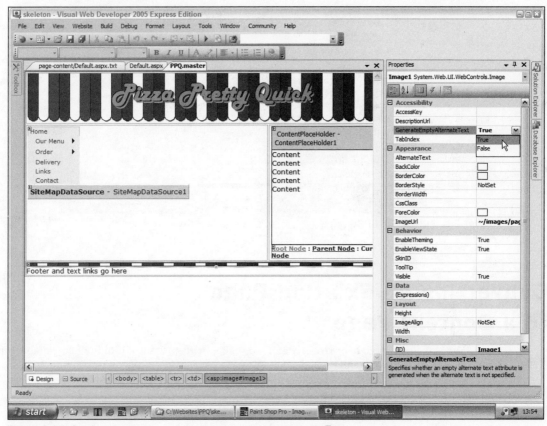

Figure 2-27: Setting the GenerateEmptyAltText **property to True**

The reason for using an ASP.NET Image control for the page-rule.gif *file is that it is not part of the informational content of the page, and so the attributes on the rendered control should indicate this to specialist page readers. The accepted way is to include the attribute* alt="" *(an empty string), but the ASP.NET controls do not generate this attribute automatically—even when you do not provide a value for the* Alt *property. However, certain ASP.NET controls in version 2.0 (such as the* Image *control) do provide the* GenerateEmptyAltText *property, which adds this attribute when set to* True.

10. Save and close the Master Page (PPQ.master) and go back to the Default.aspx Content Page. Select View in Browser from the File menu, or click the Start Debugging (green arrow) button on the toolbar. Your first page is now part of the PPQ Web site! Figure 2-28 shows the result.

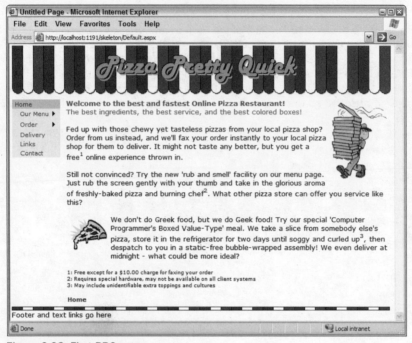

Figure 2-28: First PPQ page

Converting an Existing Page to a Content Page

In Chapter 1, you created a page named TestMenu.aspx that extracts values from the PPQ database in SQL Server 2005 Express Edition and displays these values in a GridView control (see Figure 2-29). In this section of the chapter, you will convert this into a Content Page and use it in the Master Page you have just created.

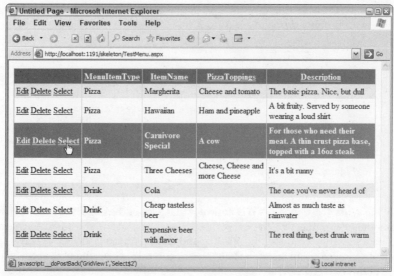

Figure 2-29: The pizza menu page from Chapter 1

1. Open the page `TestMenu.aspx`, and switch to Source view. The first task is to tell ASP.NET that this will now be a Content Page. Place the input cursor after the end of the `Language` attribute in the `@Page` directive, and press the Spacebar (see Figure 2-30).

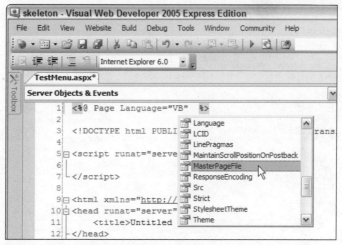

Figure 2-30: Telling ASP.NET this will now be a Content Page

2. Select the `MasterPageFile` attribute name from the drop-down list, type an "equals" sign (=) and a double quotation mark ("), and VWD offers a list of Master Pages in the current project from which you can choose. Select `PPQ.master` (see Figure 2-31).

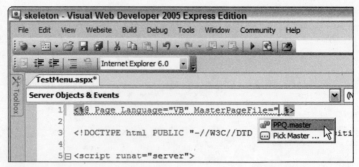

Figure 2-31: Selecting PPQ.master

3. Now the syntax checking in VWD indicates that a lot of the page is invalid. Delete everything except the @Page directive, the <asp:GridView>, control and the <asp:SqlDataSource> control declarations—but including the opening and closing <html>, <head>, <body>, and other HTML elements. Now you can insert the only type of control that is valid at the root level of a Content Page, namely an ASP.NET Content control. As soon as you start typing, a drop-down list displays the valid options and you can select for the asp:Content control entry (see Figure 2-32).

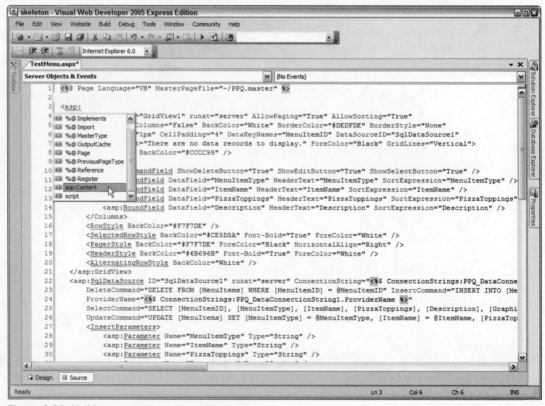

Figure 2-32: Valid asp:Content **control options**

4. The IntelliSense feature helps you add the appropriate attributes to the `Content` control declaration, and you should end up with this:

```
<asp:Content runat="server" ContentPlaceHolderID="ContentPlaceHolder1">
```

A closing `</asp:Content>` tag is also inserted, and you must move this to the end of the page, after the `GridView` and `SqlDataSource` control declarations. Then, save the page, and view it in the browser to see the results (shown in Figure 2-33). As you can see, our original page now fits in well with the new PPQ site.

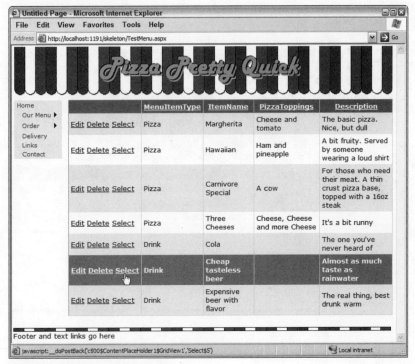

Figure 2-33: Revised PPQ page

Checking for Accessibility

You have built a Master Page and two Content Pages in this chapter, and they look okay when viewed in Internet Explorer. The next step is to ensure that they work properly in other browsers as well. Unfortunately, it is not easy to test your page with other browsers when using the VWD built-in Web server because it responds to local requests only. However, you can set up alternative browsers by selecting Browse With. . . from the File menu in VWD and adding your favorite Web browser to the list. You can even make it the default browser for viewing pages. Unfortunately, this does not work with some text-based user agents that cannot provide the correct authentication information when accessing the VWD Web server.

The other solution is to deploy the application, as it now stands, to another server that has IIS and SQL Server available — and that can be accessed from any location and by any browser or page reader for testing. The database files, PPQ_Data.MDF and PPQ_Data_Log.MDF, can be attached to a SQL Server 2000 or 2005 database server, and the connection string in the Web.Config file changed to point to this server.

As an example, after installing the application as it now stands on a separate server and accessing it with the IBM Home Page Reader (HPR), you can see the effects of the accessibility additions to the pages (see Figure 2-34). The "Skip To" links you added to the top of the Master Page are seen as hyperlinks (underlined) in the middle window. This window shows the text that HPR is currently reading aloud to the user. Therefore, if the user is browsing the site and has already grasped the layout of the pages, he or she can skip directly to the navigation bar or to the page content from the top of every page as it loads.

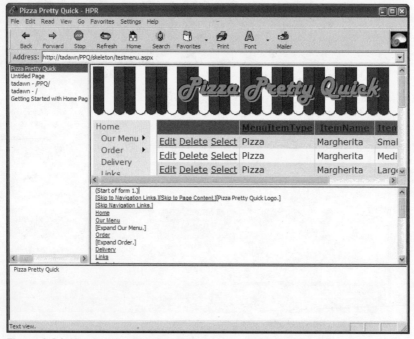

Figure 2-34: Viewing the Example Pages in the IBM Home Page Reader

Notice also that the Menu control implements a "Skip To" link of its own automatically ("Skip Navigation Links"), as well as providing the option to expand an item in the static section of the menu if it contains links on other nonvisible ("fly-out menu") levels. Typically, the ASP.NET 2.0 server controls will provide the basic level of accessibility, as you can see in Figure 2-34.

You can download an evaluation version of the IBM Home Page Reader (and buy a copy) at www-306.ibm.com/able/solution_offerings/hpr.html.

Summary

This chapter has taken the first steps in designing and building the Pizza Pretty Quick (PPQ) Web site. You saw some of the issues for consideration, such as providing accessibility for all users, managing globalization, and multilingual requirements. You also discovered some of the core design/implementation issues such as planning your strategy for navigation between the site pages, and provision for access to the data that drives the site.

Then the chapter moved on to topics that are more practical by demonstrating how to create a Master Page in ASP.NET 2.0. This section helped you to get used to the VWD interface and editing features, as well as showing just how powerful and yet user-friendly it really is. The Master Page you created contains extra accessibility features, a range of different categories of controls (both HTML elements and server controls), and several images. You saw how the Properties window, task panes, and wizards make it easy to configure the page content and fine-tune the appearance.

Then you saw how easy it is to create Content Pages that take advantage of the Master Page, and just how quickly and simply you can convert an existing ASP.NET Web Form page into a Content Page as well. By the end of the chapter, you had two pages working on the new PPQ Web site.

In summary, the topics covered in this chapter were:

❑   Designing a Web site

❑   Building and using a Master Page and Content Page

❑   Converting an existing page to a Content Page

❑   Checking for accessibility

In Chapter 3, you will look in more detail at the design of the database for the PPQ Web site, and some other ways that you can extract and display data from the database.

Building the PPQ Database

You saw in Chapter 1 how Visual Web Developer (VWD) makes it easy to display and update data stored in a database. You simply dragged a table from the database onto a page, and VWD created all the controls and code required to make this work. In Chapter 2, you used this page as a Content Page within the Master Page you created. However, it is now time to look in more detail at how to design, build, and use a database to drive your Web site or Web application.

In this chapter, you will see the design decisions taken when creating the database for the Pizza Pretty Quick (PPQ) site. These decisions follow an approach that is reasonably standard, common wherever you work with a relational database, and can easily be adapted and extended to suit your own particular situation. Once the design is complete, the tools within VWD allow you to create this database.

> *The example shown in this book uses SQL Server 2005 Express Edition, although the database tools in VWD will work with any other relational database for which .NET drivers or providers are available. This includes SQL Server, Oracle, or any OLE-DB- or ODBC-enabled database that provides managed code drivers.*

In this chapter, you will:

❑ See the design of the PPQ database

❑ Use VWD to create and modify a database

❑ Build a page to extract data from related tables

By the end of this chapter, you will understand how to create a database suitable for your own Web sites, and be able to extract and display data it contains.

Designing the PPQ Database

Database design is both an art and a science, although the science part is generally the most relevant. There are rules that govern the process of design, including a series of steps called *normalization* that ensure you have the optimum structure for the tables in your database. However, you must also balance this process with the way that you intend to use the data. In some cases, the normalization rules can divide your data across more tables than is strictly necessary when taking into account the data content and the way you will use it.

The example application stores data about only two "things." These are the items that are for sale (pizzas and drinks) and the orders placed by customers. In database design terms, these "things" may be referred to as *entities*. Therefore, the design process starts with two entities: a *menu* and an *order*. Obviously, each order consists of one or more items, each being an item from the menu, and so you can reflect this in a diagram (see Figure 3-1).

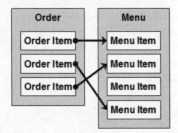

Figure 3-1: The entities for which the database will hold data

Now you can think about the individual items of data that you want to store for each entity. For a menu item, these will probably be the type of item (pizza or drink), the name, some description, the size, and the price. For an order, you will probably need to store the customer's name and address, and the items he or she ordered.

Storing the Menu Items Data

Looking first at the menu items, a simple approach to the table design for holding data about pizzas might look like this:

ItemType	ItemName	Toppings	Description	Small Price	Medium Price	Large Price
Pizza	Margherita	Cheese, Tomato	The basic pizza	6.50	7.50	9.50
Pizza	Hawaiian	Ham, Pineapple	Tropical taste	6.75	7.75	9.75
Drink	Cola	[no value]	Crisp and tasty	2.25	3.25	3.75

This table could also hold data about other menu items, such as drinks, by leaving the `Toppings` column empty. Moreover, there could be many more "size-price" columns, depending on the number of different sizes available for all the menu items. However, there are fundamental issues here with regard to *normalization*. Any change to the range of sizes means changing the table structure, while several of the columns in each row might be empty.

Applying the Rules of Normalization

This is where the rules of normalization come into play. The first rule states that a row must not contain repeating groups. You must convert this design into *first normal form* by removing the repeated information. Therefore, the table should instead contain a row for each size of each menu item, like this:

ItemType	ItemName	Toppings	Description	Size	Price
Pizza	Margherita	Cheese, Tomato	The basic pizza	Large	9.50
Pizza	Margherita	Cheese, Tomato	The basic pizza	Medium	7.70
Pizza	Margherita	Cheese, Tomato	The basic pizza	Small	6.50

However, each pizza or drink will be available in more than one size, so there will be a row in the table for each one. This means repeating any data that is the same for each type of pizza or drink, such as the name, toppings (if any), and description. After all, a Hawaiian pizza still has ham and pineapple toppings whether it is a small, medium, or large size. The second rule of normalization states that you must remove data repeated in multiple rows and place it in a separate linked table.

Converting the design to *second normal form,* therefore, means moving the repeated columns into a new table and then linking them to the corresponding rows in the existing table. A numeric key column implements this link. The existing table stores a primary key for each row (the values in the `MenuItemID` column of Table 3-1), and the new table also contains this key. The value in each row of the new table, `SizeAndPrice` (see Table 3-2), is set to the value of the corresponding row in the `MenuItems` table (see Table 3-1) to link the new table rows with the original table rows.

Table 3-1: MenuItems Table

MenuItemID	MenuItemType	ItemName	Toppings	Description
1	Pizza	Margherita	Cheese, Tomato	The basic pizza
2	Pizza	Hawaiian	Ham, Pineapple	Tropical taste
3	Drink	Cola	[no value]	Crisp and tasty

Table 3-2: SizeAndPrice Table

fkMenuItemID	ItemSize	ItemPrice
1	Large	9.50
1	Medium	7.70
1	Small	6.50
2	Large	9.75
2	Medium	7.75
2	Small	6.75
3	16 fl.oz.	2.25
3	32 fl.oz.	3.75

Specifying that a column is the primary key of a table also ensures that duplicate rows cannot be inserted that have the same value for this key. However, there can be more than one row in the child table with the same value for the foreign key, because this is how the parent (primary key) row links to multiple child (foreign key) rows.

MenuItemID is the primary key for the MenuItems table (shown as shaded), and is, therefore, unique for each item. There will be only one row in this table for each item (each pizza or drink), irrespective of the size. The SizeAndPrice table will contain a row for each size for each item in the MenuItems table, and the column named fkMenuItemID (the prefix "fk" indicates to the developer that it is a foreign key column) will contain the value of the primary key (MenuItemID) from the row it pertains to in the MenuItems table.

Because there will potentially be more that one row for each value of fkMenuItemID, this column alone cannot be the primary key for the SizeAndPrice table. However, the combination of fkMenuItemID and ItemSize will be unique for each row, and so these two columns together will form the primary key for this table (shown as shaded). Setting the primary key prevents the insertion of more than one row into the table with the same primary key value(s), and so helps to maintain integrity of the data.

Applying the Remaining Normalization Rules

The third rule of normalization states that data in the row should not depend on anything other than the primary key of the table. In the example, the values for the ItemType column of the MenuItems table (in the example, these are "Pizza" and "Drink") may be the same for several rows. However, it may be that there are several other types of item available as well. Placing them into the MenuItems table makes it hard if you just want to fetch a list of these types, and it also causes data to be repeated. If you wanted to change the description from "Pizza" to something else, you would have to change every row.

In *third normal form*, the `ItemType` column would contain a key value that linked to a separate table. This separate table would contain one row for each item type, with the key value and the description. While this is the ideal, however, it makes it more difficult to extract the type description of each item (for example, if you wanted to include "Pizza" or "Drink" in the output). With a limited number of types as in this example, you may choose to ignore third normal form, as is the case with the example in this book.

MenuItemID	MenuItemType	ItemName	Toppings	Description
1	1	Margherita	Cheese, Tomato	The basic pizza
2	1	Hawaiian	Ham, Pineapple	Tropical taste
3	2	Cola	[no value]	Crisp and tasty

fkMenuItemID	ItemSize	Item Price
1	Large	9.50
1	Medium	7.70
1	Small	6.50
2	Large	9.75
2	Medium	7.75
2	Small	6.75
3	16 fl.oz.	2.25
3	32 fl.oz.	3.75

fkMenuItem	Description
1	Pizza
2	Drink

There are actually five rules of normalization. The final two help to optimize the data structure and produce the most ideal data format, but at the expense of extra complexity that you will probably not require in your application. Generally, you will apply only the first three rules as described here.

The rules for normalization are the work of E. F. (Ted) Codd working at IBM in the early 1970s, and there are many articles and resources on the Web that explore these rules in depth. Microsoft publishes two at `http://support.microsoft.com/kb/164172/EN-US/` *and* `http://support.microsoft.com/kb/100139/EN-US/`. *Search the Web for "Codd normalization rules" to see more.*

Storing the Orders Data

The second entity that the database must store is order information. The database stores each order placed by a customer. In a real application, you will probably include data on registered customers and parts of the order process. However, in this simple example, you will store only the details of each order as a customer places it.

As with the menu items data, the first approach to the design of the table might be:

Name	Address	Zip Code	Date	Itemi	Qty1	Item2	Qty2	...
J.Smith	3 High St.	123-456	3/7/2005	2	1	3	2	...
C.Sing	NE 4th, 219	222-345	4/5/2005	1	1	3	1	...

However, this obviously suffers the same problem as you saw with the `MenuItems` table. It contains repeated groups of columns (item and price), which not only limit the number of different items on each order to some specific preset amount (the number of item/quantity column pairs in each row) but also results in a lot of empty columns in row where the customer orders only one or two items.

In first normal form, the table contains multiple rows for each order, with an `OrderID` identifying the order that the item belongs to, and the `fkItemID`, `Size`, and `Qty` columns indicating details of this item on the order. The `fkItemID` column relates the ordered item to the rows in the `MenuItems` table (it contains the value of the key from the `MenuItems` row that describes the item). The `Size` column contains the size that the customer selected, as listed in the `SizeAndPrice` table. There will potentially be multiple rows for each order, with the same `OrderID`, and so this column cannot be used as a primary key:

OrderlD	Name	Address	ZipCode	Date	fkltemID	Size	Qty
10	J.Smith	3 High St.	123-456	3/7/2005	2	3	1
11	C.Sing	NE 4th, 219	222-345	4/5/2005	1	1	1
11	C.Sing	NE 4th, 219	222-345	4/5/2005	3	1	2

Again, there are issues here in that there may be multiple rows where there is more than one item on an order, but the `Name`, `Address`, `ZipCode`, and `Date` are the same (i.e., are repeated) for all the rows on the same order.

In second normal form, there is only one row for each order in the `Orders` table (see Table 3-3), and the `OrderID` column becomes the primary key for the table. Each row contains data related only to this order (such as the customer, delivery details, and date), and not data about the individual items (the order lines) for this order.

Table 3-3: Orders Table

OrderID	Name	Address	ZipCode	OrderDate	DeliveryCharge	TotalValue
10	J. Smith	3 High St.	123-456	3/7/2005	3.50	15.50
11	C.Sing	NE 4th, 219	222-345	4/5/2005	5.00	24.25

Notice that this table includes a column for the total cost of the order, even though you can calculate this at any time by adding the individual order item row totals and the delivery charge. This actually contravenes the third rule of normalization, but makes it considerably easier to display order data when required.

If the customer data were stored in other tables, you would instead use a key value in the `Orders` *table that links the order to the appropriate customer. This would remove the repeated name and address details from each order row where the same customer places more than one order.*

The OrderItems Table

The details of each item on a specific order are stored in the `OrderItems` table. In theory, this table needs only to contain the links (the key values) to relate the ordered item to the appropriate rows in the `Orders` and `MenuItems` tables, the size selected by the customer, and the quantity they ordered. However, again it makes it much easier when working with the data to be able to display the item name without having to look it up in the `MenuItems` table.

Therefore, although it contravenes the third rule of normalization, the final design for the `OrderItems` table (see Table 3-4) contains links through the key values to the `Orders` (see Table 3-3) and `MenuItems` table (see Table 3-1), the item size and name as text, the quantity ordered, and the value for just this item on the order. Notice how the first three columns are now required for the primary key (the `OrderID` column). No combination of fewer columns can provide a unique value for this row — for example, the customer could order both a small and a large Hawaiian pizza.

Table 3-4: OrderItems Table

OrderID	fkMenuItemID	ItemSize	ItemName	Quantity	LineValue
10	2	3	Hawaiian	1	9.75
10	3	1	Cola	1	2.25
11	1	2	Margherita	1	7.50
11	3	3	Margherita	2	9.50
11	3	1	Cola	2	2.25

This table structure reduces the repeated content seen in the original design for storing the order data, but still allows easy display of the order details. For example, you can see that by displaying the contents of the appropriate `Orders` table row, followed by the linked rows in the `OrderItems` table, you could easily build a page such as that shown in Figure 3-2, which shows the completed order details page in the example application.

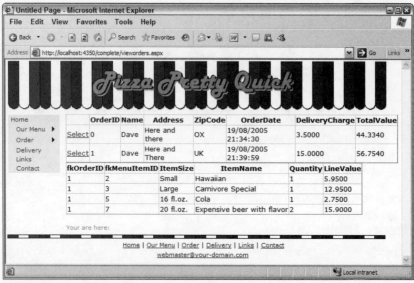

Figure 3-2: The completed order details page in the example application

The Final Database Design

Having learned about the design for the database in the example PPQ application, you will see how to build it in the next section of this chapter. However, before then, it is worth briefly summarizing the final design.

Figure 3-3 shows the tables as they appear in a database diagram (generated by the Database Explorer in VWD). You will see how to create and view diagrams like this later in this chapter. Notice that there is an extra column named `GraphicFileName` in the `MenuItems` table. This is used to store the name of the image (`.gif`) file for that item.

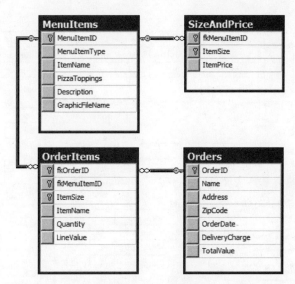

Figure 3-3: The final database design for the PPQ application

You can see in Figure 3-3 relationships drawn between the columns that link each table, with a "key" at one end and an "infinity" symbol at the other end. These indicate that the column in each row at the "key" end is the primary key of that table, and so the values in that column will be unique. The column at the "infinity" end of the relationship can contain more than one row with the matching key value — this is a *one-to-many* relationship. This is what supports application of the normalization rules by allowing removal of repeated data from one table and placement in a linked table.

Figure 3-4 shows an example of the kinds of values stored in the tables. It also shows how the key values link the tables together to maintain the required data model (not all links are shown as arrows). The shaded columns are the primary keys for each table. You can see that, for example, C. Sing living on NE 4th Street has ordered both a Medium and a Large Margherita pizza, and a 16 fl.oz. Cola. The total value of the order, including the 5.00 delivery charge, is 24.25.

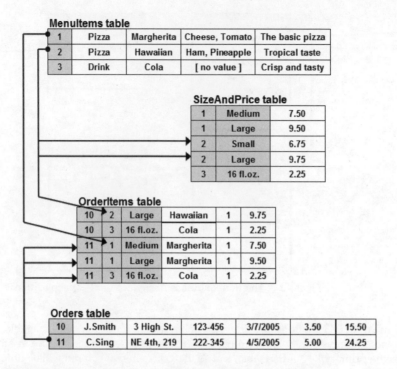

Figure 3-4: An example of row values for the database tables

This data model simplifies the data-storage requirements of the example application, while providing plenty of opportunity to demonstrate data access and storage techniques. It does not follow all the rules for ideal data normalization, but it does provides a reasonable balance between data-storage efficiency and ease of display. While the rules of normalization provide the science of database design, this achievement of balance is where the art comes into play. In your own applications, you will find that achieving this balance becomes easier as you get familiar with the way that ASP.NET works, and how the ways that the data is used affect design decisions.

Creating and Modifying Databases in VWD

Visual Web Developer (VWD) contains several features that make it easy to work with a database, including the Database Explorer window that you first saw in Chapter 1. When you open the example PPQ site in VWD, it attaches the database provided in the examples to SQL Server Express Edition and displays the contents of this database in the Database Explorer window. If the Database Explorer window is not visible, open it from the View menu, or press Ctrl-Alt-S.

If you are following the examples in these chapters, and working with the `skeleton` version of the application, you will see three tables in the Database Explorer window (the version of the application in the `complete` folder contains more tables that you will build yourself in this chapter).

Figure 3-5 shows the three tables expanded to display the names of the columns they contain.

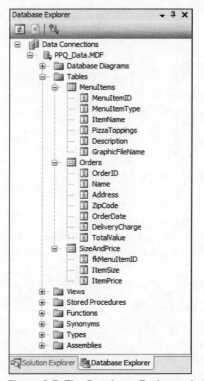

Figure 3-5: The Database Explorer window

If you right-click on a table in the Database Explorer window, you will see a context menu that provides several options for managing the database and the table (see Figure 3-6). This includes adding a new table, trigger, or query, viewing the definition of the selected table, viewing the table's data content, and copying or deleting the table. You can also refresh the display if the database has changed, and display the properties of the table.

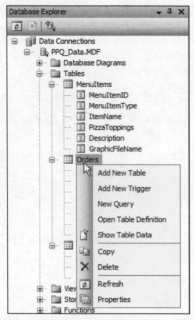

Figure 3-6: Some of the actions available in the Database Explorer window

The Table Designer Window

When you select the Open Table Definition option from the context menu or from the Data menu on the main toolbar, VWD displays the Table Designer. This is where you create and modify the structure of the tables in the database, set the primary key(s), and specify the properties for each column.

Figure 3-7 shows two copies of the Table Designer open, one each for the MenuItems table on the left and the Orders table on the right. You can see how you specify the data type (varchar(25), for example, simply means a 25-character string value), and whether the column can contain NULL values, for each column in the tables.

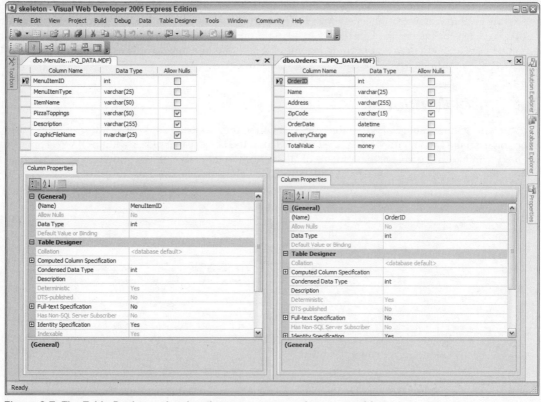

Figure 3-7: The Table Designer showing the `MenuItems` **and** `Orders` **tables**

The first column, named `MenuItemID`, is selected in the `MenuItems` table and the properties for this column are shown in the lower section of this window. This is the primary key of the table, as indicated by the key symbol in the column name grid at the top of the window. It is also an `Identity` (auto-number) column, and so the `Identity Specification` property value is `Yes`. The `Identity Increment` and `Identity Seed` properties, which you find by expanding the `Identity Specification` entry, are set to `1` (the default values), which means that as a row is added to this table the `MenuItemID` will be set automatically to the next available positive number.

The `Orders` table displayed in the right-hand window also shows the data types for each column, and indicates that the `OrderID` column is in the primary key. In this table, there is a column named `OrderDate` that is specified as of type `datetime`, and two columns — `DeliveryCharge` and `TotalValue` — that will contain `money` (currency) values.

These last three columns also have a default value set, which is inserted into the row if the user does not provide a value when creating a new row. The `OrderDate` column (selected in Figure 3-7) has the value `(getdate())` for the `Default Value or Binding` property. This means that the SQL Server function named `getdate` will insert the current date into the column for a new row. The `DeliveryCharge` and `TotalValue` columns have a default value of zero set.

The Query Window

If you select Show Table Data from the context menu in the Database Explorer window (or select this option from the Data menu when a table is selected in the Database Explorer window), VWD opens the Query window and displays the contents of all the rows in that table. When building pages that display data, this is a good way to see what a table actually contains (see Figure 3-8).

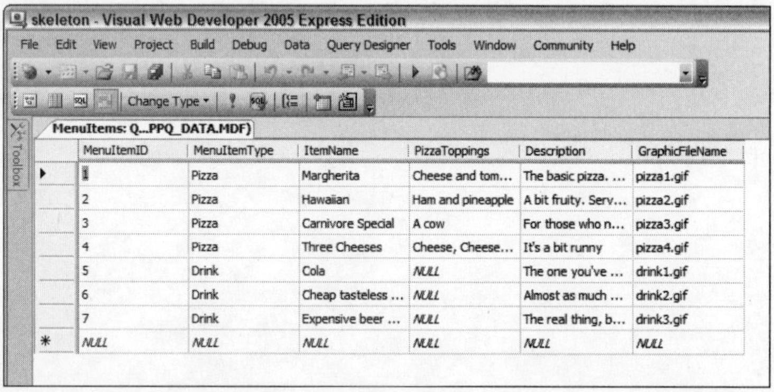

Figure 3-8: Viewing the data in a table from the Database Explorer window

In fact, this is the same window as you saw in Chapter 1 when you experimented with creating a query to extract data from a database table. The three buttons at the top left of the main window switch the display so that it shows the Diagram pane (the tables from which the data is extracted), the Criteria pane (where the columns included in the query are specified and any filtering is applied), and the SQL pane (which displays the SQL statement used to extract the data). Try opening all these panes to see how VWD is able to display the contents of a database table (see Figure 3-9).

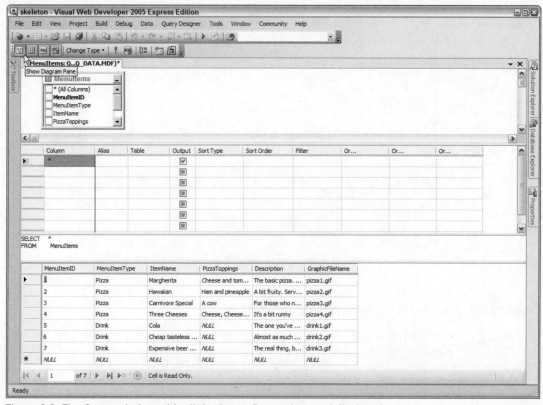

Figure 3-9: The Query window with all the "panes" turned on and displayed

Creating a New Database

In the next section, you will build the remaining table required for the PPQ Web site, and then construct the relationships between this and the other tables already provided in the example database. If you were starting completely from scratch, you would first have to create a new database. For this, you would right-click the top-level entry in the Solution Explorer window (*not* the Database Explorer window!) that shows the path to your Web site and select Add New Item... from the context menu. In the Add new Item dialog that appears, select SQL Database and specify the name, then click Add. This opens the Database Explorer window for the new database, where you can add the tables and other objects you require.

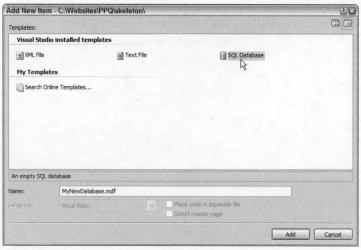

Figure 3-10: Creating a new database in SQL Server Express Edition

Creating the PPQ OrderItems Table

This chapter devoted considerable space to discussing database design issues. It has also looked at how VWD supports database development. In this section, you will create the remaining table required by the PPQ Web site. The MenuItems, SizeAndPrice, and Orders tables are provided in the example database. The one missing table is the OrderItems table.

1. Open the Database Explorer window (press Ctrl-Alt-S if it is not visible) and right-click on the Tables entry. Select Add New Table from the context menu that appears (see Figure 3-11).

Figure 3-11: Database Explorer window

2. This opens the Table Designer window (see Figure 3-12), ready for you to specify the columns for the new table. Type in the column name **fkOrderID**, and select the int data type from the drop-down list. Make sure that you clear the Allow Nulls checkbox as well.

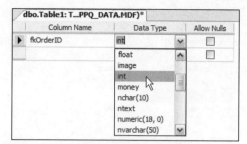

Figure 3-12: Table Designer window

The prefix fk is the accepted way to indicate that this column contains a foreign key. When the rows in two tables are related through key values within specific columns of the tables, the value of the primary key in the parent table row is used in the child table rows that match that parent row. These values in the child table are the foreign keys, and so the column is generally referred to as a foreign key column.

3. Now continue by defining the remaining columns for the OrderItems table. These are:

Column Name	Data Type	Allow Nulls
fkMenuItemID	int	no
ItemSize	varchar(50)	no
ItemName	varchar(50)	yes
Quantity	int	no
LineValue	money	no

You should see the result shown in Figure 3-13.

dbo.Table1: T...PPQ_DATA.MDF)*		
Column Name	Data Type	Allow Nulls
fkOrderID	int	☐
fkMenuItemID	int	☐
ItemSize	varchar(50)	☐
ItemName	varchar(50)	☑
Quantity	int	☐
LineValue	money	☐
		☐

Figure 3 -13: OrderItems data

4. Now you can set the specific properties of the columns in the new table. Select the Quantity column, and in the Column Properties section at the bottom of the Table Designer window find the entry for Default Value or Binding. This is the value for this column in new rows where no specific value is provided when the row is created. Type the value **1** for this property, as shown in Figure 3-14. Then select the LineValue column, and set the Default Value or Binding property value to zero.

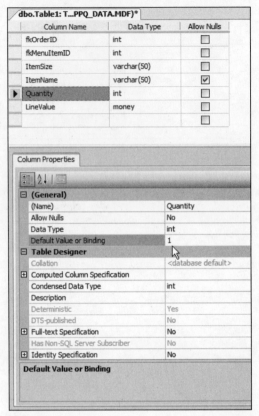

Figure 3-14: `Default Value or Binding` **property**

5. The next step is to specify the primary key for the new table. You will recall from the earlier discussion of the database design that this table requires the first three columns to produce a unique value suitable for the primary key. Click on the square gray row selector button at the extreme left of the first column, (`fkOrderID`) and hold the Shift key down while clicking on the row selector for the third column (`ItemSize`) so that the top three columns in the list are selected. Then click the Set Primary Key button on the toolbar (as shown in Figure 3-15), or right-click and select Set Primary Key from the context menu. Alternatively, you can select the Set Primary Key option from the main Table Designer menu. Whichever method you choose, a key symbol appears on the rows to indicate that, together, they form the primary key for this table.

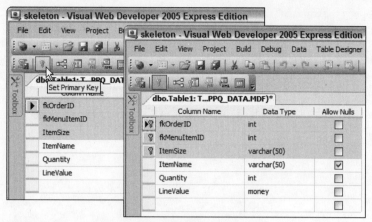

Figure 3-15: Selecting the Set Primary Key button

6. The primary key will automatically ensure that rows will appear in the order of the values in the three columns that form the primary key, unless you specify otherwise in a query. However, sometimes it is useful to create indexes on other columns to speed up processing of queries. For example, if you intend to execute many queries against this table that use the value in the ItemName column, you might want to create an index on it. To do this, right-click anywhere inside the Table Designer window and select Indexes/Keys from the context menu (as shown in Figure 3-16), or select Indexes/Keys from the main Table Designer menu.

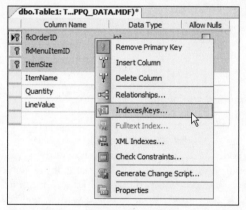

Figure 3-16: Selecting Indexes/Keys from the context menu

7. This opens the Indexes/Keys dialog, which shows the index named `PK_Table1` that was created automatically when the primary key was set on the table. Click the Add button at the bottom of the Indexes/Keys dialog to create a new index named `IX_Table1`. Make sure that this new index is selected and go to the `Columns` property in the right-hand window. The first column in the table is selected by default, so click the "three dots" (. . .) button to open the Index Columns dialog and select the `ItemName` column. The default sort order is `Ascending`, as shown in Figure 3-17, which is what you want. You can change this if you want items indexed in reverse order (for example, with a column containing dates or monetary values).

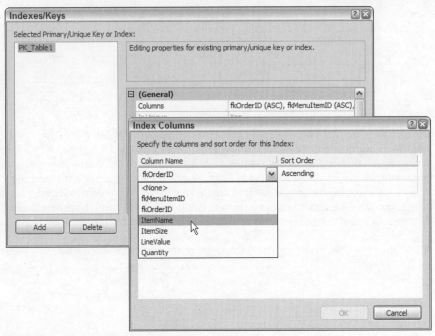

Figure 3-17: Ascending sort order

8. Click OK to close the `Index Columns` dialog and go back to the Indexes/Keys dialog (see Figure 3-18). Notice the `Is Unique` property of the new index. Because multiple rows in the table can contain the same value for `ItemName` (the name of the item ordered), and can also contain `NULL` values (because you did not turn this off in the column designer window), the values will not be unique, and so the index cannot be unique either. The `Is Unique` property must be `No`. For a primary key column, however, or any other column where you specify only unique values can exist, you could create a unique index.

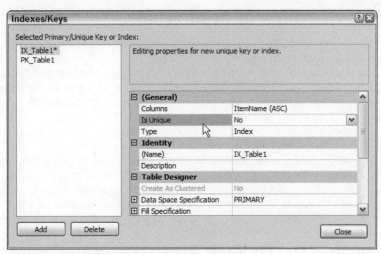

Figure 3-18: Indexes/Keys dialog

An index can be created over multiple columns if required. In the `Index Columns` *dialog, you just add more columns to the grid in the same way as you add columns to the table in the Table Designer window. Click in the empty row below the last Column Name and another drop-down list appears allowing you to select the other columns that will be part of the index. If you go to the Indexes/Keys dialog and select the* `PK_OrderItems` *index, you will see the three columns that form this index in the* `Columns` *property of the index. You can create as many indexes as you like on a table, but each one has an effect on performance when you add or remove rows in the table. Therefore, you should only create indexes that you will use regularly in queries or when extracting data.*

9. Now you can save the new table definition by clicking the Save button on the main toolbar, or by selecting Save Table1 or Save All from the File menu. A dialog appears asking for the name of the new table. Enter **OrderItems** and click OK. The new table appears in the Data Explorer window (see Figure 3-19).

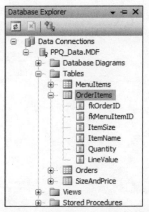

Figure 3-19: New table in Data Explorer window

Defining Relationships between Tables

You have now completed the tables for the PPQ database, but there is still the task of defining the *constraints* that implement the relationships between these tables. Just because you created a primary key and a foreign key column in your tables does not mean that SQL Server will respect this. It will freely allow you to add rows to the child table where the foreign key value does not match any parent row primary key, and remove parent rows where there are existing matching child rows.

Both of these situations will cause the data to be inconsistent, because *orphan rows* (that is, child rows with no matching parent row) will exist. Constraints prevent this happening by checking for the presence of matching primary key and foreign key values in the rows before allowing new child rows to be added or parent rows to be deleted. In doing so, they help to maintain *referential integrity* of the data. In VWD, you create constraints by specifying the relationships between tables — using either the Table Designer or a database diagram. The easier way is to use a database diagram, but before exploring this in more detail, the following section shows briefly how it is done in the Table Designer.

Defining Relationships in the Table Designer

With a table open in the Table Designer, you can right-click on the Designer window and select Relationships to open the Foreign Key Relationships dialog. This shows any constraints and relationships defined for the selected table. Click Add to a new relationship then select the `Tables and Columns Specification` property in the right-hand window of this dialog and click the three dots (. . .) button to open the Tables and Columns dialog (see Figure 3-20).

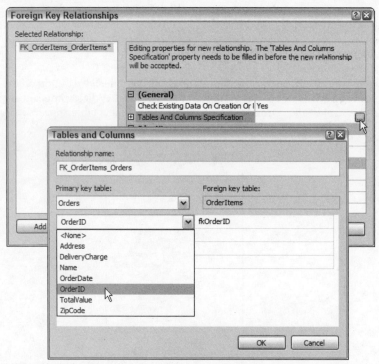

Figure 3-20: Setting the Tables and Columns Specification for a table relationship

In the Tables and Columns dialog, you specify the primary key table, and select the column in that table that contains the primary key for this relationship. Then you select the column in the current table that contains the foreign key. After clicking OK, the Foreign Key Relationships dialog shows the properties of the new relationship. Notice how the `Tables and Columns Specification` indicates a relationship between the `Orders` and `OrderItems` tables (see Figure 3-21), using the `OrderID` primary key and the `fkOrderID` foreign key columns.

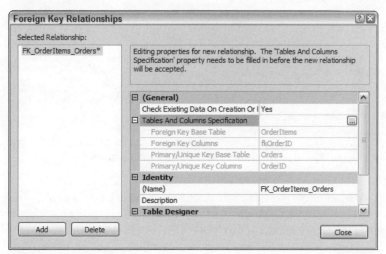

Figure 3-21: Viewing the `Tables and Columns Specification` **for a table relationship**

Relationships also control how the database will react to changes to the rows in the parent table. This includes deletion of existing parent rows, and (although it is not good practice to do so) changes to the primary key values in the parent table rows. The three options for the Delete Rule and Update Rule (see Figure 3-22) are:

Rule Action	Deleted Parent Row	Updated Primary Key in Parent Row
Cascade	Any related rows in the child table are deleted.	The value in the foreign key column of any related child rows is updated to the new primary key value.
Set Null	The value in the foreign key column of any related child rows is deleted so that the column contains NULL.	The value in the foreign key column of any related child rows is deleted so that the column contains NULL.
Set Default	The value in the foreign key column of any related child rows is replaced by the default value for that column if one is specified, or NULL otherwise.	The value in the foreign key column of any related child rows is replaced by the default value for that column if one is specified, or NULL otherwise.

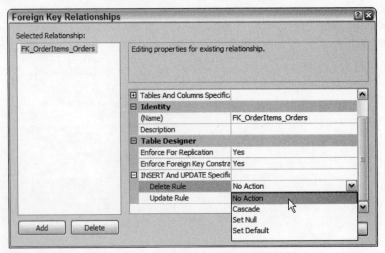

Figure 3-22: The Delete Rule and Update Rule Actions

In general, you should avoid ever changing the value of a primary key in any existing row, and handle deletes to a parent table in your code so that you correctly manage the deletion of linked child rows. Doing this means that you can leave the Delete Rule and Update Rule set to No Action. However, the other actions can prove useful in maintaining data integrity in cases where you do not directly manage updates and deletes in your code, for example when using a database row editor or client database tool such as Microsoft Access. The rules will allow you to edit and delete rows, while still maintaining database integrity.

Defining Relationships with a Database Diagram

Having seen the principles of relationships between tables in a database, you will now add the two relationships required for the PPQ database. You created a new table named OrderItems earlier in this chapter, and this table must be related to the existing tables to force referential integrity to be maintained when orders are added, updated, or deleted. You will create these relationships using a database diagram, and you will see that this makes the process much easier than using the Table Designer discussed in the previous section.

1. In the Database Explorer window, right-click on the database diagrams entry and select Add New Diagram (see Figure 3-23).

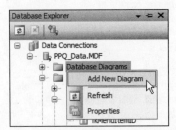

Figure 3-23: Selecting database diagrams in the Database Explorer

2. The Database Diagram window opens, together with the Add Table dialog. Click on `MenuItems`, hold down the Shift key, and click on `SizeAndPrice` to select all four tables. Then click Add (see Figure 3-24).

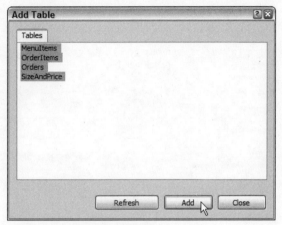

Figure 3-24: Add Table window

3. You will see the four tables appear in the Database Diagram window. You will probably have to drag them around to get a tidy layout like that shown in Figure 3-25. Notice that there is an existing relationship between the `SizeAndPrice` table and the `MenuItems` table. This is already present in the example database. You can click on the joining line that represents the relationship and drag it around to get a neat display — it is a good idea to position it so that it points to the appropriate columns in the table as in Figure 3-25. The Database Designer does not do this automatically.

Figure 3-25: Joining line

4. To create a relationship between tables, you drag the primary key column from one table onto the foreign key column in the other table. You need to create a relationship between the MenuItems table and the OrderItems table, so click on the gray "row selector" button at the left-hand end of the MenuItemID column in the MenuItems table, and then drag it onto the row selector in the fkMenuItemID column in the OrderItems table. This opens both the Foreign Key Relationship and the Tables and Columns dialogs (see Figure 3-26).

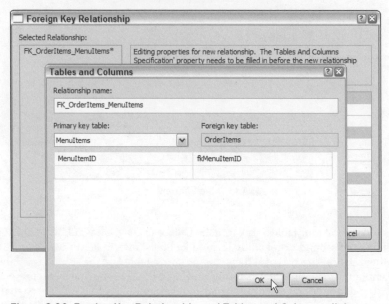

Figure 3-26: Foreign Key Relationship and Tables and Columns dialogs

5. Notice that VWD automatically selects the correct tables and columns in this dialog (see Figure 3-26) — it does not do this when you open the Foreign Key Relationship dialog from the Table Designer. All you need do is confirm that it has selected the correct tables and columns in the Tables and Columns dialogs (if you dragged the correct columns in the diagram window, it will have done so), and click OK. Then, in the Foreign Key Relationship dialog, click OK to create the new relationship (see Figure 3-27).

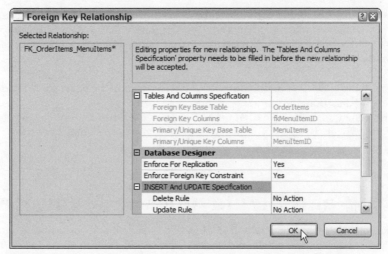

Figure 3-27: Automatically selecting the correct tables and columns

6. Now repeat the process to create a relationship between the Orders and OrderItems tables. Drag the OrderID column in the Orders table onto the fkOrderID column in the OrderItems table, and click OK in the Tables and Columns and Foreign Key Relationship dialogs. The result will be a diagram like that shown in Figure 3-28.

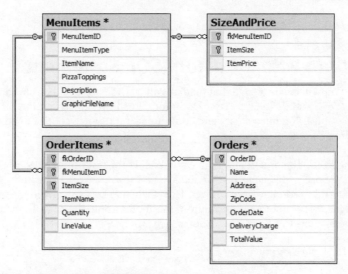

Figure 3-28: Table relationships

7. Now close the Database Diagram window. You will be prompted to save the diagram (you can accept the default name). The Database Diagram window then adds the constraints that implement the new relationships to the `MenuItems`, `OrderItems`, and `Orders` tables, and prompts you to save these changes to the tables.

You now have all the tables you require for the PPQ Web site, and the next step is to add a page that displays the menu data from the `MenuItems` and `SizeAndPrice` tables. However, this is not as straightforward as the technique you saw in Chapter 1 of just dragging the table onto a page, because the data must come from two related tables. To finish this chapter, you will see how to create a page that accesses data in more than one table.

Extracting and Displaying the Menu Items

In this final section of the chapter, you will create a simple page that extracts all the data from the `MenuItems` and `SizeAndPrice` tables, and displays it in a grid. Because the data is in two tables, you will need to join the tables together to get the rows you need. There are a few ways of doing this, all based on a SQL statement that implements a table join. You will see three possibilities in the remainder of this chapter:

❑ Using a custom SQL statement

❑ Using a stored procedure

❑ Using a database view

The first of these naturally leads to the other two, as you will see later in the chapter.

Extracting Data with a Custom SQL Statement

In this example, you will create a page that displays all the items available from the PPQ site, using the two tables `MenuItems` and `SizeAndPrice`. These contain all the data about the PPQ menu, but as it is divided over two tables, you must create and configure a data source control to access and combine this data into the correct format.

1. Open the `skeleton` project and add a new Web Form to it using the New File . . . option on the File menu. Specify the name **TestMenu2.aspx** for the new Web Form in the `Add New Item` dialog, and click Add to add it to your project. Then switch to Design view in the main editing window, and drag a `SqlDataSource` control from the Toolbox onto the page. In the pop-up SqlDataSource Tasks pane, select Configure Data Source (see Figure 3-29).

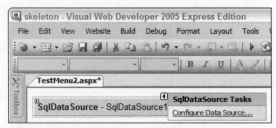

Figure 3-29: Selecting Configure Data Source

2. This starts the Configure Data Source Wizard. In the first page, select the existing connection string (see Figure 3-30). This connection string was automatically created and added to the project when you carried out the examples in Chapter 1. It is actually stored in the `Web` `.config` file for the application.

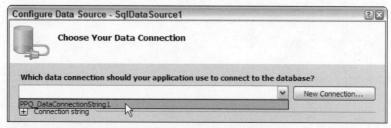

Figure 3-30: Selecting an existing connection string

3. The next page in the wizard allows you to select the object in the database that will provide the data for the `SqlDataSource` control. However, you can select only one table (as shown in the left-hand side of Figure 3-31). You need to include data from two tables, so select the option to specify a custom SQL statement or stored procedure, and click Next.

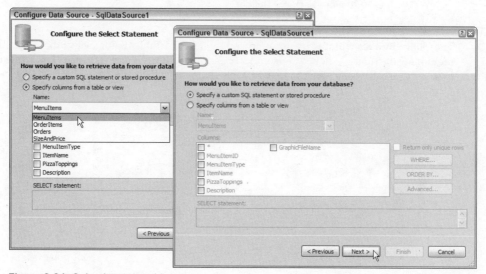

Figure 3-31: Selecting one table

4. The next page in the wizard allows you to type in or create the SQL statement you need. The easiest way to build a SQL statement if you are not familiar with SQL is through the Query Builder. Click the Query Builder . . . button in the wizard (see Figure 3-32).

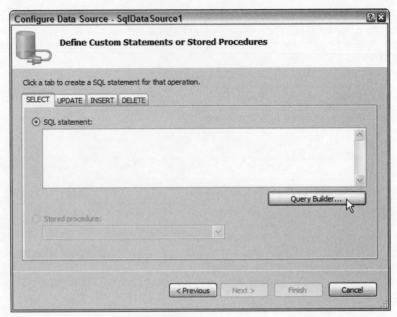

Figure 3-32: Using the Query Builder

5.   The Query Builder window opens, followed by the Add Table dialog. Select the two tables you require for the query—MenuItems and SizeAndPrice. Hold down the Ctrl key while clicking to select more than one item in the Add Table dialog (see Figure 3-33).

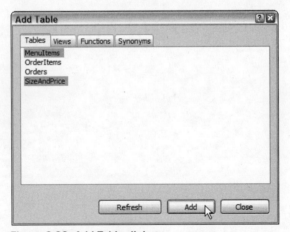

Figure 3-33: Add Table dialog

6. The two tables now appear in the top section of the Query Builder window. However, the relationship between them is not enforced. This allows you to create a relationship for this query that differs from the one in the database that is there to maintain referential integrity. To create the relationship you need for this query, click on the `MenuItemID` column in the `MenuItems` table, and drag it onto the `fkMenuItems` column in the `SizeAndPrice` table (see Figure 3-34).

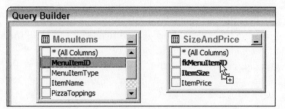

Figure 3-34: Dragging the `MenuItemID` **column**

7. You will see the relationship between the two tables appear in the Query Builder window. Select all the columns in the two tables except for the two "`* (All Columns)`" entries and the `fkMenuItemID` foreign key column (see Figure 3-35). You can either tick the boxes in the tables, or drag the columns onto the Criteria grid below them.

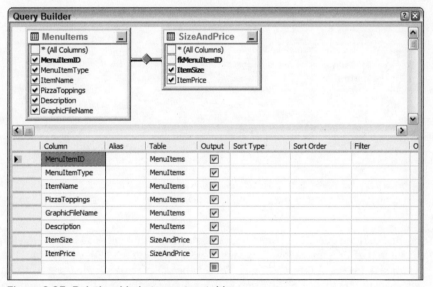

Figure 3-35: Relationship between two tables

Right-clicking the diamond-shaped "icon" on the link opens a context menu where you can change the properties of the relationship. The default for a relationship is an `INNER JOIN` on the tables, which means that a row will be included in the results only if there is both a parent row and a child row with the same value for the columns that provide the relationship. In this example, a row will be present in the results only if there is a row in the `SizeAndPrice` table with the same key value in the `fkMenuItemID` column as it exists in the `MenuItemID` column of a row in the `MenuItems` table.

However, you can specify that the query will retrieve all the rows from one of the tables (irrespective of whether there is a matching row in the related table), and leave the columns empty where there is no matching row in the other table. This kind of relationship is a LEFT JOIN *or a* RIGHT JOIN, *depending on which table provides all of its rows. The context menu options allow you to specify "Select All Rows from MenuItems" or "Select All Rows from* SizeAndPrice." *However, you need the default* INNER JOIN *in this example, so you do not need to change any of the properties.*

8. Now you can specify the sort order for the results. In the SortType column of the Criteria grid, select Descending for the MenuItemType column, Ascending for ItemName, and Ascending for ItemPrice. The Query Builder automatically sets the SortOrder column as you specify the sort type, but you can change the order if you wish. In this case, the results will be sorted first by descending item type ("Pizza" then "Drink"), then by name, then by ascending price (see Figure 3-36).

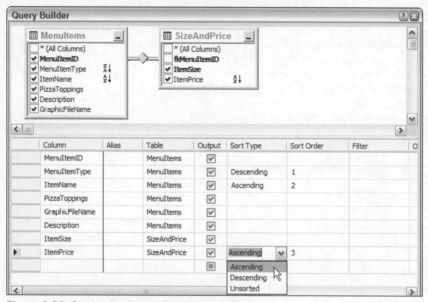

Figure 3-36: Sorting by descending item type

9. As you build the query, the equivalent SQL statement that will be executed to extract the data is shown in the SQL pane below the Criteria grid. You can see in Figure 3-37 the columns that are included in the result (in the SELECT clause), the tables that provide the data (in the FROM clause, including the INNER JOIN), and the ordering of the resulting rows (in the ORDER BY clause). Click the Execute Query button at the bottom of the Query Builder window to see the results. You have succeeded in creating a list of all the items on the menu of the PPQ Web site, even though they are stored in two separate tables!

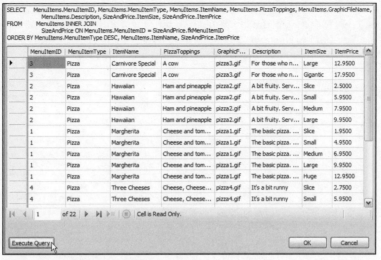

```
SELECT   MenuItems.MenuItemID, MenuItems.MenuItemType, MenuItems.ItemName, MenuItems.PizzaToppings, MenuItems.GraphicFileName,
         MenuItems.Description, SizeAndPrice.ItemSize, SizeAndPrice.ItemPrice
FROM     MenuItems INNER JOIN
         SizeAndPrice ON MenuItems.MenuItemID = SizeAndPrice.fkMenuItemID
ORDER BY MenuItems.MenuItemType DESC, MenuItems.ItemName, SizeAndPrice.ItemPrice
```

	MenuItemID	MenuItemType	ItemName	PizzaToppings	GraphicF...	Description	ItemSize	ItemPrice
▶	3	Pizza	Carnivore Special	A cow	pizza3.gif	For those who n...	Large	12.9500
	3	Pizza	Carnivore Special	A cow	pizza3.gif	For those who n...	Gigantic	17.9500
	2	Pizza	Hawaiian	Ham and pineapple	pizza2.gif	A bit fruity. Serv...	Slice	2.5000
	2	Pizza	Hawaiian	Ham and pineapple	pizza2.gif	A bit fruity. Serv...	Small	5.9500
	2	Pizza	Hawaiian	Ham and pineapple	pizza2.gif	A bit fruity. Serv...	Medium	7.9500
	2	Pizza	Hawaiian	Ham and pineapple	pizza2.gif	A bit fruity. Serv...	Large	9.9500
	1	Pizza	Margherita	Cheese and tom...	pizza1.gif	The basic pizza. ...	Slice	1.9500
	1	Pizza	Margherita	Cheese and tom...	pizza1.gif	The basic pizza. ...	Small	4.9500
	1	Pizza	Margherita	Cheese and tom...	pizza1.gif	The basic pizza. ...	Medium	6.9500
	1	Pizza	Margherita	Cheese and tom...	pizza1.gif	The basic pizza. ...	Large	9.9500
	1	Pizza	Margherita	Cheese and tom...	pizza1.gif	The basic pizza. ...	Huge	12.9500
	4	Pizza	Three Cheeses	Cheese, Cheese...	pizza4.gif	It's a bit runny	Slice	2.7500
	4	Pizza	Three Cheeses	Cheese, Cheese...	pizza4.gif	It's a bit runny	Small	5.9500

|◄ ◄ | 1 | of 22 | ► ►| ►| | ■ | Cell is Read Only.

Execute Query   OK   Cancel

Figure 3-37: SQL statement execution

10. Click OK in the Query Builder window to go back to the Configure Data Source Wizard. You will see that it now contains the SQL statement you just created, so you can click Next to continue (see Figure 3-38).

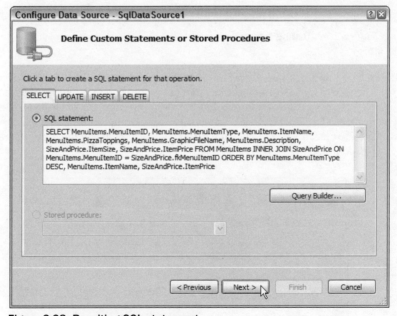

Configure Data Source - SqlDataSource1

Define Custom Statements or Stored Procedures

Click a tab to create a SQL statement for that operation.

SELECT | UPDATE | INSERT | DELETE

◉ SQL statement:

```
SELECT MenuItems.MenuItemID, MenuItems.MenuItemType, MenuItems.ItemName,
MenuItems.PizzaToppings, MenuItems.GraphicFileName, MenuItems.Description,
SizeAndPrice.ItemSize, SizeAndPrice.ItemPrice FROM MenuItems INNER JOIN SizeAndPrice ON
MenuItems.MenuItemID = SizeAndPrice.fkMenuItemID ORDER BY MenuItems.MenuItemType
DESC, MenuItems.ItemName, SizeAndPrice.ItemPrice
```

Query Builder...

◯ Stored procedure:

< Previous | Next > | Finish | Cancel

Figure 3-38: Resulting SQL statement

11. In the next page of the Configure Data Source Wizard, you can test the query you entered (see Figure 3-39). In fact, you already tested it in the Query Builder window, but this page is useful because you can test the query if you created it by selecting a table, or typed the SQL statement you want directly into the "SQL statement:" text box in the previous page of the wizard.

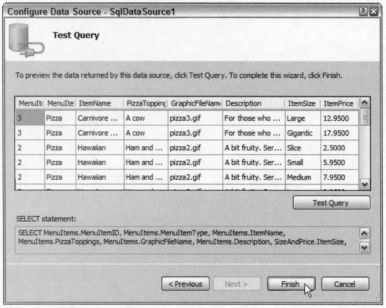

Figure 3-39: Testing a query

12. Click Finish in the Configure Data Source Wizard, and you are back in the editing window in VWD. The next stage is to add a control to display the data that the `SqlDataSource` will return, so drag a `GridView` control from the Toolbox onto the page. In the GridView Tasks pane that appears, choose `SqlDataSource1` — the `SqlDataSource` control you just configured (see Figure 3-40). You can also use the Auto Format . . . option to change the appearance of the `GridView` control.

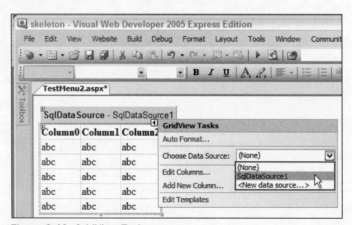

Figure 3-40: GridView Tasks pane

13. Now press the F5 key, or click the Run icon on the main VWD toolbar, and you will see the rows that are returned by the custom SQL statement you created displayed in the `GridView` control (see Figure 3-41). This proves that it is possible to reassemble the data from separate tables at any time to get the set of rows you want. The rules of normalization that you followed in the design of the database give the benefits of improved storage efficiency within the database and simplified data updates (you can clearly see the repeated data in Figure 3-41). Yet you can still extract data in the format and structure you need using a custom SQL statement.

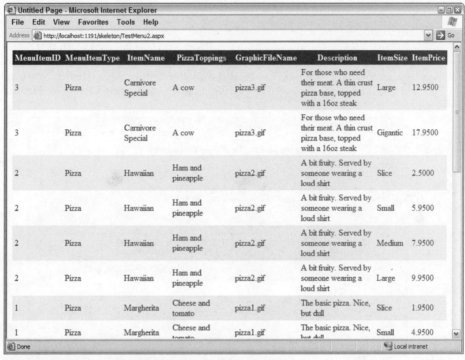

Figure 3-41: Rows returned by the custom SQL statement

Creating a Stored Procedure

The previous example used a SQL statement to extract the data required for the `GridView` control. However, this is not generally the best technique for a production application. If you switch to Source view, you will see that the SQL statement is stored in the page as the value of the `SelectCommand` attribute of the `SqlDataSource` control.

Instead, you can use a stored procedure to extract the data you want. A *stored procedure* is, as the name suggests, a query stored within the database that returns the results required to create the output you want. This approach hides the structure of the database and tables from the user, as they just execute the stored procedure and get back a rowset (a series of rows of data) or whatever result the stored procedure is designed to generate. It is also more efficient because the database server can precompile the stored procedure, and reuse the compiled code. In addition, in enterprise-level databases, the administrator can set access permissions on the tables so that users can only run a stored procedure, and not access the data in the tables directly.

There are also benefits from separating the user interface code (the Web Form) from the data access code when using a stored procedure. Providing that the stored procedure returns the same results, the actual structure of the underlying tables can change as required — without requiring any changes to the pages that access the data.

A stored procedure that returns a rowset is, effectively, just a query. The code in the stored procedure is one or more SQL statements or other commands (called Transact SQL or T-SQL). You can use the same SQL statement you generated with the Query Builder in the Configure Data Source Wizard to create a stored procedure for the example page you saw in the previous section.

1. Start the Configure Data Source Wizard from the Configure Data Source link in the SqlDataSource Tasks pane (opened from the arrow icon that appears when you mouse over the `SqlDataSource` control in `Design` view). Click Next until you get to the "Define Custom Statements or Stored Procedures" page, and copy the custom SQL statement you created with the Query Builder to the clipboard by highlighting it and pressing Ctrl-C (see Figure 3-42).

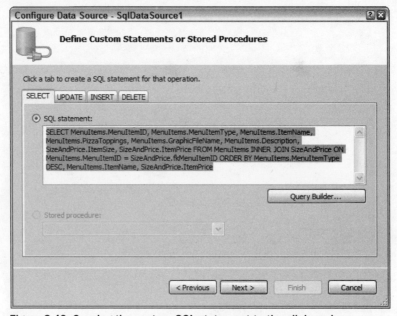

Figure 3-42: Copying the custom SQL statement to the clipboard

2. Now click Cancel to close the Configure Data Source Wizard, go to the Database Explorer window, right-click the `Stored Procedures` entry, and select Add New Stored Procedure from the context menu that appears (see Figure 3-43).

Figure 3-43: Selecting Add New Stored Procedures

3. This opens the stored procedure editor in the main window, and you can paste the SQL statement into the procedure outline that is provided. The text in green is just comments or placeholders (the characters "/*" and "*/" are comment delimiters in a stored procedure) and can be ignored for now. Make sure you change the name of the stored procedure in the first line to dbo.usp_GetAllMenuItems, as shown in Figure 3-44.

```
dbo.StoredPro...PQ_DATA.MDF)*  TestMenu2.aspx
CREATE PROCEDURE dbo.usp_GetAllMenuItems
   /*
   (
   @parameter1 int = 5,
   @parameter2 datatype OUTPUT
   )
   */
AS
   /* SET NOCOUNT ON */

SELECT MenuItems.MenuItemID, MenuItems.MenuItemType,
       MenuItems.ItemName, MenuItems.PizzaToppings,
       MenuItems.GraphicFileName, MenuItems.Description,
       SizeAndPrice.ItemSize, SizeAndPrice.ItemPrice
FROM MenuItems INNER JOIN SizeAndPrice
     ON MenuItems.MenuItemID = SizeAndPrice.fkMenuItemID
ORDER BY MenuItems.MenuItemType DESC,
         MenuItems.ItemName, SizeAndPrice.ItemPrice

RETURN
```

Figure 3-44: Changing the name of the stored procedure

The prefix dbo *for the stored procedure name indicates that the owner of the stored procedure (within the database) is the built-in default system user. The actual name you use to refer to the procedure later will generally not include this prefix. The characters "*usp*" at the start of the name is a convention that indicates this is a "user" stored procedure (as opposed to a "system" stored procedure). System stored procedures start with "*sp*" or "*xp*" and so using a different prefix makes it easier to see which stored procedures are yours and which were created by VWD or the database itself.*

4. Save the new stored procedure and close the stored procedure window. Then, in the Configure Data Source Wizard, change the settings in the "Define Custom Statements or Stored Procedures" page to specify "Stored procedure:" as the source of the data, and select the new stored procedure in the drop-down list (see Figure 3-45).

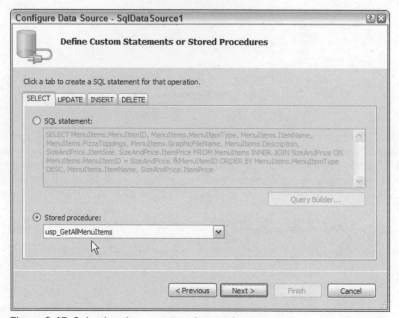

Figure 3-45: Selecting the new stored procedure

5. Now click Next and then Finish to complete the Configure Data Source Wizard and go back to the TestMenu2.aspx page in VWD. You will see that the page looks the same, and you can run it to prove that you get exactly the same results. However, if you now switch to Source view, you will see that the SelectCommand attribute of the SqlDataSource control just specifies the name of the stored procedure.

Using a View Instead of a Table or Stored Procedure

Another approach to exposing data from more than one table as a single rowset for display using the controls in VWD and ASP.NET 2.0 is through a *database view*. You create a view in much the same way as you do a stored procedure. Right-click the entry named Views in the Database Explorer window and select Add New View from the context menu that appears.

This opens a Query Builder window, where you add the tables and specify the columns and sorting order just as you did when creating a custom SQL statement. Alternatively, you can just copy the custom SQL statement from the Configure Data Source Wizard (as in the previous example) and paste it into the SQL pane of the Query Builder. Then save the new view as AllMenuData.

Now, if you work through the Configure Data Source Wizard again in the page you used for the previous example, you can specify that the data will come from a table or a view, and select the new view you just created (see Figure 3-46). This displays all the columns in the view, and you can select the ones you want. For the purpose of this example, you should select all of them.

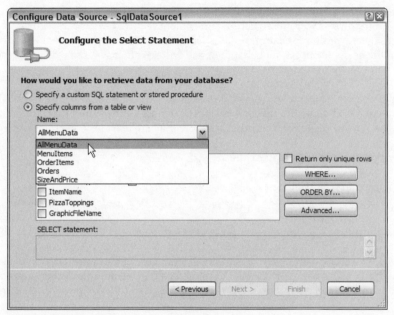

Figure 3-46: Specifying a view as the data source

Now, when you go back to the TestMenu2.aspx page, it looks just the same. You can run the page, and again there is no difference from what you saw using a custom SQL statement or a stored procedure. However, now the data is coming from a view, and if you switch to Source view you will see that the SelectCommand attribute of the SqlDataSource control specifies the SQL statement SELECT * FROM [AllMenuData]. This means that SQL Server executes the SQL statement you specified to create the view, and then returns all the columns. The structure of the database is hidden from the user, and SQL Server can even cache the results of executing the SQL statement that creates the view.

Summary

In this chapter, you have seen the process of designing a simple database to support an application such as the Pizza Pretty Quick (PPQ) example Web site. You saw how the principles of normalization can be applied to a table structure that, at first, appears to be obvious, so that storage and processing efficiency are optimized. It also means that there is no need to perform multiple updates when one item of data changes, as redundant and unnecessary repeated data is removed from the tables.

After settling on a final design for the PPQ example database tables, you saw how you can use the tools provided in VWD to build tables, set the properties, and create relationships between them. These are the fundamental tasks for working with a database, and VWD is a great environment for accomplishing them all.

With the database complete, you then saw how you can take the data split over multiple tables and reassemble it into rowsets with the structure and content required to power the pages of the site. In this chapter, you saw only a simple example — a list of all the menu items complete with description, size, and price. In the next and subsequent chapters, you will see other ways of extracting the data, assembling it into rowsets, and using it to create more attractive and useful pages.

The chapter ended with a discussion of the different ways you can expose data from a database. The three fundamental techniques are through custom SQL statements, stored procedures, and database views. You saw how to create each of these, and how they are used in VWD to power your Web pages.

In summary, the topics of this chapter were:

- ❑ Designing the PPQ database
- ❑ Using VWD to create and modify a database
- ❑ Building a page to extract data from related tables

In Chapter 4, you will see a lot more ways to display data using the controls available in VWD and ASP.NET 2.0. You will also see how to create nested data output, and how other types of data display controls and templates can be used to build more attractive and useful data-driven pages.

Accessing and Displaying Data

In the previous chapters, you have glimpsed some of the power of Visual Web Developer (VWD) and ASP.NET 2.0. Using just drag-and-drop techniques, and the VWD wizards, you have built the initial parts of the example PPQ Web site without writing any code, and without having to know anything other than the basics of HTML and Web page design. Yet, the pages contain interactive content such as fly-out menus, and data extracted from a database—that you can even edit within the page!

This demonstrates just how productive the combination of VWD and ASP.NET is. However, while you can build quite complex pages, and even whole Web sites, without ever having to look at the code that VWD creates, it is still a good idea to understand at least the basics of what is happening when you build pages like this. It helps you to adapt the code that VWD produces to maximize performance and to extend the capabilities of the pages.

In this and the next chapter, you will explore just one area where an appreciation of the workings of ASP.NET can help you build better pages. In this chapter, you will see:

❑   How the data source and data display controls in ASP.NET work

❑   How templates can improve the display of data

❑   How you can use other types of data display controls

To start the chapter, you will see how you can improve the output generated by the test pages you created at the end of Chapter 3, which display the pizzas and drinks available from the PPQ Web site.

Data Source and Data Display Controls

In Chapter 1, you saw how VWD and ASP.NET can automatically create a page that displays rows from a database, and allow you to select, edit, and delete the rows in the database table.

Figure 4-1 shows this page as you last saw it at the end of Chapter 2. You created it simply by dragging a table from the Database Explorer in VWD onto the page and then setting some properties using the GridView Tasks pane, such as enabling paging, selection, editing, and deleting of rows.

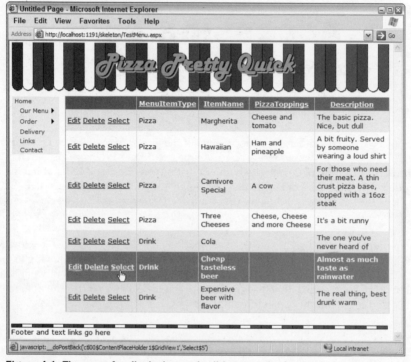

Figure 4-1: The page for displaying and editing rows in the `MenuItems` table

In Chapter 3, you saw how you can join two tables in the database together, then extract and display the data from these two tables. In this case, you used the Configure Data Source Wizard to set the properties of the data source control to which the `GridView` control is bound. The `GridView` control automatically extracts the rows from the data source control and displays them in the resulting page (see Figure 4-2).

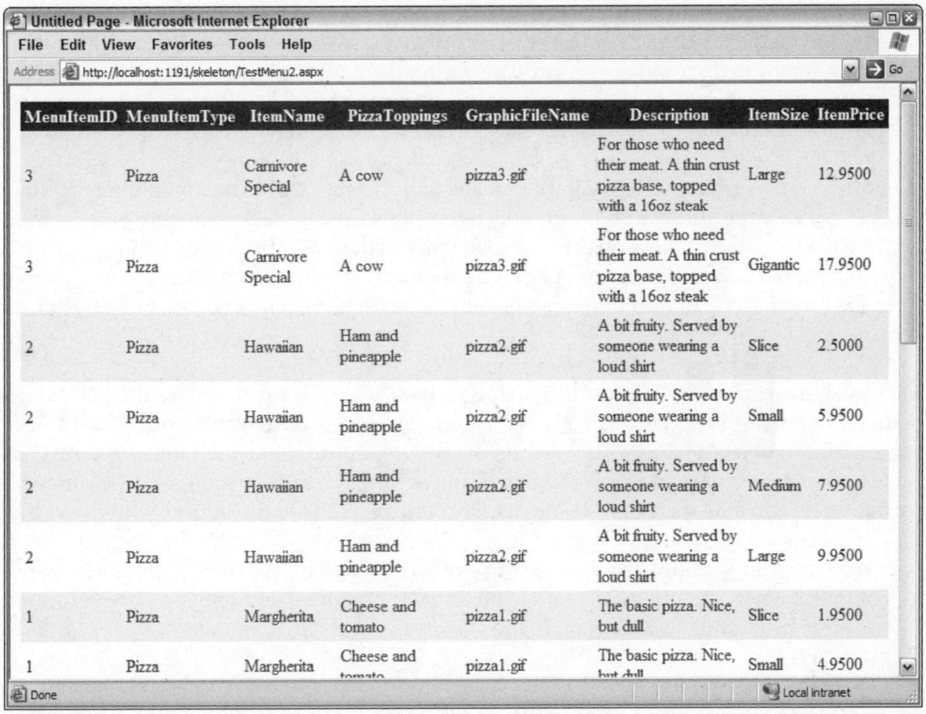

MenuItemID	MenuItemType	ItemName	PizzaToppings	GraphicFileName	Description	ItemSize	ItemPrice
3	Pizza	Carnivore Special	A cow	pizza3.gif	For those who need their meat. A thin crust pizza base, topped with a 16oz steak	Large	12.9500
3	Pizza	Carnivore Special	A cow	pizza3.gif	For those who need their meat. A thin crust pizza base, topped with a 16oz steak	Gigantic	17.9500
2	Pizza	Hawaiian	Ham and pineapple	pizza2.gif	A bit fruity. Served by someone wearing a loud shirt	Slice	2.5000
2	Pizza	Hawaiian	Ham and pineapple	pizza2.gif	A bit fruity. Served by someone wearing a loud shirt	Small	5.9500
2	Pizza	Hawaiian	Ham and pineapple	pizza2.gif	A bit fruity. Served by someone wearing a loud shirt	Medium	7.9500
2	Pizza	Hawaiian	Ham and pineapple	pizza2.gif	A bit fruity. Served by someone wearing a loud shirt	Large	9.9500
1	Pizza	Margherita	Cheese and tomato	pizza1.gif	The basic pizza. Nice, but dull	Slice	1.9500
1	Pizza	Margherita	Cheese and tomato	pizza1.gif	The basic pizza. Nice, but dull	Small	4.9500

Figure 4-2: The page from Chapter 3 that joins the `MenuItems` and `SizeAndPrice` tables

It is obvious that the combination of a data source control and a `GridView` control is responsible for connecting to the database, extracting the data, and displaying it. In this section of the chapter, you will explore this relationship in a little more depth, so that you can take advantage of the extended capabilities it offers for improving the appearance and efficiency of the process.

The Object-Oriented and Event-Driven Architecture

ASP.NET is an object-oriented and event-driven programming environment. In fact, the whole .NET Framework is built up of code classes that, when instantiated, create the objects you use in your pages. These objects include the ASP.NET `Page` itself, and the various controls (such as `Image`, `Hyperlink`, `Menu`, `DataGrid`, and `SqlDataSource`) that you have used so far in the example PPQ site. Each of these objects was instantiated by a declaration visible in the ASP.NET page in Source view, for example:

```
<asp:SqlDataSource ID="SqlDataSource1" runat="server"
   ConnectionString="<%$ ConnectionStrings:PPQ_DataConnectionString1 %>"
   SelectCommand="SELECT * FROM [AllMenuData]">
</asp:SqlDataSource>
```

As objects, each one can expose properties, methods, and events. The SqlDataSource declared in this code exposes properties such as ID, ConnectionString, and SelectCommand, and these can be set (as you can see in the preceding code) simply by declaring them as attributes on the element in the page. Methods that the objects expose allow you to execute specific functionality. For example, you can force a data display control to bind to and display its source data by calling the DataBind method of that control.

The event-driven nature of ASP.NET simply means that the objects that make up the ASP.NET platform expose events when specific actions occur. Effectively, they send a message to any other objects that are listening for that event, and these objects can then react to the event by executing the appropriate code. As an example, a Button control on a Web page will raise a Click event when clicked and the page is submitted to the server. Code in the page can register to receive this event, and react to it by, for example, displaying a message in the page.

The pages you have created so far (which include a data source control such as the SqlDataSource, and a data display control such as the GridView) depend on the event-driven architecture of ASP.NET 2.0. When the client requests a page, a series of events occurs within the page framework. Any data source controls on the page handle (react to) this event by fetching the data specified by the properties of the control, and then call a method of the data display control to create the output you see on the page.

In Chapter 5, you will see how you can react to events exposed by the GridView control, and even other types of objects such as the ASP.NET Page itself. In later chapters, you will see how you can create your own classes that plug into, and work with, the classes in the .NET Framework.

About the GridView Control

The examples you have seen so far that use a GridView control all depend on this control automatically generating the output structure as a series of columns, one for each column in the original data source that you want to display in the page. In fact, this is a simplification of the situation because VWD generates a design-time declaration for the columns you see in the output.

The GridView control has a property named AutoGenerateColumns, which is True by default. If you have a SqlDataSource in the page that has its ID property set to MySqlDataSource, you can display all the columns it contains automatically by simply declaring a GridView control in the source of the page like this:

```
<asp:GridView ID="MyGrid" runat="server" DataSourceID="MySqlDataSource" / >
```

The GridView control will create a BoundField control for each column in the data source. This column displays the contents of the column as text, irrespective of the data type in the underlying data source. For example, the number 12, which could represent the size of a pizza in inches or the price in dollars, is displayed as the text string "12". The one exception is where the source column is a SQL bit type, which can hold only the values True or False. In this case, the GridView control displays the column contents as a checkbox.

When editing is enabled in a `GridView` control, as you saw in the example at the end of Chapter 1 (see Figure 4-1 earlier in this chapter), the control displays links that change the selected row into edit mode where the `BoundField` columns display the content in a text box. You can edit this value, and then save this new value back to the database. The `GridView` and `SqlDataSource` controls work together to enable this behavior automatically. For a `bit` column, you can change the setting of the checkbox, and save the new setting back to the database.

There are also other data display controls you can use to display and edit data. These include the `DetailsView` and `FormView` controls that are new in ASP.NET version 2.0, and the `DataList` and `Repeater` control originally introduced in version 1.0. You will see examples of these controls later in this chapter and in subsequent chapters.

Using Different Column Types in a GridView

When you add a `GridView` control to the page in VWD, it turns off the `AutoGenerateColumns` feature, and instead creates the code to implement the columns in the original data source. This allows you to change the column types used for each column in the data source to produce a display that is more in line with your requirements. You will explore this feature now to see some of the things that are possible.

1. Open the page `TestMenu2.aspx` that you built in Chapter 3. Mouse over the `GridView` control. Then open the GridView Tasks pane, and click the Edit Columns . . . link (see Figure 4-3).

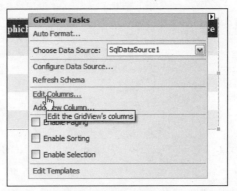

Figure 4-3: Clicking Edit Columns . . . in the GridView Tasks pane

2. This opens the Fields dialog for the `GridView` control. In the top left is a list of the available field types, with the existing fields that contain values from the database shown as being of the `BoundField` type. Under this list is the "Selected fields" list, which shows the fields in the source data for which there are columns in the `GridView` control. As you select each field in this list, notice the properties that appear in the right-hand list. The `ItemName` field is selected in Figure 4-4, and you can see that the `DataField` property indicates that it is bound to the `ItemName` column within the source data. Also notice that VWD automatically turns off the "Auto-generate fields" option (which corresponds to the `AutoGenerateColumns` property of the `GridView` control), and declares the fields you can see in this dialog.

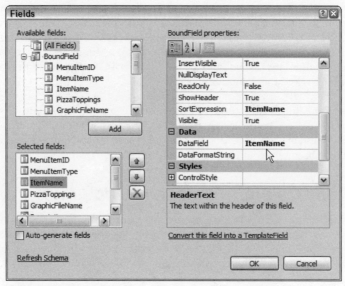

Figure 4-4: Viewing properties for the ItemName field

3.   Select the GraphicFileName column in the "Selected fields" list, and click the button next to the list to remove this column (see Figure 4-5). Then repeat this to delete the MenuItemID column.

Figure 4-5: Removing the GraphicFileName column

4.   Select the ImageField type in the "Available fields" list, and click the Add button. You will see a new ImageField appear in the "Selected fields" list, with its properties shown in the right-hand list (see Figure 4-6).

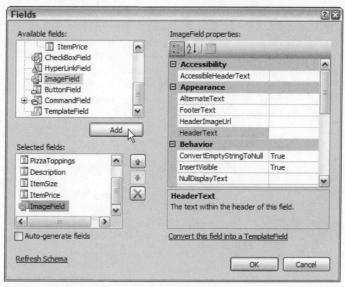

Figure 4-6: Viewing the properties of the `ImageField` **type**

5. Now you can set the properties of the new `ImageField` column. This column type will generate an ASP.NET `Image` control in each row. In the Data section of the list of properties, set the `DataAlternateTextField` property to the name of the column that will provide the data to set the `AlternateText` property of the `Image` control (used to create the `alt` attribute when the page is displayed). Use the `ItemName` column for this. Then set the `DataImageUrlField` property to the name of the column that will provide the data to set the `ImageUrl` property of the `Image` control (the path to the image file to be displayed). Use the `GraphicFileName` column for this, which contains the names of the `.gif` image files (see Figure 4-7).

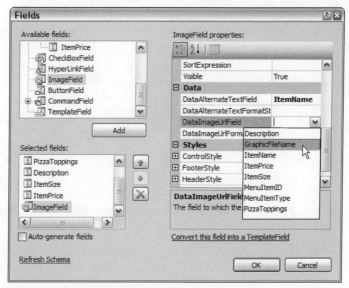

Figure 4-7: Selecting `GraphicFileName`

6. The MenuItems table contains just the filename of the images for the menu page, and not the full path. The images are, in fact, in a subfolder named images. To get the correct path in the ImageUrl property of each Image control, you must also set the DataImageUrlFormatString property of the new ImageField column to the format string images/{0} (see Figure 4-8). This format string will cause the column value to be set to the text in the string, but with the place-holder {0} replaced by the value from the column that you specified for the DataImageUrlField property. Therefore, you will get — for example — images/pizza2.gif as the value of the ImageUrl property for the second pizza row.

Figure 4-8: Setting the DataImageUrlFormatString property

7. There are some more properties you should set for the new ImageField column. Set the NullImageUrl property by selecting it and clicking the three dots (. . .) button that appears. Select the image file blank.gif from the images folder. This is the image that will be displayed if there is no value in the column that normally provides the value for the ImageUrl property and prevents the user seeing a "broken image" in the page in this case. Notice that VWD precedes the file you select with the tilde (~) character. This signifies the root folder of the site and makes sure that the correct path to the image is used, even if you move the page to a subfolder afterwards. Set the ShowHeader property to False, so there is no header displayed for this column. Finally, set the AccessibleHeadertext property to Picture of item. This text will be used as an abbr attribute of the column when the page is displayed, making it possible for users of specialist nonvisual user agents to more easily tell what the column contains.

8. Now go to the "Selected fields" list and use the up arrow button to move the new column to the top of the list so that it is displayed as the first column of grid (see Figure 4-9).

Figure 4-9: Moving the new column to the top of the list

9. That completes the new ImageField column, so go back to the "Available fields" list and select the HyperlinkField type. Click Add so that a new field of this type is added to the end of the Selected fields" list (see Figure 4-10).

Figure 4-10: Adding a new field

10. In the properties for the new `HyperlinkField`, set the `Text` property to `Search`. This is the text to display in this column for *every* row. If you want the text of a hyperlink to be different in each row, and reflect the data in the underlying data source, you set the `DataTextField` property to name of the column containing the text for the hyperlink, and optionally the `DataTextFormatString` property. These properties work in the same way as the `DataImageUrlField` and `DataImageUrlFormatString` properties you set for the `ImageField` column in step 6. Set the `Target` property to the value `blank` (from the drop-down list) to force the page that opens from the hyperlink to appear in a new browser window.

11. Set the `DataNavigateUrlFields` property to the value `MenuItemType, ItemName`. You can click this property entry and open the String Collection Editor dialog using the three dots (. . .) button that appears, or simply type the value directly. This property holds a list of the columns in the source data that will be referenced when building the URL of the hyperlink to be displayed in this column. Then set the `DataNavigateUrlFormatString` property to the value `www.google.com/search?q={0} {1}` (see Figure 4-11). This URL will allow users to search the Google Web site for more information about the items on the PPQ menu. The two placeholders in the string are replaced for each row by the values from the two columns specified as the `DataNavigateUrlFields` property.

Figure 4-11: Setting the value of the
`DataNavigateUrlFormatString` **property**

12. The final change to the columns in the `GridView` control is to specify the formatting of the `ItemPrice` column. At present, this just displays as a number, such as `12.9500` (as you saw in Figure 4-2 earlier in this chapter). You can specify a format string for the `DataFormatString` property of the column to change this, and the obvious choice is currency format using the format string `{0:c}`, as shown at the bottom of the `Fields` dialog in Figure 4-12. However, this depends on the regional settings of the server, and you may prefer to be more precise about the actual currency symbol to display by using the format string `$ {0:F2}`, as shown in Figure 4-12.

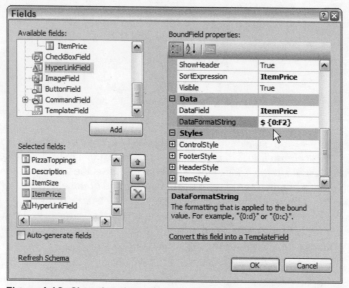

Figure 4-12: Changing the `DataFormatString` property

Chances are that the prices stored in your database are in a specific currency, such as U.S. dollars. In this case, using the `{0:c}` format string means that the currency symbol and number format depends on the regional settings of the server, whereas the value in the table is always U.S. dollars. Therefore, it is always wise to consider using format strings that specify the currency symbol, and format the remainder of the numeric value with a fixed number of decimal places. The format string `$ {0:F2}` forces a U.S. dollar currency symbol to appear, with the value formatted to two decimal places.

13. Now you can click OK to close the fields dialog, and run the page to see the results. Figure 4-13 shows that the first column now contains an image of the item in the menu, and the final column contains a Search link. If you hover over this link, you will see the target URL appear in the status bar of the browser, in this case `http://www.google.com/search?q=Pizza Hawaiian`. Also notice the formatting of the values in the `ItemSize` column.

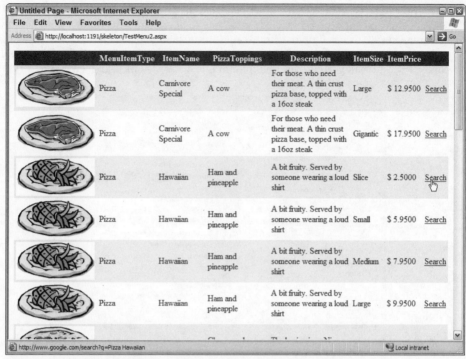

Figure 4-13: Image inserted into first column and hyperlink in final column

There are plenty of other properties for the columns that you can set to experiment with changing the appearance of the GridView output. For example, you can set or change the header text (or use an image), or apply specific formatting to the contents. However, there are other ways that you can exert even more control over the appearance, as you will see next.

Using Data Display Control Templates

The previous section showed how you can change the way the GridView control displays the data exposed by a data source control. You replaced the standard BoundField control for some of the columns with an ImageField and a HyperlinkField, so that the output contains images and links to other pages. You also changed the format of the text in the result, so that the price displays with the appropriate currency symbol.

However, these are not the only ways to generate custom output in a GridView or other data display controls. You can, instead, replace the BoundField with a TemplateField and generate the entire output you require yourself. A TemplateField allows you to specify the entire content for a column, using other controls and text to create the appearance you require.

1. With the page `TestMenu2.aspx` still open from the previous example, open the GridView Tasks pane, and click the Edit Columns . . . link to open the Fields dialog. Remove all the columns in the "Selected fields" list except for the `GraphicFileName`, `Description`, and `Search` columns. Then select the `Description` column and click the link at the bottom right of the `Fields` dialog to convert this column into a `TemplateField` (see Figure 4-14).

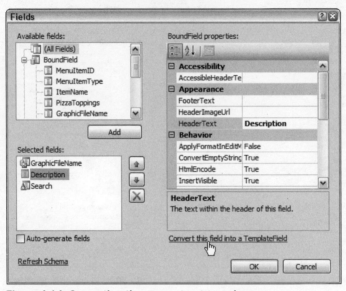

Figure 4-14: Converting the `Description` column

2. Click OK to close the Fields dialog, and go back to the GridView Tasks pane. Click the Edit Templates link, as shown in Figure 4-15.

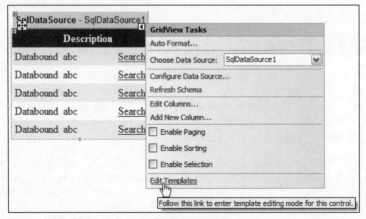

Figure 4-15: Clicking the edit Templates link

3. This changes the GridView Tasks pane into template editing mode. The pane now shows a list of the templates that are available for the control, listed by column name. There is only one `TemplateField` column in your `GridView` control — the column named `Description` at index 1 (the second column in the control because the index starts at zero), as shown in Figure 4-16. Select the `ItemTemplate`, and the control displays an editing panel that contains a `Label` control.

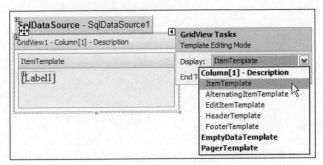

Figure 4-16: Selecting `ItemTemplate`

The Template Editing Mode pane opens showing the `ItemTemplate` by default. Normally the edit area is empty, but there is a `Label` here in this case because you converted the existing `Description` column (which used a `Label` control to display the contents) into a `TemplateField`. If you select the `EditItemTemplate` from the drop-down list, you will see that there is a `TextBox` in this template. Again, this is because you converted the existing `Description` column into a `TemplateField`. Data display controls display the contents of the appropriate template depending on which mode they are in, and so the `TextBox` displays only in the row that is in edit mode. The remaining rows display the `Label` control.

4. Close the GridView Tasks pane, and select the `Label` control. Open the Label Tasks pane using the small arrow icon that appears and click the Edit DataBindings . . . link (see Figure 4-17).

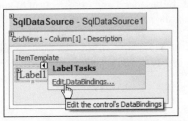

Figure 4-17: Clicking the Edit DataBindings. . . link

5. This opens the Label1 DataBindings dialog. The column itself is not bound to any specific column in the source data, but this dialog allows you to bind the controls you place in the templates for this `TemplateField` to the columns in the source data. The `Label` control in the `ItemTemplate` for this column has its `Text` property bound to the `Description` column in the source data, as you can see in Figure 4-18. There is no `Format` provided, but this feature allows you to specify a format string just like those you used in the previous example to change the way the value is displayed. You can even specify your own custom binding statement for this column if you prefer.

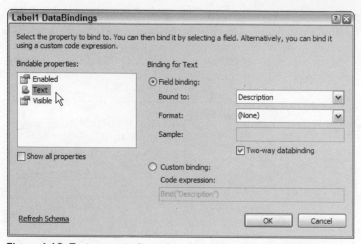

Figure 4-18: Text property bound to the `Description` column

Usually, you will bind the `Text` property of a control to the column in the underlying data source. However, you can bind other properties, such as the `NavigateUrl` of a `Hyperlink` control, or the `AlternateText` property of an `Image` control. Notice that you can display all the properties of a control by setting the checkbox below the "Bindable properties" list.

6.   The binding of the `Label` control's `Text` property to the source data, in this example, is a *two-way binding* (because you converted the `BoundColumn` to a `TemplateColumn`). The code expression is `Bind("column-name")`. This means that any changes to the value in the control (for example if it were a `TextBox`) will be pushed back into the database automatically. As you are just displaying data in this page, you can untick the checkbox in the `Field binding` section of the dialog to specify one-way binding.

7.   Click OK to close the `Label1 DataBinding` dialog, and close the `Label Tasks` pane. Now you will add more controls to the `ItemTemplate` section to specify how the source data will display in this column. Drag a `Label` control from the Toolbox into the ItemTemplate editing area, and use the Edit DataBindings . . . link on the Label Tasks pane to open the DataBindings dialog for this control. Select the `ItemName` column in the "Bound to" drop-down list. Notice that, by default, this is *not* a two-way binding, and so the code expression is `Eval("column-name")`, as shown in Figure 4-19.

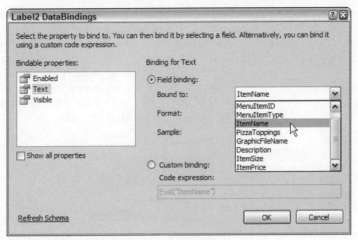

Figure 4-19: Binding for `ItemName` column

8. Drag another `Label` control from the Toolbox onto the ItemTemplate editing area. Bind this control (`Label3`) to the `PizzaToppings` column, but this time add a format string by typing the text **generously topped with {0}** into the Format section of the DataBindings dialog (see Figure 4-20).

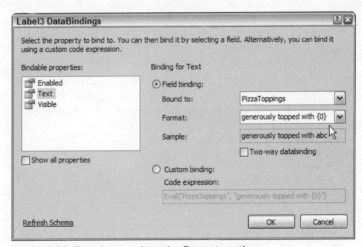

Figure 4-20: Entering text into the Format section

9. Continue by adding two more `Label` controls to the `ItemTemplate`. Bind one (`Label4`) to the `ItemSize` column. Bind the other (`Label5`) to the `ItemPrice` column, and type **$ {0:F2}** into the Format box to ensure that the price is displayed with a dollar symbol and two decimal places (as in the previous example). Then, rearrange the `Label` controls by dragging them into position in the `ItemTemplate`, and typing text and carriage returns between them to get the layout shown in Figure 4-21 — you can drag the border of the control to give yourself more room inside the template editing area. Then change the text size, and the color and style, using the controls on the VWD Formatting toolbar if you wish.

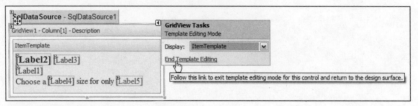

Figure 4-21: Arranging `Label` controls

10. Now, click the End Template Editing link in the GridView Tasks pane, and open the Properties window for the `GridView` control (right-click on it and select Properties from the context menu). Change the `GridLines` property to `Vertical` and the `ShowHeader` property to `False`. Then run your page to see the results. As you can see in Figure 4-22, the output is no longer just a table of values, but a page where you have exerted complete control over how the values extracted from the source data appear.

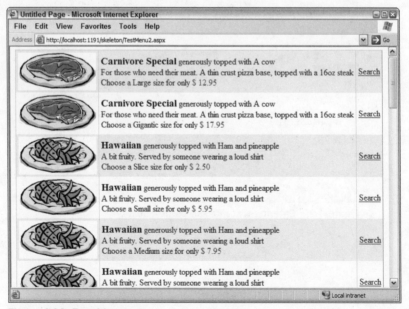

Figure 4-22: Resulting page

Look at the list of drinks toward the end of the page, and you will see why we specified a format string for the PizzaToppings *column, but typed the other text that you see directly into the* ItemTemplate *section. Where there is no value (*NULL*) for a column, the format cannot be applied and the bound control displays nothing. This means that for drinks (which have* NULL *for the* PizzaToppings *column), the text "*generously topped with . . .*" does not appear at all.*

The DetailsView and FormView Controls

All of the examples you have seen so far use the GridView control. This is, however, just one of the controls available for displaying the data exposed by a data source control. The GridView control, as you have seen, displays a grid of rows and columns, giving you a view of the data that corresponds directly to the original data table. You can change this by using different column types, or with templates, but the underlying structure of the output is still rows and columns, with one row for each row in the source data.

Two of the other new data display controls in ASP.NET 2.0 display the data one row at a time, with the individual columns laid out like a "form." They provide links that allow you to move from one page or row to the next one, the previous one, the first one, or the last one. This form-based view of the data often makes it easier to see what a row that has a large number of columns contains. The individual values can be displayed with separate labels for each one, laid out vertically as fields from one row rather than as a series of horizontally arranged columns.

The two controls that provide this type of output are the DetailsView and FormView. The difference between them is that the DetailsView control, like the GridView control, can automatically generate the fields and display the content from the associated data source control. The FormView control, on the other hand, provides no automatic display support other than the navigation between rows, and you must create the entire content of the display form using templates. However, these templates work in just the same way as you saw for the GridView control in the previous section.

Other display controls for rowset data are the DataList and Repeater. The DataList and Repeater controls do not support automatic row selection, editing, paging, or sorting. The DataList control generates an HTML table with one row containing a single cell for each row in the source data. You provide details of the data items from the source data, and how they are to be displayed, for each row. The Repeater control is even simpler. It generates repeated output using a template that you create, without providing any other support for formatting or layout. All it does is output to the browser the contents of the template once for each row in the data source.

Using a DetailsView and FormView Control

You will see most of the data source controls used in the PPQ example site. However, to help you become familiar with the different types, this example demonstrates the use of the DetailsView and FormView controls.

1. In the `TestMenu2.aspx` page you used in the previous example, click on the `GridView` control and press the Delete key to remove it from the page. Then drag a `DetailsView` control from the Data section of the Toolbox and drop it onto the page just below the existing `SqlDataSource` control. In the DetailsView Tasks pane, select the existing data source (named `SqlDataSource1`) in the Choose Data Source drop-down list (see Figure 4-23).

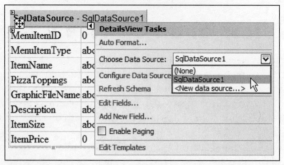

Figure 4-23: Selecting the existing data source

2. Now click the Auto Format link in the DetailsView Tasks pane, and select one of the formats that are available from the list in the Auto Format dialog that appears. Then, back in the DetailsView Tasks pane, tick Enable Paging and you will see the navigation links appear below the control (see Figure 4-24).

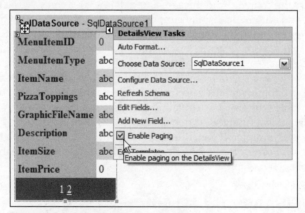

Figure 4-24: Selecting Enable Paging

3. Now drag a `FormView` control from the Data section of the Toolbox onto the page, placing it below the `DetailsView` control. Repeat the preceding steps to specify the existing `SqlDataSource` as the data source for the `FormView` control (you can bind more than one control to a single data source), apply an auto-format to it, and enable paging. The `FormView` control looks quite different from the `DetailsView` control (see Figure 4-25).

MenuItemID: 0
MenuItemType: abc
ItemName: abc
PizzaToppings: abc
GraphicFileName: abc
Description: abc
ItemSize: abc
ItemPrice: 0

1 2

Figure 4-25: `FormView` **control**

In fact, VWD has added a lot of content to the `FormView` *control for you. This allows it to be used straight away, without requiring you to edit and populate the templates. If you switch to* `Source` *view, you will see that the* `DetailsView` *contains a series of* `BoundField` *controls, just as you saw used with the* `GridView` *control. For the* `FormView` *control, VWD has created an ItemTemplate, EditItemTemplate, and InsertItemTemplate section, and populated these with controls to display all the columns, and even allow editing of all the columns (with the exception of the primary key column) in the source data.*

4. Run the page, and again you see the differences between the two controls. The `DetailsView` control at the top displays the contents using an HTML table to lay out the captions and values, and adds row-level formatting. The `FormView` control simply contains the text generated by the default templates that VWD created (see Figure 4-26).

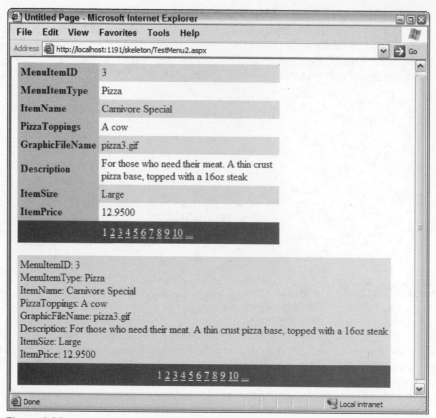

Figure 4-26: `DetailsView` **control and** `FormView` **control with text generated by the default templates**

5.   Back in Design view, open the DetailsView Tasks pane, and click the Edit Fields link. You see the same Fields dialog as you did with the `GridView` control. You can add, remove, format, and change the types of the columns in the `DetailsView` control in just the same way as you saw earlier in this chapter with the `GridView` control. However, there is no Edit Fields link in the FormView Tasks pane, because it does not support the field controls. Instead, you must switch to template editing mode where you add, remove, change, and format the controls in each of the templates, just as you did in the previous example with a `TemplateField` (see Figure 4-27). The only difference is that, in the `FormView` control, the templates make up the entire content of the output, whereas a `TemplateField` in a `GridView` control just specifies the appearance for that column.

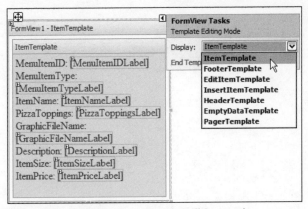

Figure 4-27: Switching to template editing mode

The DetailsView and FormView controls in this example do not support editing or inserting new rows because they are bound to a query that does not allow updates to be pushed back into the database. Recall that the query used by the SqlDataSource control in this page joins two tables and returns rows from both. If you use a query that returns rows from a single table, or from an updateable database view, the Tasks panes for the DetailsView and FormView controls will allow you to turn on the editing and inserting of new rows, and will automatically handle the whole process for you just like the GridView control does.

Summary

This chapter has concentrated on the techniques available within VWD for creating pages that display data from a relational database. It is often important to know a little more about how a technology works to be able to get the best from it, and ASP.NET and VWD are certainly no exception. This chapter explored the basics of the ASP.NET event-driven architecture, and the way that this provides the ability to react to events in your own pages and code.

Equally important, for developers working with relational or XML data (which includes the vast majority of developers at some time or another), is a basic grasp of what the data source controls in ASP.NET actually do. You saw some details in this chapter, and you will see more in subsequent chapters.

However, the bulk of the chapter was concerned with the use of *templates* in the data display controls such as the GridView. You tend to discover, surprisingly quickly, that the standard output generated by the data display controls in ASP.NET often does not give you exactly what you want. Instead, you will find yourself increasingly using templates to achieve exactly the required results, and this chapter showed just how powerful this feature is.

Toward the end of the chapter, you saw some of the other data display controls — including the DetailsView and FormView controls that are new in version 2.0 of ASP.NET. These controls provide a view of data that was not easily obtainable in previous versions, allowing users to scroll easily through a set of rows, and even update the data, if you decide to expose this feature.

Chapter 5 continues this theme of accessing and displaying data, extending it to include nested data display and working with XML data. It also looks at creating reusable content as user controls.

Displaying Nested and XML Data

In Chapter 4, you looked in detail at how VWD provides support for building data-driven pages and Web sites through the new data source controls and data display controls. You saw how easy it is to connect to a database, extract and display data, and even perform updates to that data.

In this chapter, you will see some more ways that you can use data in your Web pages. The first main topic is the creation of pages that more closely represent the requirements of many every-day situations, such as displaying details of orders or (as in this case) the items on a menu. This generally involves working with more than one table of data and, as a result, the best way to display this data by using a "nested" approach to the layout.

However, data does not always come from a database. Increasingly, applications are using XML to pass data from one place to another, and store it as a disk file. ASP.NET contains controls that make displaying this kind of data easy, as you will see in this chapter.

The third and final topic in this chapter is an approach you can use to create reusable content for your Web applications and Web sites. ASP.NET provides a feature called user controls that allows you to generate independent sections of pages or code, which are easy to insert into other pages.

So, the topics for this chapter are:

❑   How you can build nested displays of data from multiple tables

❑   How you can display XML data, rather than data from a relational database

❑   How you can create reusable sections of a page as user controls

To start the chapter, you will continue your investigation of displaying relational data by discovering techniques for creating nested displays using data binding.

Building Nested Data Displays

Chapter 4 discussed the various ways that data exposed by a data source control can be bound to a range of data display controls, such as the GridView, DetailsView, and FormView. Each control displays all of the source data rows—either all at once in a "grid," or one row at a time in a "form." This approach is fine if the data source you use contains all the columns required for the output, and the result requires only these columns. However, what happens when you want to display data that comes from separate tables, yet you do not want to repeat the output for every row in both tables?

To make it easier to see what the issue here is, consider the situation with the rowset containing the pizza menu items that you have been working with so far. To get the sizes and prices into each row, you use a stored procedure, database view, or custom SQL statement to join the MenuItems and SizeAndPrice tables together. The result is a rowset containing a row for each of the rows in the SizeAndPrice table, with the columns from the MenuItems table added to it and populated with the appropriate values from the linked rows in the MenuItems table (see Figure 5-1).

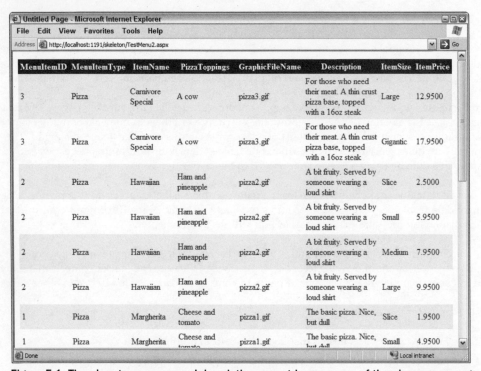

Figure 5-1: The pizza type, name, and description repeat in every row of the pizza menu page

A more natural way to display this type of information is by repeating just the items that are different in each row.

This could be as simple as removing the repeated data from the rows and leaving them empty. However, a much more common requirement, and the one you will implement here, is to use nesting to create a list of the nonrepeated items within a list of the repeated items. In other words, the main list will only contain the items that are unique in the `MenuItems` table. Within each of these rows, however, will be another nested list of the sizes and prices for that particular menu item (see Figure 5-2).

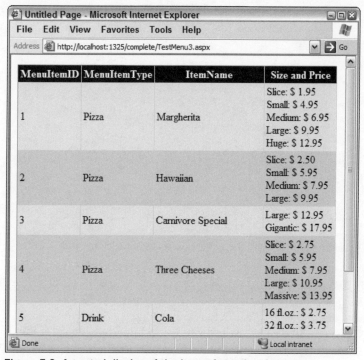

Figure 5-2: A nested display of the items from the pizza menu

This is a much more natural way of displaying data from two related tables, where the child tables contain multiple linked rows for each row in the parent table. It applies to many situations other than a menu, for example when displaying an order that contains more than one "order line" (more than one item). The parent table contains the details of the order (such as the address and delivery charge), while each related child row contains details of one item on that order.

Creating Nested Data Displays Declaratively

In this example, you will build the page you have just seen in Figure 5-2, using mainly drag-and-drop techniques and with only a few lines of code. You will create it using the code-behind approach, where the executable code for the page resides in a separate file that—along with the `.aspx` page that implements the interface—uses the partial classes feature in .NET version 2.0 that allows a single class to be divided across separate files. This makes it easier for one or more people to work independently on either the code or the interface section of the page.

1. Select New File . . . from the File menu, or right-click on the root entry in the Solution Explorer window and select Add New Item . . . to open the Add New Item dialog. Select Web Form, and change the filename to TestMenu3.aspx. Be sure to tick the "Place code in separate file" checkbox near the bottom of the dialog, and then click Add (see Figure 5-3).

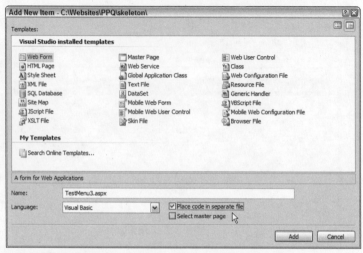

Figure 5-3: Clicking the checkbox, and then clicking Add

2. VWD creates two new files, and adds them to the project. If you look in the Solution Explorer window (see Figure 5-4), you will see these two files. TestMenu3.aspx contains the interface code, and automatically opens in the main editing window. TestMenu3.aspx.vb contains the executable code for the page, which you will examine later in this example.

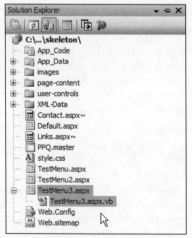

Figure 5-4: Two new files appearing in the Solution Explorer window

3. Switch to Design view, and drag a `SqlDataSource` control from the Toolbox onto the page (`TestMenu3.aspx`) that is open in the Editing window. Select Configure Data Source in the SqlDataSource Tasks pane to start the Configure Data Source Wizard. Select the entry `PPQ_DataConnectionString1` for the connection string in the first page of the wizard, and click Next. In the Configure the Select Statement page, select "Specify columns from a table or view," and select the `MenuItems` table. In the Columns: list, select the `MenuItemID`, `MenuItemType`, and `ItemName` columns (see Figure 5-5).

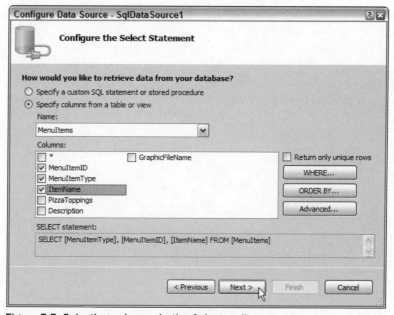

Figure 5-5: Selecting columns in the Columns: list

4. Click Next. Test the query if you wish, and click Finish to close the Configure Data Source Wizard. Then drag a `GridView` control from the Toolbox onto the page. In the GridView Tasks pane, select `SqlDataSource1` in the Choose Data Source: list, and apply an Auto Format of your choice. Now, click the Add New Column . . . link in the GridView Tasks pane, as shown in Figure 5-6.

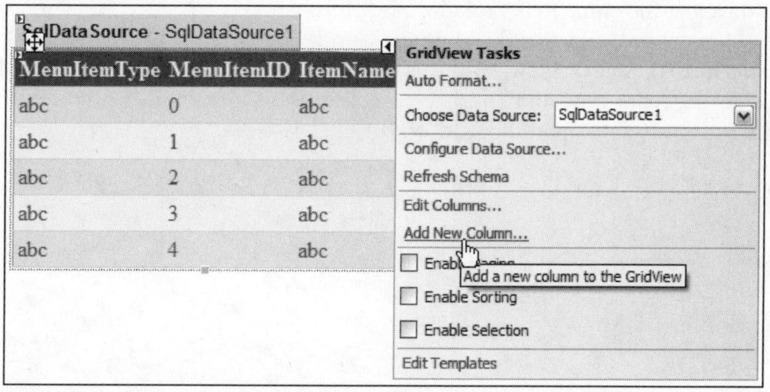

Figure 5-6: Selecting Add New Column . . .

5. This opens the Add Field dialog. Choose a `TemplateField` in the list at the top of the dialog, and enter **Size and Price** as the Header Text (see Figure 5-7).

Figure 5-7: Add Field dialog

6. This adds a new `TemplateField` as the last column of the `GridView` control. Click OK to close the Add Field dialog, and click the Edit Templates link at the bottom of the GridView Tasks pane to switch this pane into Template Editing Mode. You will see the new column named `Size and Price` and the templates that are available for it. Select the `ItemTemplate`, as shown in Figure 5-8.

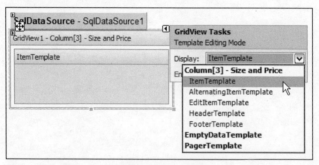

Figure 5-8: Template Editing Mode pane

7. Whatever you place in this template will appear in this column of every row in the `GridView` control at run time. Therefore, you need to add controls into this template that will fetch the rows from the `SizeAndPrice` table that match the `MenuItemID` value in the current row of the `GridView`. Drag a `SqlDataSource` from the Toolbox into the template-editing area, and select Configure Data Source in the SqlDataSource Tasks pane to start the Configure Data Source Wizard. Select the entry `PPQ_DataConnectionString1` for the connection string in the first page of the wizard, and click Next. In the Configure the Select Statement page, select "Specify columns from a table or view," but this time select the `SizeAndPrice` table. In the Columns: list, select the `ItemSize` and `ItemPrice` columns, as shown in Figure 5-9. Then click the WHERE . . . button to open the Add WHERE Clause dialog.

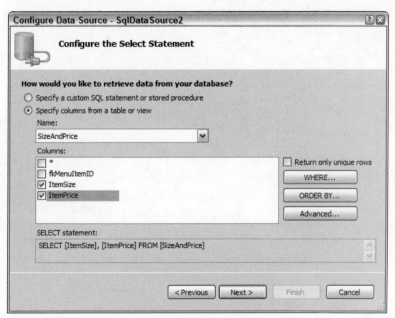

Figure 5-9: Selecting columns from the Columns: list

You must add a WHERE clause (a criteria) to the SQL statement so that only the rows matching the current menu item are returned. The data source controls allow you to add parameters to the SQL statement, and these can even be populated with the appropriate value dynamically at run time. For example, you can use a ControlParameter automatically populated with the value from, say, a DropDownList so that the rows returned by the query match the currently selected value in this list. However, things are not that simple with a GridView control, as you will see in the next step.

8. The Add WHERE Clause dialog (shown in Figure 5-10) allows you to select a Column in the source data that the query generates, an Operator (such as equals), and a Source for the value to compare to the specified column contents. The Source specifies the type of parameter to create and there are several types available. You can take the value from another control on the page, a value in the query string, a posted form value, a value from a cookie, or a value from the user's session or profile. In the example you are building now, it would be tempting to add a parameter that takes its value from the current row in the GridView control, as shown in Figure 5-10.

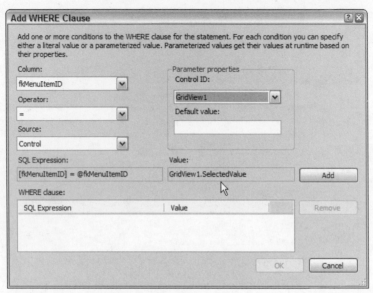

Figure 5-10: Add WHERE Clause dialog

9. Unfortunately, this will not produce the required result. If you look at the Value: that the wizard proposes, you can see that it will come from the `SelectedValue` property of the `GridView` control. The problem is that, when simply displaying data, the rows in the `GridView` control are not actually "selected." Only one row can be in "selected mode" in a `GridView`, as you may recall from the example in Chapter 1 that demonstrates selection and editing in a `GridView` control. Instead, you must add a "normal" parameter (one that is not automatically populated) to the SQL statement, and then set the value of this parameter using code at run time. Confusingly, to create a parameter of this type, you select None in the Source: list of the Add WHERE Clause dialog, as shown in Figure 5-11. You should also leave the Value: (in the "Parameter properties" section of the dialog) empty. After setting these values in the Add WHERE Clause dialog, click the Add button. You will see them appear in the SQL Expression and Value section at the bottom of the list (you can add multiple criteria in this dialog). Then click OK to close the dialog and return to the Configure Data Source Wizard.

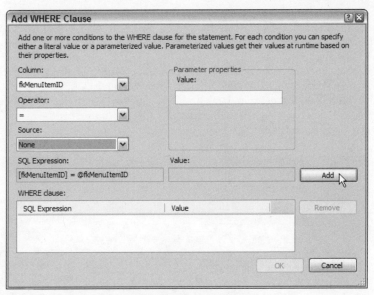

Figure 5-11: Selecting None in the Source: list

10. Back in the Configure Data Source Wizard, you can now specify the sorting of the rows by adding an ORDER BY clause to the SQL statement. Click the ORDER BY . . . button to open the Add ORDER BY Clause dialog. Select the ItemPrice column, and check that the order is set to Ascending. You can see the final SQL statement at the bottom of this dialog, with the WHERE and ORDER BY clauses you have just created (see Figure 5-12).

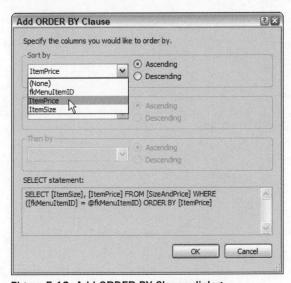

Figure 5-12: Add ORDER BY Clause dialog

Notice that the WHERE *clause specifies that the* fkMenuItemID *column (in the* SizeAndPrice *table) must be equal to a parameter named* @fkMenuItemID. *This is the default naming convention. When using SQL Server, parameter names should always start with the* @ *character.*

11. Click OK to close the Add ORDER BY Clause dialog, and click Next in the main Configure Data Source Wizard window. Now you can test your query. Click the Test Query button, and — because there is a parameter in the SQL statement — the Parameter Values Editor dialog opens showing the name and type of each parameter that is required by the query. Enter a value between 1 and 7, and click OK (see Figure 5-13).

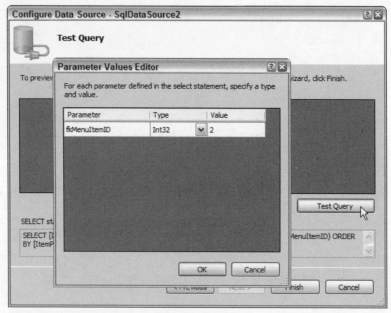

Figure 5-13: Parameter Values Editor dialog

12. You will see that the result contains only the rows that have the value you entered in their fkMenuItemID column (see Figure 5-14). After viewing the results, click Finish to complete the Configure Data Source Wizard.

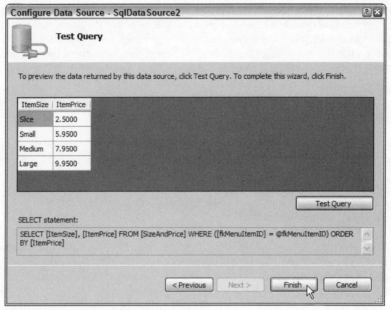

Figure 5-14: SELECT statement results

13. Back in the main VWD editing window, you can now add the list control that you will bind to the SqlDataSource control you just configured. Only a line break is required between each item in the list, and so the obvious choice is the lightweight and simple Repeater control. Drag a Repeater control from the Toolbox and drop it into the ItemTemplate editing area. In the Repeater Tasks pane, select the new SqlDataSource (named SqlDataSource2) in the Choose Data Source list (see Figure 5-15).

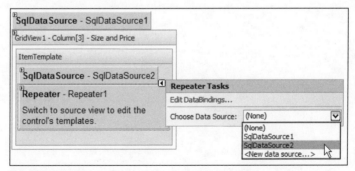

Figure 5-15: Choose Data Source drop-down list

14. The `Repeater` control depends on templates to provide all of its content and yet is one of the few controls that does not provide a design-time interface for editing its templates. As you can see in Figure 5-15, you must switch to Source view and manually enter the templates and content. Find the `<asp:Repeater>` control declaration, and insert the following ItemTemplate declaration (as shown highlighted in Figure 5-16):

```
<ItemTemplate>
  <%#Eval("ItemSize")%>: <%#Eval("ItemPrice", "$ {0:F2}")%><br />
</ItemTemplate>
```

The `Repeater` control generates a copy of the ItemTemplate contents at run time for each row in the source data rowset. The content you just added consists of two `Eval` statements, which display the values from the specified columns of the current row, and some literal text (the ":" and a space) plus an HTML line break. Notice that the second `Eval` statement also specifies a format string (like that you saw in previous examples), so the value will appear with a dollar sign and two decimal places.

Looking at the source of the page (in Figure 5-16), you can see the declaration of the second `SqlDataSource` *control (with* `ID="SqlDataSource2"`*) within the* `ItemTemplate` *of the* `GridView` *control. Nested inside the* `SqlDataSource` *is a* `SelectParameters` *section that contains the parameter you added to the SQL statement in the Configure Data Source Wizard.*

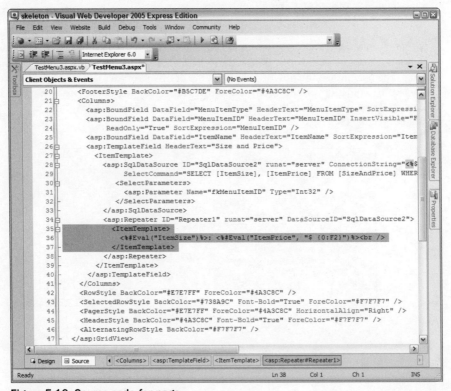

Figure 5-16: Source code for page

15. If you run the page now, you will see nothing in the `Size` and `Price` column. This is because the `SqlDataSource` in the ItemTemplate of the `GridView` control cannot match any rows in the `SizeAndPrice` table — the value of the `@fkMenuItemID` parameter is empty. To set the value, you need to write some code that will execute as each row of the `GridView` is bound to its data source (a row from the `MenuItems` table). Recalling how you learned in the previous chapter that ASP.NET controls raise events, you will not be surprised to discover an event that provides just the opportunity you need. The `GridView` control raises a `RowDataBound` event after it has collected the data from the data source for each row, and is ready to create the output. Go to the Solution Explorer window and open the code-behind page named `Testmenu3.aspx.vb`. In the two drop-down lists at the top of the main VWD editing window, select the `GridView` control (`GridView1`), and the `RowDataBound` event, as shown in Figure 5-17.

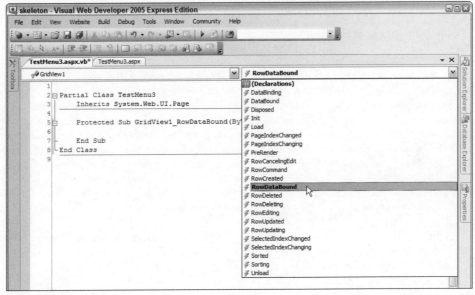

Figure 5-17: Selecting the `RowDataBound` **even**

16. An outline of the event handler routine appears in the page (see Figure 5-17), to which you can then add your own code (see Figure 5-18). The code you require is:

```
If e.Row.RowType = DataControlRowType.DataRow Then

  Dim ds As SqlDataSource = CType(e.Row.FindControl("SqlDataSource2"),
    SqlDataSource)

  ds.SelectParameters("fkMenuItemID").DefaultValue =
    GridView1.DataKeys(e.Row.RowIndex).Value
End If
```

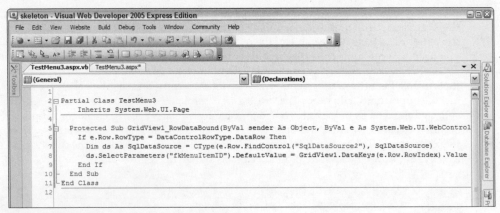

Figure 5-18: Outline of event handler routine

The code used here looks complicated, but has a simple task to accomplish. It first checks what type of row this is by looking at the `RowType` *property of the row — referenced through the arguments passed to the event handler (it might be a data row, a header row, or a footer row). If it is a data row, it will contain the* `SqlDataSource` *and* `Repeater` *controls. The code uses a method of the* `Row` *object named* `FindControl` *to get a reference to the* `SqlDataSource` *control in this row. Then it extracts the value of the* `MenuItemID` *column for the current row from the* `DataKeys` *collection (VWD automatically sets the* `DataKeyNames` *property of the* `GridView` *control to the primary key column(s) in the source rowset, which populates the* `DataKeys` *collection). The value of the parameter named* `fkMenuItemID` *in the* `SelectParameters` *collection of the* `SqlDataSource` *control in this row is then set to the* `MenuItemID` *value for this row, causing it to extract the matching rows from the* `SizeAndPrice` *table.*

17. Click Save to save the two files, and then run your page to see the results. As you can see in Figure 5-19, the `Repeater` control now generates a list of values from the `SizesAndPrices` table for each row in the `MenuItems` table.

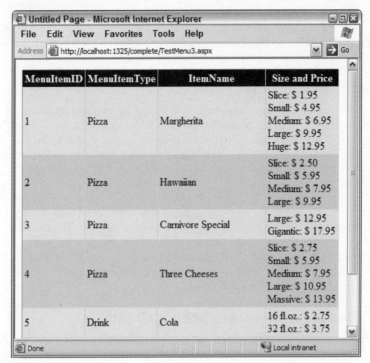

Figure 5-19: Results of `Repeater` control generating a list of values

Writing Code to Access and Display Nested Data

The example you have just seen works but is not particularly efficient. There are two reasons for this, one of which can benefit many of your other data access pages, and one that pertains directly to the display of nested data. To understand both of these issues, you need to know a little about how data access works in .NET. This includes the way that ASP.NET accesses data through the data source controls, and the way that the data is stored in memory and used to populate the data display controls.

This leads on to the concept of writing your own data access code that builds up the data structures required to bind to the data display controls. This also allows you to take control of the data in specific situations that require it and thereby create much more efficient pages for your Web sites. In later chapters, where you look at the process of extracting and updating data in the database as users place orders, you will see that writing your own data access code is the only option.

Yes, you can still take advantage of data source controls in most cases and then simply extend the capabilities when required for many other cases (as you saw in the previous example in the "Creating Nested Data Displays Declaratively" section). However, there will always be that case where writing custom data access code is the only way, or by far the most efficient way, to achieve the desired result.

The DataReader and DataSet Objects

The fundamentals to understanding data access in .NET are the two objects `DataSet` and `DataReader`. The `DataSet` is the default storage approach used by the data source controls in ASP.NET. A `DataSet` is an in-memory store than can contain one or more tables (rowsets) of data, and optionally the relationships between the tables. The `DataSet` uses an object called a `DataAdapter` to connect to the database and extract the rows, and the `DataAdapter` can push changes made to the data within the `DataSet` back into the database tables.

The alternative approach involves fetching the data using a `DataReader`. A `DataReader` is more like a "pipe" that connects the database server to the consumer of the data. The database server executes the SQL statement or stored procedure to generate the results rowset, and the `DataReader` streams this rowset to the control in your ASP.NET page in read-only, forward-only fashion. Reopening the `DataReader` and reexecuting the query is the only way to reread the data. Changes to the data cannot be stored or pushed back into the database.

Using a DataReader with a Data Source Control

By default, when a `SqlDataReader` fetches its data from the database, it stores this data in memory in a `DataSet` (i.e., `SqlDataSource` not `SqlDataReader`). This allows the control to do clever tricks such as caching the data to reduce server loading (you configure this through the properties of the control), and supporting features such as paging, selection, and editing.

However, creating a `DataSet` and storing it in memory is less efficient than simply streaming the data from the database and using it to populate the data display control. If the page is only displaying the data, and does not allow caching, paging, selection, or editing, you can improve performance by changing the data source control to use a `DataReader` rather than a `DataSet`. This simply involves setting the `DataSourceMode` property of the data source control, as shown in Figure 5-20. To show the Properties dialog, you can right-click on the data source control and select Properties from the context menu that appears.

Figure 5-20: Setting a data source control to use a `DataReader` instead of a `DataSet`

As an example, the previous example in the section "Creating Nested Data Displays Declaratively" uses several data source controls. As the page executes, the `GridView` control binds to the `DataSet` exposed by the first `SqlDataSource` control on the page and generates a grid row for each row in the

MenuItems table. Each of these rows also contains a SqlDataSource control, which you placed in the ItemTemplate of the TemplateField of the GridView control. As each row is bound to its source row, the SqlDataSource control in that row fetches a DataSet containing the child rows from the SizeAndPrice table that match the current parent row in the MenuItems table.

This proliferation of DataSet instances, even though they are all quite small (having only a few rows each), means multiple calls to the database server, and multiple objects instantiated. Simply by changing the properties of the SqlDataSource controls to use a DataReader instead of a DataSet will help to reduce the processing overhead, even though it cannot prevent the multiple data access operations. Just set the DataSourceMode property of the two SqlDataSource controls in the example page to DataReader instead of DataSet.

Generating a Single DataSet with Relationships

You can take an even better approach to data access for nested data binding. It depends on the ability of a DataSet to hold multiple tables and the relationships between them. The idea is to populate the DataSet with all of the rows you want to display from both the MenuItems and SizeAndPrice tables, so that only one data access operation is required to create the entire nested display. The process of creating the DataSet requires more server resources than using a DataReader, but there is only one request to the database. If the database is on a separate server, as is usually the case in enterprise-level applications, this alone can provide a big performance boost.

After fetching the data, you then create a relationship within the DataSet that corresponds to the relationship between the MenuItems and SizeAndPrice tables within the database. Relationships (implemented as DataRelation object instances) expose the CreateChildView method that allows on demand extraction from the DataSet of sets of SizeAndPrice rows that match a specific MenuItems parent row. These child rows then populate the nested Repeater control.

1. Open the page PPQ.master from the Solution Explorer window and switch to Design view. Right-click within the ContentPlaceHolder control at the right of the main section of the page, and select Add Content Page from the context menu that appears (see Figure 5-21).

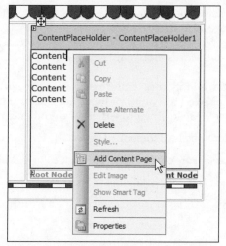

Figure 5-21: Selecting Add Content Page

145

2. Switch to Design view, drag a DataList control from the Toolbox, and drop it into the Content section of the new page. Click the Property Builder . . . link in the DataList Tasks pane that appears to open the DataList1 Properties dialog. Check that you have the same settings for your DataList control as those shown in Figure 5-22.

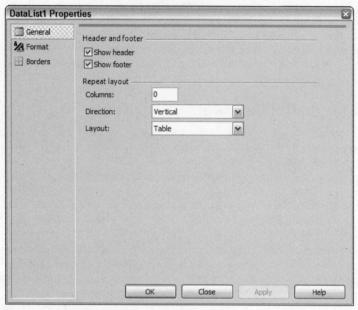

Figure 5-22: DataList1 Properties pane

Notice that the DataList can lay out its contents (the repeated items) in columns and fill these columns either vertically or horizontally. This particular feature makes the DataList control ideal for pages where you need multicolumn lists. Meanwhile, on another note, it might seem confusing having two different Properties windows—a dialog that opens from the Property Builder link and a normal window that lives at the edge of the screen. In fact, they just offer two different ways to set the properties of the control. The Property Builder dialog you see here makes it easier to specify the format for the templates within a list control such as the DataList.

3. The Format page of this Properties dialog makes it easy to specify the style for the templates in a list control. Enter or select the value for the Header of your DataList control as shown in Figure 5-23. Then set the following properties for the other templates:

❑   Footer: Horizontal Alignment = Center

❑   Normal Items: Fore color = #284775, Back color = White

❑   Separators: Horizontal Alignment = Center

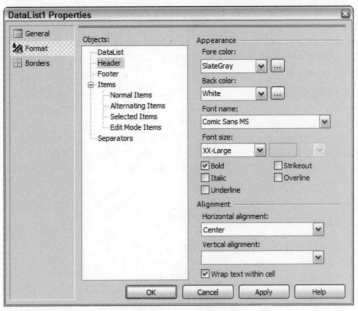

Figure 5-23: Format page of Properties dialog

4. Click OK to close the Properties dialog and select Edit Templates from the DataList Tasks pane. Select Header Template, type in the header text Our Stone-Baked Menu and press Return. Then, drag an Image control from the Standard section of the Toolbox into the template editing area below this text. Right-click on the Image control and select Properties to open the Properties window. Set the GenerateEmptyAlternateText property to True, and then select the ImageUrl property entry. Use the three dots (...) button to open the Select Image dialog, and select the image named menu-spacer.gif from the images subfolder. Your Header Template should now resemble Figure 5-24.

Figure 5-24: Header template

5. Now, select Footer Template in the DataList Tasks pane, and add an `Image` control to this template as you did in the previous step, setting the same properties. You do not need to add any text to this template because it will just appear at the end of the list of menu items. Then select Separator Template in the DataList Tasks pane and add another `Image` control there, with the same properties.

6. The final task for the `DataList` control is to create the content for the ItemTemplate section. This contains an `Image` control to display a picture of the menu item, some `Label` controls to display details of the item, and a `Repeater` control to display the sizes and prices available for that item (as shown in Figure 5-25). This is similar to the ItemTemplate you created in the previous example, and so — rather than working through each step — you can use the section of code provided in the file `Menu.aspx.txt` in the `page-content` subfolder of the examples.

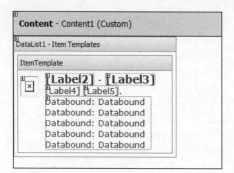

Figure 5-25: ItemTemplate section

7. Switch to Design view, use the Edit Templates link in the DataList Tasks pane to show the list of templates, and select the ItemTemplate. You should have an ItemTemplate, as shown in Figure 5-26.

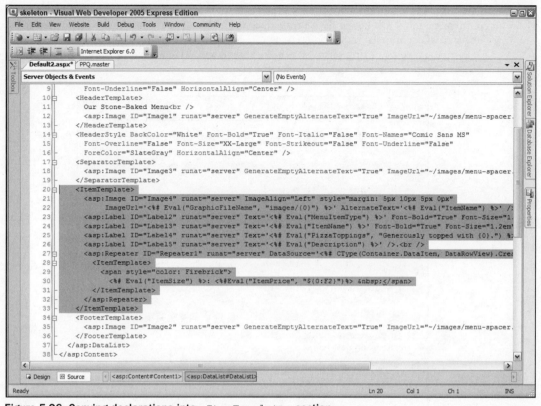

Figure 5-26: Copying declarations into `<ItemTemplate>` section

8. One other addition to the code is required. At the top of the page, directly after the `Page` directive, add `Import` directives to import the classes in the `System.Data` and `System.Data.SqlClient` namespaces. As shown in Figure 5-27, add the lines:

```
<% @Import Namespace="System.Data" %>
<% @Import Namespace="System.Data.SqlClient" %>
```

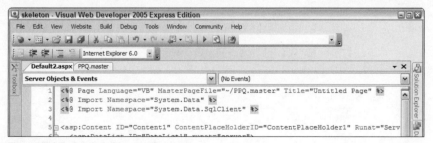

Figure 5-27: Adding lines to the code

9. Now go back to Design view, drag a `Label` control from the Toolbox, and drop it into the
`Content` control just below the `DataList` control. This `Label` will only be used to show any
errors that occur in the data access code you will write, so set the `Text` property of this `Label`
control to an empty string so that it is not visible when there is no error. You should now have a
Content section in your page that looks like Figure 5-28.

Figure 5-28: Content section in page

10. Before going any further, you can rename the page. When you create a Content Page directly from
a Master Page (by right-clicking within the `ContentPlaceHolder` control and selecting Add
Content Page as you did in this example), the page name appears as `Default2.aspx` or something
similar. Save and close your new page and, in the Solution Explorer window, right-click the page
name and select Rename from the context menu. Name the page `ShowMenu.aspx`, as shown in
Figure 5-29.

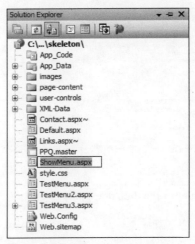

Figure 5-29: Renaming the page

11. The next step is to add the code that accesses the database, extracts the data, and binds it to the `DataList` and `Repeater` controls to create the menu page. The Content Page you are creating uses the code inline approach by default (if you want to use code-behind, you must create a new Web Form and then add the `<asp:content>` elements and convert it into a Content Page as you did with the `TestMenu.aspx` page in Chapter 2). Double-click on the new page `ShowMenu.aspx` in Solution Explorer to open it in the editor again in Source view. At the top of the main editing window, select the `Page` object and the `Load` event in the two drop-down lists, as shown in Figure 5-30. VWD adds a `<script>` section to the page, and inserts into it the outline of a `Page_Load` event handler like this:

```
<script runat="server">
  Protected Sub Page_Load(ByVal sender As Object, ByVal e As System.EventArgs)

  End Sub
</script>
```

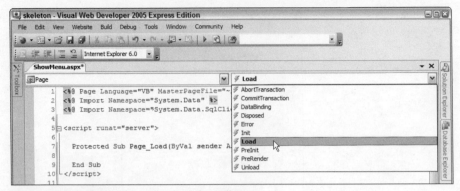

Figure 5-30: Selecting from the drop-down lists

12. Open the file `ShowMenu.aspx.vb.txt` from the `page-content` subfolder, and copy the contents into this event handler. This saves you a lot of typing, though you might like to type in at least a few of the lines of code yourself to see the way that VWD provides pop-up tooltips and auto-complete for object properties and method names. Figure 5-31 shows the result.

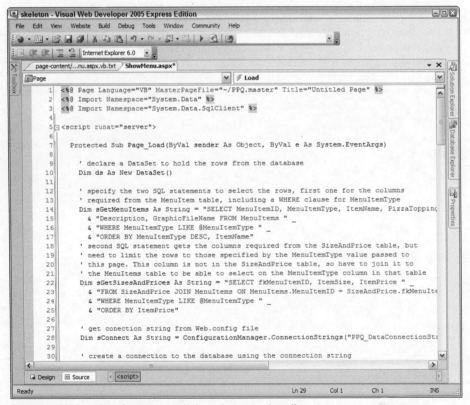

Figure 5-31: Results of copying code into the event handler

13. Now, run the page to see what you have created, as shown in Figure 5-32. Because you have not provided a value for the item type in the query string, the menu shows — by default — all of the items in the `MenuItems` table. However, if you use the links on the fly-out menu on the left of the page (`Our Menu | Pizzas` or `Our Menu | Drinks`), you will see that the page displays only the items that match that selection for the `MenuItemType`. You will see how all this works when you examine the code in the new page in the next section of this chapter.

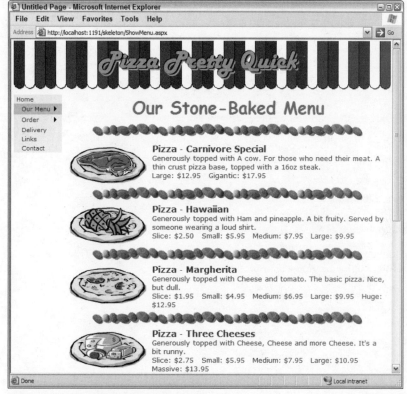

Figure 5-32: Seeing the completed page

How the Code in the ShowMenu.aspx Page Works

Quite a lot of the detailed workings of the page you just built were omitted when you copied the control declarations and code provided as separate files into your page. To understand how the example works, this section describes the code and the way that the nested data binding is implemented. The code in the `Page_Load` event handler runs when the page loads each time, and fills a `DataSet` with two tables from the database.

Note that we have added some line breaks into the following listings. In VB.NET, you can break a line of code over two lines by adding a space and an underscore to the end of the first line.

The first steps are to create an empty `DataSet` object instance and then declare the SQL statements that extract the data. You can build these statements using the Query Builder in VWD. They include a `WHERE` clause that specifies a value for the `MenuItemType` (which can be "Pizza" or "Drink" in this example), and they sort the rows as required for display in the page. Notice that the second SQL statement has to join the two tables together to be able to include a `WHERE` clause that specifies the `MenuItemType` column:

```
' declare a DataSet to hold the rows from the database
Dim ds As New DataSet()

' specify the two SQL statements to select the rows, first one for the columns
' required from the MenuItem table, including a WHERE clause for MenuItemType
Dim sGetMenuItems As String = "SELECT MenuItemID, MenuItemType, ItemName, " _
    & " PizzaToppings, Description, GraphicFileName FROM MenuItems " _
    & "WHERE MenuItemType LIKE @MenuItemType " _
    & "ORDER BY MenuItemType DESC, ItemName"
' second SQL statement gets the columns required from the SizeAndPrice table, but
' need to limit the rows to those specified by the MenuItemType value passed to
' this page. This column is not in the SizeAndPrice table, so have to join it to
' the MenuItems table to be able to select on the MenuItemType column in that table
Dim sGetSizesAndPrices As String = "SELECT fkMenuItemID, ItemSize, ItemPrice " _
    & "FROM SizeAndPrice JOIN MenuItems " _
    & "ON MenuItems.MenuItemID = SizeAndPrice.fkMenuItemID " _
    & "WHERE MenuItemType LIKE @MenuItemType " _
    & "ORDER BY ItemPrice"
...
```

Next, the connection string can be extracted from the `Web.config` file. This is the same connection string as used in all the previous examples:

```
...
' get conection string from Web.config file
Dim sConnect As String = ConfigurationManager.ConnectionStrings( _
                    "PPQ_DataConnectionString1").ConnectionString
...
```

To populate a `DataSet` with rows from a database, you need a `SqlDataAdapter`. This object uses a `SqlConnection` to connect to the database, and so the code next creates a new `SqlConnection` instance using the connection string. A `SqlDataAdapter` is then created using the `SqlConnection` and the first of the SQL statements declared earlier:

```
...
' create a connection to the database using the connection string
' the Using statement ensures that the connection is closed and
' disposed automatically after use
Using con As New SqlConnection(sConnect)

    ' create a SqlDataAdapter using the SqlConnection object
    ' and the first SQL SELECT statement declared earlier
    Dim da As New SqlDataAdapter(sGetMenuItems, con)
    ...
```

Specifying the ItemType for the Query

The page must be able to show all of the menu items, or just a subset of pizzas or drinks. When the page is opened, a query string may be added to the URL — for example: `ShowMenu.aspx?type=pizza`. This means that a parameter is required to pass the specified value to the `SqlDataAdapter`, so that it can pass it to the database when executing the SQL statement. The code creates this parameter next, specifying that it will hold a String value of length up to 10 characters. The value from the query string is then extracted (using the ASP.NET `QueryString` collection), and the wildcard character "%" added to the end. If there is no value in the query string, just the "%" character — when sent to the database — will ensure that all rows are returned:

```
...
' create a SqlParameter to hold the type of menu items to show
Dim param As New SqlParameter("@MenuItemType", SqlDbType.VarChar, 10)

' get the item type specified when the page was opened from the query string
' it will force the SelectCommand to select only the required rows, or all
' of the rows if there is no value in the query string (% means match anything)
param.Value = Request.QueryString("type") & "%"

' add the parameter to the SelectCommand used by the SqlDataAdapter
da.SelectCommand.Parameters.Add(param)
...
```

Fetching the Rows from the Database

The next section of code fetches the rows from the database and creates two new tables in the `DataSet`, by calling the `Fill` method of the `SqlDataAdapter` and specifying the target `DataSet` and the name of the table. After fetching the first rowset from the `MenuItems` table, it changes the SQL statement and fetches the rows from the `SizeAndPrice` table. The same parameter, used both times, selects only the appropriate rows that match the item type from the query string:

```
...
Try

    ' fetch the MenuItems rows into the DataSet as a new table
    da.Fill(ds, "MenuItems")

    ' change the SQL statement in the SelectCommand of the
    ' SqlDataAdapter to the one that selects the SizeAndPrice rows
    da.SelectCommand.CommandText = sGetSizesAndPrices

    ' fetch the SizeAndPrice rows into the DataSet as another new table
    da.Fill(ds, "SizeAndPrice")

Catch ex As Exception

    ' if there is an error, display the message and stop execution here
    Label1.Text = "ERROR: " & ex.Message
    Exit Sub

End Try

End Using
...
```

155

Notice how a `Try..Catch` construct traps any error that may occur and displays the error message from the resulting `Exception` instance in the `Label` control you placed below the `DataList` control in the page.

Creating the Relationship in the DataSet

Now the code can create the relationship between the two tables in the `DataSet`. It creates a reference to the primary key column (`MenuItemID` in the `MenuItems` table) and the foreign key column (`fkMenuItemID` in the `SizeAndPrice` table), and then creates a new `DataRelation` instance named `MenuLink` using these two column references. This relationship is then added to the `DataSet`:

```
...
' create a relationship between the two tables in the DataSet
' first get references to the primary key in the MenuItems table
' and the foreign key in the SizeAndPrice table
Dim pkcol As DataColumn = ds.Tables("MenuItems").Columns("MenuItemID")
Dim fkcol As DataColumn = ds.Tables("SizeAndPrice").Columns("fkMenuItemID")

' now create the relationship within the DataSet
Dim dr As New DataRelation("MenuLink", pkcol, fkcol)

' add this relationship to the Relations collection of the DataSet
ds.Relations.Add(dr)
...
```

Binding the List Controls to the DataSet

The final step is to bind the `DataList` in the page to the table named `MenuItems` in the `DataSet`. This is achieved by setting the `DataSource` and `DataMember` properties of the `DataList` control and calling its `DataBind` method. In fact, this is just what the `SqlDataSource` control you saw in earlier examples does behind the scenes when you use it to populate a data display control:

```
...
' bind the MenuItems table to the DataList control to display the rows
DataList1.DataSource = ds
DataList1.DataMember = "MenuItems"
DataList1.DataBind()
```

This process populates the `DataList` control, causing it to display the menu items in the `Image` and `Label` controls you placed in the various templates of this control. However, it does not explain how the nested `Repeater` control in each row of the `DataList` obtains its values. To understand this part of the process, you need to look at the declaration of the `Repeater` control. This is the declaration you used:

```
<asp:Repeater ID="Repeater1" runat="server"

    DataSource='<%# CType(Container.DataItem,
                       DataRowView).CreateChildView("MenuLink") %>'>
  <ItemTemplate>
    <span style="color: Firebrick">
      <%# Eval("ItemSize") %>: <%#Eval("ItemPrice", "${0:F2}")%>  </span>
  </ItemTemplate>
</asp:Repeater>
```

Notice the `DataSource` attribute. The code you see in the data binding statement gets a reference to the `Container`, which is the data-binding context for the current row in the `DataList`. The `DataItem` property of the `Container` returns a reference to the `DataRow` within the `DataSet` table that provides the data for this row in the `DataList`. This `DataRow` is converted (cast) into an instance of the `DataRowView` class, which exposes a method named `CreateChildView`. This method takes the name of a `DataRelation` within the `DataSet`, and returns only the rows that match the primary key in the current row.

This "child view" set of rows is, of course, just what you want to bind to the nested `Repeater`. Inside the `ItemTemplate` of the `Repeater`, the data binding statements extract the `ItemSize` and `ItemPrice` values from each row in the child view and display them separated by a nonbreaking space character, and with the price preceded by a dollar sign and formatted to two decimal places (see Figure 5-33).

Pizza - Hawaiian
Generously topped with Ham and pineapple. A bit fruity. Served by someone wearing a loud shirt.
Slice: $2.50   Small: $5.95   Medium: $7.95   Large: $9.95

Figure 5-33: The Result of the nested binding in the `ShowMenu.aspx` **page**

You have now seen two different approaches to creating a Web page using nested data binding. One approach uses the data source controls, while the second and more efficient approach means that you have to write code yourself to populate a `DataSet` and bind it to the data display controls in the page. Even though VWD provides a great drag-and-drop environment for building ASP.NET pages without writing any code (or even needing to know about code at all), you can see that there are situations where knowledge of how ASP.NET works, and how to get better performance by writing code yourself, brings benefits. You will see this again in subsequent chapters.

User Controls and Binding to XML Data

To complete this chapter, you will see two more examples that use data source controls and data display controls. This time, however, the data comes not from a relational database, but from XML disk files. The first example takes the data from the `delivery.xml` file, which contains details of the delivery areas and delivery costs for the PPQ Web site. You will see how this data can be exposed through an `XmlDataSource` control, and bound to a `GridView` control for display in the page.

The second example uses the `Web.sitemap` file that you met in Chapter 2. The `Menu` and `SiteMapPath` controls in the Master Page for the PPQ site use this file — which contains a list of the pages in the site, their URL, and a description of each one. The example you will see here creates a series of text links from this file, for display at the foot of every page in the site to provide better accessibility for specialist user agents (as discussed in Chapter 2 in the section "Building and Using a Master Page and Content Page"). In addition, to demonstrate another useful feature of ASP.NET, you will build this page as a `User Control`, which you can reuse in other pages within the site or in other Web sites that you build.

Building the Delivery Costs Page

The page that displays the delivery costs is relatively simple. However, it takes its data not from a relational database (as you have seen so far), but from an XML disk file named `delivery.xml`, stored in the XML-Data subfolder of the PPQ site. The good news is that you can use a data source control to access this data, and then bind a data display control to this data source control to display the data—in much the same way as you did with a `SqlDataSource` control and the `GridView` control in previous examples.

The file `delivery.xml` looks like this:

```
<?xml version="1.0" encoding="utf-8" ?>
<ppq-delivery-areas>
  <delivery-area id="1" name="Uptown" delivery-cost="2.5" />
  <delivery-area id="2" name="Downtown" delivery-cost="3.5" />
  <delivery-area id="3" name="Middletown" delivery-cost="3" />
  <delivery-area id="4" name="Out of town" delivery-cost="5.5" />
  <delivery-area id="5" name="Wrong side of the tracks" delivery-cost="7.5" />
  <delivery-area id="6" name="Out of State" delivery-cost="15" />
</ppq-delivery-areas>
```

An `XmlDataSource` control can read this file and expose it as a rowset to which a `GridView` control (and other list controls) can be data-bound. However, life is not always as simple as this, as you will see in this example.

1. Open the `PPQ.master` page in Design view, right-click on the `ContentPlaceHolder` control, and select Add Content Page. Switch the new page to `Design` view, and save it as `Delivery.aspx` using the Save Default2.aspx As . . . option on the File menu. Now drag an `XmlDataSource` control from the Data section of the Toolbox onto the page, and select Configure Data Source from the XmlDataSource Tasks pane. Click the Browse. . . button next to the "Data file:" text box, and select the file `delivery.xml` from the XML-Data subfolder (see Figure 5-34).

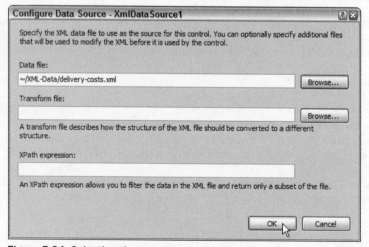

Figure 5-34: Selecting the `delivery.xml` file

2. Click OK, and then drag a `GridView` control from the Toolbox onto the page. In the GridView Tasks pane, select `XmlDataSource1` in the Choose Data Source drop-down list, and the `GridView` shows the values of the attributes in each of the `<delivery-area>` elements. Apply an Auto Format of your choice, and then select Edit Columns . . . in the GridView Tasks pane (see Figure 5-35).

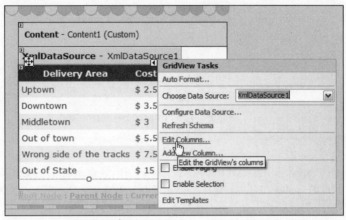

Figure 5-35: Selecting Edit Columns . . . in the GridView Tasks pane

3. Remove the first column (named `id`) by clicking on it in the Selected fields: list and clicking the button next to this list. Select the `name` column and change the `HeaderText` property to `Delivery Area`. Then select the `delivery-cost` column and change the `HeaderText` property to just `Cost`. This final column contains a value for the delivery cost and should be displayed as a currency amount, so enter the format string `$ {0:F2}` you used in previous examples for the `DataFormatString` property (see Figure 5-36).

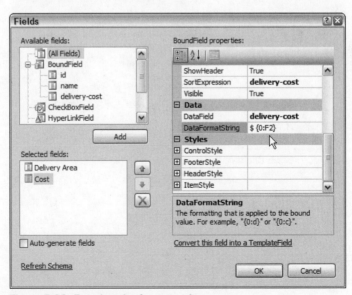

Figure 5-36: Entering the format string

4. Now, run the page to see the results. You have values in the `GridView` control, but the `Cost` column is not formatted correctly (see Figure 5-37). This is because the values in the attributes of the XML file are text strings and not numeric types, as they are when you extract data from a database.

Delivery Area	Cost
Uptown	$ 2.5
Downtown	$ 3.5
Middletown	$ 3
Out of town	$ 5.5
Wrong side of the tracks	$ 7.5
Out of State	$ 15

Figure 5-37: Improperly formatted
`Cost` **column**

5. Go back to Design view, select the `GridView` control, and open the GridView Tasks pane. Select Edit Columns . . . and, in the Fields dialog, select the `Cost` column in the Selected fields: list. Click the link to "Convert this field into a TemplateField" (see Figure 5-38), and then click OK.

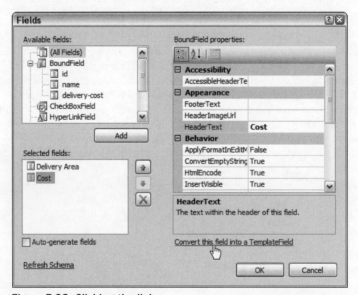

Figure 5-38: Clicking the link

6. Now switch to Source view and look at the code that VWD has created, shown in the following listing. As expected, it has added a `TemplateField` to the declaration of the `GridView` control, replacing the `BoundField` for the `Cost` column. It uses the `Bind` statement to bind the values in the XML attributes to the `Label` and `TextBox` controls (even though you cannot switch to edit mode against an `XmlDataSource` control). The format string you specified is there but has no effect on the string data in the attribute.

```
<asp:TemplateField HeaderText="Cost" SortExpression="delivery-cost">
  <ItemTemplate>
    <asp:Label ID="Label1" runat="server"
               Text='<%# Bind("delivery-cost", "$ {0:F2}") %>'>
    </asp:Label>
  </ItemTemplate>
  <EditItemTemplate>
    <asp:TextBox ID="TextBox1" runat="server"
                 Text='<%# Bind("delivery-cost") %>'>
    </asp:TextBox>
  </EditItemTemplate>
</asp:TemplateField>
```

7. The only solution is to change the binding statement to one that does provide the output format you need. If you write a custom function in code (you will see more on this topic in subsequent chapters) that creates and returns the value you want to display, you can call this function from here using the following:

```
Text='<%# MyFunction(XPath("@delivery-cost")) %>'>
```

This simply collects the value from the attribute that would have been bound to the `Label` control (using the `XPath` statement and specifying the attribute named `delivery-cost`) and passes this value to your custom function. Whatever the function returns is displayed in the page. However, here is an even easier solution — you can include a single code statement that creates the value directly within the data-binding section (within the `<%#` and `%>` delimiters). The following statement creates the required result by specifying a dollar currency symbol and then applying the `Format` method of the `String` class to the result of parsing the value of the attribute into a number of type `Double`:

```
"$ " & String.Format("{0:F2}", Double.Parse(XPath("@delivery-cost")))
```

In your page (see Figure 5-39), delete the `<EditTemplate>` section and modify the `<ItemTemplate>` section so that it looks like this:

```
<asp:TemplateField HeaderText="Cost" SortExpression="delivery-cost">
  <ItemTemplate>
    <asp:Label ID="Label1" runat="server"

               Text='<%# "$ " & String.Format("{0:F2}",
                         Double.Parse(XPath("@delivery-cost"))) %>'>
    </asp:Label>
  </ItemTemplate>
</asp:TemplateField>
```

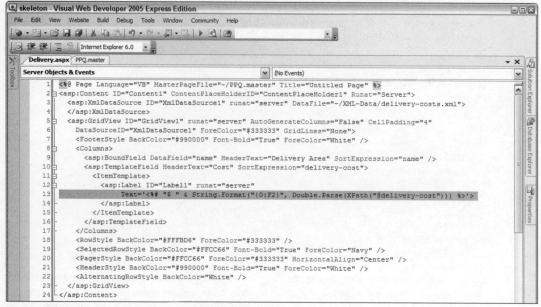

Figure 5-39: Deleting a section and modifying a section

8. Now click "run" on the main toolbar, or press F5, to see the results. As you can see in Figure 5-40, the delivery costs are now properly displayed in currency format. This is yet another example of why it is often useful to understand and be able to use custom code when building your pages — and leaving it to VWD to do the hard work of generating the rest of the page!

Delivery Area	Cost
Uptown	$ 2.50
Downtown	$ 3.50
Middletown	$ 3.00
Out of town	$ 5.50
Wrong side of the tracks	$ 7.50
Out of State	$ 15.00

Figure 5-40: Delivery costs displaying in the proper format

Building the Text Links User Control

In Chapter 2, you saw the Web.sitemap file that provides the data from the Menu and SiteMapPath controls in the Master Page of the PPQ example site. At the end of that chapter, you had a working page — but with only a placeholder for the footer and page text links at the bottom (see Figure 5-41).

Figure 5-41: The placeholder for the footer and text links

The task here, then, is to create a section of content that automatically displays the links from the main navigation bar, but simply as text links suitable for users of all types of specialist browser. These links will be created dynamically from the `Web.sitemap` file, so that changes to the layout of the site in this file are reflected in the page footer links. However, the navigation menu is hierarchical, and you probably want to display only the main pages (those at the top level of the menu and not those on the fly-out sections); otherwise, there will be too many links to assimilate easily.

Converting the XML with an XSLT Style Sheet

The main problem is that the `Web.sitemap` file has an unusual structure — one that makes it impossible to bind directly to an `XmlDataSource` control. Some of the nodes have been removed from the following listing, but you can clearly see that there is a single "Home" node (`Default.aspx`) within the root node. Within the "Home" node are several other nodes that are displayed at the top level of the menu, but are child nodes of the "Home" node. Each of these nodes can also have child nodes, which represent the items on the "fly-out" sections of the menu.

```xml
<?xml version="1.0" encoding="utf-8" ?>
<siteMap xmlns="http://schemas.microsoft.com/AspNet/SiteMap-File-1.0" >
   <siteMapNode url="Default.aspx" title="Home" description="Home Page">
     <siteMapNode url="ShowMenu.aspx" title="Our Menu"
                 description="View our menu">
       <siteMapNode url="ShowMenu.aspx?type=pizza" title="Pizzas"
                 description="View our pizza range" />
       <siteMapNode url="ShowMenu.aspx?type=drink" title="Drinks"
                 description="View our range of drinks" />
     </siteMapNode>
     <siteMapNode url="Order.aspx" title="Order" description="Place an order">
       ... more nodes here ...
     </siteMapNode>
     ... more nodes here ...
   </siteMapNode>
</siteMap>
```

To use an `XmlDataSource` control, the Extensible Markup Language (XML) must provide a structure where all the nodes that are to be treated as a set or collection are at the same level of the hierarchy. In other words, you need a document that looks like this:

```xml
<?xml version="1.0" encoding="utf-8" ?>
<footerLinks>
   <siteMapNode url="Default.aspx" title="Home" description="Home Page" />
   <siteMapNode url="ShowMenu.aspx" title="Our Menu"
                 description="View our menu" />
   <siteMapNode url="Order.aspx" title="Order" description="Place an order" />
       ... more nodes here ...
</footerLinks>
```

An Extensible Style Language Translation (XSLT) style sheet can perform this conversion. There is not enough room in this book to provide a tutorial for XSLT, but the next listing shows the style sheet so that you can see what it is trying to achieve. XSLT works by processing templates, which can execute other templates in turn for each node in the current context. This style sheet selects the root `<sitemap>` element in the original `Web.sitemap` file and then processes it. This processing involves selecting first the "Home" `<siteMapNode>` element, and then all of its child `<siteMapNode>` elements (but not any other descendant `<siteMapNode>` elements). For each element it processes, it simply copies that element to the output.

```
<xsl:stylesheet version="1.0" xmlns:xsl="http://www.w3.org/1999/XSL/Transform"
                xmlns:wsm="http://schemas.microsoft.com/AspNet/SiteMap-File-1.0">

<xsl:template match="/">
  <footerLinks>
    <xsl:apply-templates select="//wsm:siteMap" />
  </footerLinks>
</xsl:template>

<xsl:template match="wsm:siteMap">
  <xsl:apply-templates select="./wsm:siteMapNode" />
  <xsl:apply-templates select="./wsm:siteMapNode/wsm:siteMapNode" />
</xsl:template>

<xsl:template match="wsm:siteMapNode">
  <xsl:copy-of select="." />
</xsl:template>

</xsl:stylesheet>
```

This process does not remove the descendant child nodes within each of the nodes it processes, but they have no effect on the operation of the `XmlDataSource` control. The important point is that all of the nodes required for the links in the footer are now at the top level of the XML document. The style sheet you have just seen, named `FooterLinksTransform.xsl`, is in the `user-controls` folder of the examples.

Creating the User Control

This section describes the steps for creating the user control that implements the text links and footer section for the pages in the PPQ site.

1. Go to the Solution Explorer window, and select the folder named `user-controls`. Right-click, and select Add New Item . . . to open the Add New Item dialog (doing this from a folder in the Solution Explorer window means that the new item will be created within the selected folder, rather that at the root of the Web site). Select Web User Control, change the filename to `FooterLinks.ascx`, and click Add (see Figure 5-42).

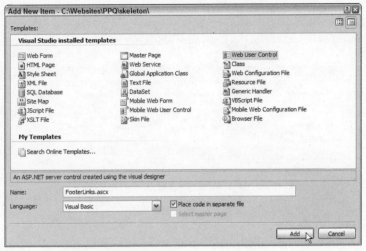

Figure 5-42: Add New Item dialog

2. Switch to Design view, and drag an XmlDataSource control from the Data section of the Toolbox onto the page. Click Configure Data Source in the XmlDataSource Tasks pane that appears to open the Configure Data Source dialog. Click the Browse . . . button next to the "Data file" text box to open the Select XML File dialog, change the "Files of type" list at the bottom to All Files (*.*). Then select Web.sitemap and click OK (see Figure 5-43). Notice that VWD adds the tilde character (~) to the start of the filename to indicate that it is in the root folder of the Web site's ASP.NET application.

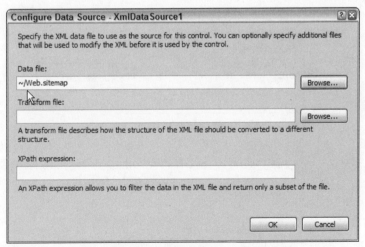

Figure 5-43: Tilde character (~) at beginning of filename

3. Click the Browse . . . button next to the "Transform file" text box to open the Select XML Transform File dialog. Select `FooterLinksTransform.xsl` from the `user-controls` subfolder (see Figure 5-44), and click OK. Then click OK again to close the Configure Data Source dialog.

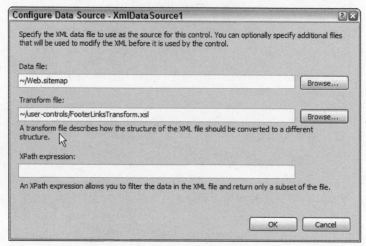

Figure 5-44: Filling in the Transform File dialog

4. Drag a `Div` control from the HTML section of the Toolbox onto the page, and then drag a `Repeater` control from Data section of the Toolbox and drop it into the `Div` control. Select XmlDataSource1 in the Choose Data Source drop-down list of the Repeater Tasks pane (see Figure 5-45).

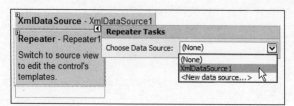

Figure 5-45: Repeater Tasks pane

5. Drag another `Div` control from the HTML section of the Toolbox onto the page, placing it below the `Repeater` control. Then drag a `Hyperlink` control from Standard section of the Toolbox and drop it into the `Div` control (see Figure 5-46).

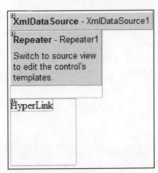

Figure 5-46: Adding a `Hyperlink` control

6. Switch to Source view, click on the first opening `<div>` element, and go to the Properties dialog. Select the `Style` property, and click the three dots (...) button to open the Style Builder dialog. In the Font page, go to the Size section in the middle of the dialog and select Specific; then enter `0.8` and select em. Then go to the Text page and select `Centered` for Alignment, Horizontal. Finally, go to the Edges page, enter 5, select px for the Padding, Top setting (see Figure 5-47), and click OK to close the Style Builder dialog. Now, click on the second `<div>` element and apply the same settings. Together, they will center the text links on the page and use a slightly smaller than standard font.

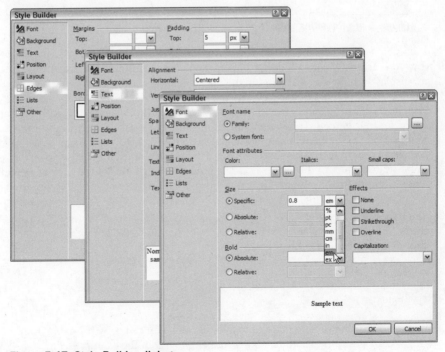

Figure 5-47: Style Builder dialog

7. Click on the opening `<asp:Hyperlink>` tag, and open the Properties dialog. Set the `Text` property to the Webmaster address you want to use for your site, set the `Tooltip` property to `Email the Webmaster`, and set the `NavigateUrl` property `mailto:your-email-address`. Remove any content (such as "Hyperlink") that VWD has inserted into the `<asp:Hyperlink>` element between the opening and closing tags. Also remove the width and height selectors that VWD adds to style attributes as the two `<div>` elements. Your code should now look something like Figure 5-48 (you can tidy up the layout and add line breaks to make it easier to read and assimilate).

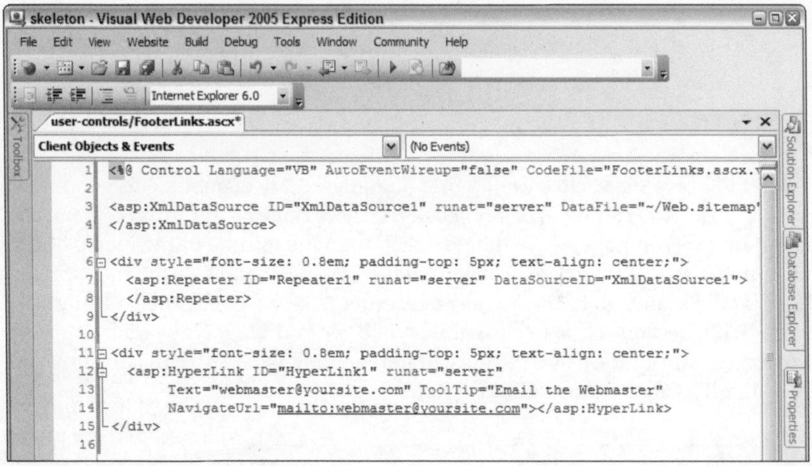

Figure 5-48: Resulting code

8. Now you can add the data binding statements that will pull the data from the `XmlDataSource` and display it in the page. To bind to the nodes in an XML file, you use the `XPath` statement (rather than `Eval` or `Bind` that you saw in earlier examples with a `SqlDataSource` control). The following listing shows the completed repeater control declaration, with the data binding statements highlighted. The statement `XPath("@url")` extracts the value of the attribute named `url` from the current element as the `Repeater` control is binding to each node in the XML document in turn. This sets the `href` attribute of a normal HTML anchor `<a>` element. Similarly, the values of the `description` and `title` attributes of the current element set the `title` attribute (the pop-up tooltip) and the text within the `<a>` and `</a>` tags that is displayed in the page.

```
<asp:Repeater ID="Repeater1" runat="server" DataSourceID="XmlDataSource1">
  <ItemTemplate>
    <a href='<%#XPath("@url")%>'
       title='<%#XPath("@description")%>'><%#XPath("@title")%></a>
  </ItemTemplate>
  <SeparatorTemplate> | </SeparatorTemplate>
</asp:Repeater>
```

To save you having to type this and to avoid errors, you can copy this code from the file named `FooterLinks.ascx.txt` in the `page-content` folder of the examples. Figure 5-49 shows what it should look like when complete.

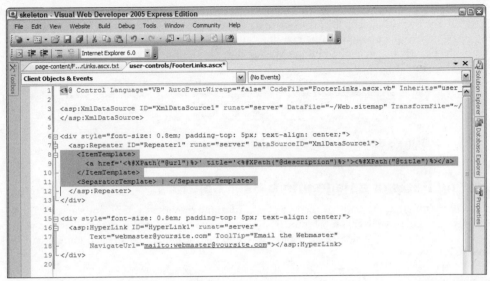

Figure 5-49: Result of adding data-binding statements

9. The final task now is to insert the new user control into the Master Page of the site where the placeholder is currently located. The easiest way to insert a user control into another page is to drag it from the Solution Explorer window into the target page. Open the page PPQ.master in Design view, and drag the file FooterLinks.ascx from the user-controls subfolder in the Solution Explorer window onto the PPQ.master page. Drop it into the bottom section of the page, next to the existing text placeholder ("Footer and text links go here"). Then delete the text placeholder. You will see the contents of your user control in the page (see Figure 5-50).

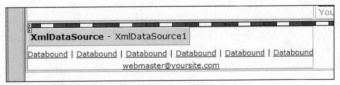

Figure 5-50: Contents of user control

10. Switch to Source view to see what VWD has done. At the top of the page, it added a Register directive that provides the link between the prefix and name of the element (tag) that will be used to insert the user control into the page, and the file containing the declaration of the user control:

```
<%@ Register Src="user-controls/FooterLinks.ascx"
            TagName="FooterLinks" TagPrefix="uc1" %>
```

Then, at the position where the control will appear on the page, it added the appropriate element:

```
<uc1:FooterLinks ID="FooterLinks1" runat="server" />
```

169

You can, of course, add these elements yourself rather than using the drag-and-drop method. To see the result, click the "run" button on the toolbar, or press F5. VWD executes the `Default.aspx` page, and the text links and footer can be seen at the bottom of the section of the page that is generated by the Master Page (see Figure 5-51).

Figure 5-51: Master Page text links and footer

Converting Parts of a Page into a User Control

Instead of creating a user control directly, as you did in the previous section, you can convert existing sections of a page into a user control quite easily. Any page content that is repeated across your pages (even if repeated only on a single page), or that would be useful in other sites you build, can be converted into a user control.

You simply copy any HTML, control declarations, or code that you want to place in the user control into a separate file. You can create this file by selecting Web User Control in the Add New Item dialog (select New File . . . from the File menu), or you can do it by removing any unwanted content from an existing Web Form (`.aspx`) page. Then change the `@Page` directive to `@Control` and save the file with the `.ascx` extension. To insert this file as a user control, just drag it from the Solution Explorer window into your target Web Form page.

> Note that a user control should not contain the `<html>`, `<head>`, or `<body>` tags, or a server-side `<form>` (a `<form>` element with the `runat="server"` attribute). Only one instance of these elements is permitted in a page, and the parent page that contains the user control should declare these elements instead. That way, you can use multiple copies of the user control in the same page if you wish.

You can only use a user control from within the same ASP.NET application, but you can copy your user control (complete with any images or other resources it uses) into another application and use it there. You will come across another example of a user control later in this book, when you see how the process of placing an order in the PPQ Web site is implemented.

Summary

In this chapter, you have investigated three topic areas. The first was a detailed look into how ASP.NET can create nested data-bound output from a relational database, both by using the data source controls and through custom code that you write yourself. The display of data in nested format might seem an esoteric topic but, in fact, it finds its way into many common scenarios. Examples range from the pizza menu you saw in this chapter to displaying details of customer orders, and even to areas such as stock location in a warehouse.

Getting the most from any programming environment generally means learning more about the tools and the underlying frameworks and languages it supports. To achieve some of the tasks in this chapter, you need to learn more about the programming techniques available within the .NET Framework—but this is no bad thing. In this chapter, you discovered more about how data access works in ADO.NET and how custom code can improve the performance of your pages.

The second topic area covered in this chapter is the way that you can handle XML data using a data source control and the same data display controls as you used earlier with relational data from a database. XML data is becoming increasingly common, and ASP.NET provides plenty of techniques for managing it. As with ADO.NET, there are plenty of classes available within the System.Xml namespace you can use to write your own custom XML data-handling routines.

Finally, this chapter showed how you can create reusable content for your Web sites as user controls. These are simply sections of HTML, code, server controls, or other content that are stored as separate files and then dropped into the target page in VWD. They provide many advantages for situations where you have repeated similar content (for example, you can edit the user control and these changes automatically appear in all the pages that use it).

In Chapter 6, you continue your exploration of the PPQ Web site, and the techniques used to build it, by moving on to the process of taking an order from a customer.

Managing and Editing Data

In the previous two chapters, we have looked at various ways of displaying data, using the data source controls and grids supplied with ASP.NET. While displaying data is a core requirement of many Web sites, there are times when you also need to allow editing, and you can use the same controls as for displaying data. In the PPQ application, users have no need to update data, but the site administrators might — to update the menu and prices.

In this chapter, we are going to see how the administrator of a site can perform edits on the data. In particular, we'll be looking at:

❑   How to modify the SqlDataSource control to allow data editing

❑   How to configure the GridView to allow data editing.

Both of these topics extend techniques you've already used, so you will find this a natural progression into your exploration of data controls.

Data Source Controls

In Chapter 4, you saw how the SqlDataControl was used to fetch data from a database by specifying a SQL command in the SelectCommand property. When the page is loaded, the SqlDataSource object opens a connection to the database and runs this command to fetch the data. The SqlDataControl also has properties that allow you to define the command to be run to modify data, which are the InsertCommand, UpdateCommand, and DeleteCommand properties. You've already seen these in action, even if you didn't realize it, when you used the test menu pages in Chapter 4 (the grid had editing capabilities).

The properties of the SqlDataSource control allow you to specify different SQL commands for different types of operation. So, we have the following properties:

❑   SelectCommand, which you use to fetch data from the database

❑   InsertCommand, which you use to insert data into the database

❑   UpdateCommand, which you use to update data in the database

❑   DeleteCommand, which you use to delete data from the database

When you drag a table from the Database Explorer and drop it onto a page, these properties are automatically set for you. But it's worth learning how to configure data sources manually.

Try It Out   Configuring the SqlDatSource Control for Editing

1.   Create a new ASP.NET Web Form called Admin.aspx, making sure to select the "Place code in a separate file" option, and switch the page to Design view.

2.   From the Data section of the Toolbox, drag a SqlDataSource control and drop it onto the page.

3.   From the SqlDataSource Tasks, select "Configure Data source . . ."

4.   On the first page of the configuration window, select PPQ_DataConnectionString1 from the data connections (see Figure 6-1), and click Next.

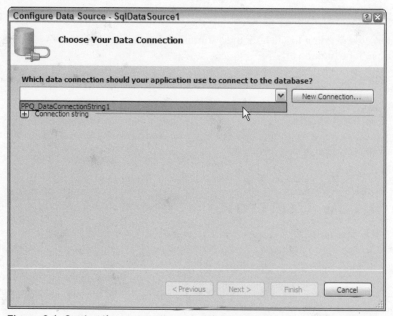

Figure 6-1: Setting the connection string for the SqlDataSource **control**

5.   To configure the Select Statement, select MenuItems from the Name list, and tick the * option (see Figure 6-2).

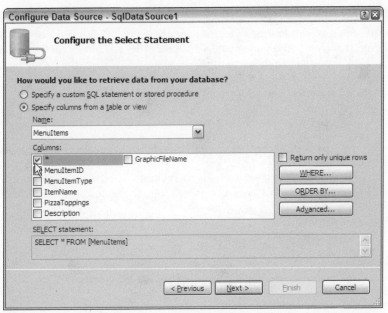

Figure 6-2: Configuring the Select Statement on a SqlDataSource control

6. Click the Advanced button. On the advanced options window, tick "Generate INSERT, UPDATE, and DELETE statements" (see Figure 6-3). Click the OK button to close this window.

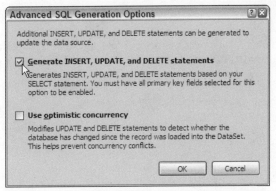

Figure 6-3: Enabling generation of the insert, update, and delete statements

7. Back on the data source configuration window, click Next and then Finish to close the window.

How It Works

Although we haven't seen this in action yet, it's worth looking at the code to see what the Configuration Wizard has done. This way, you'll understand what properties have been configured and how they relate to the wizard. If you switch the page to Source view, you will see the following code.

On the first page of the wizard, you set the connection string, detailing the database to connect to, which sets the `ConnectionString` property:

```
<asp:SqlDataSource ID="SqlDataSource1" runat="server"
  ConnectionString="<%$ ConnectionStrings:PPQ_DataConnectionString1 %>"
```

On the next page of the wizard, you set the table and columns for the `Select` command, which is what defines the data to be shown (in this case, all columns from the `MenuItems` table), and this sets the `SelectCommand` property:

```
SelectCommand="SELECT * FROM [MenuItems]"
```

Selecting the advanced options and ticking the box to automatically generate the other commands sets the `DeleteCommand`, `InsertCommand`, and `UpdateCommand` properties:

```
DeleteCommand="DELETE FROM [MenuItems] WHERE [MenuItemID] = @MenuItemID"

InsertCommand="INSERT INTO [MenuItems] ([MenuItemType], [ItemName],
[PizzaToppings], [Description], [GraphicFileName]) VALUES (@MenuItemType,
@ItemName, @PizzaToppings, @Description, @GraphicFileName)"

UpdateCommand="UPDATE [MenuItems] SET [MenuItemType] = @MenuItemType, [ItemName] =
@ItemName, [PizzaToppings] = @PizzaToppings, [Description] = @Description,
[GraphicFileName] = @GraphicFileName WHERE [MenuItemID] = @MenuItemID">
```

These define the SQL statements that will be run to delete, insert, or update data, and we'll be coming back to these in a little while. For each command that modifies data, there is also a section for the parameters:

```
<DeleteParameters>
  <asp:Parameter Name="MenuItemID" Type="Int32" />
</DeleteParameters>
<UpdateParameters>
  <asp:Parameter Name="MenuItemType" Type="String" />
  <asp:Parameter Name="ItemName" Type="String" />
  <asp:Parameter Name="PizzaToppings" Type="String" />
  <asp:Parameter Name="Description" Type="String" />
```

```
      <asp:Parameter Name="GraphicFileName" Type="String" />
      <asp:Parameter Name="MenuItemID" Type="Int32" />
   </UpdateParameters>
   <InsertParameters>
      <asp:Parameter Name="MenuItemType" Type="String" />
      <asp:Parameter Name="ItemName" Type="String" />
      <asp:Parameter Name="PizzaToppings" Type="String" />
      <asp:Parameter Name="Description" Type="String" />
      <asp:Parameter Name="GraphicFileName" Type="String" />
   </InsertParameters>
</asp:SqlDataSource>
```

To understand how all of this works, you must consider the commands and parameters together, so let's start with deleting rows.

You will be deleting only a single row at a time. Each row is unique. It contains a single menu item, identified by the ID field, which is MenuItemID (this was explained in Chapter 3). So, to delete a row, we want to run the Delete command only when the MenuItemID field matches a certain value — the ID of the row being deleted, which will be passed into the SQL statement by the SqlDataSource control. To pass a value in, we use *parameters* — this is a general programming term used to denote the passing of values to another routine. For SQL statements, the parameters are preceded by an @ sign, so @MenuItemID is the only parameter for the DeleteCommand property.

```
DeleteCommand="DELETE FROM [MenuItems] WHERE [MenuItemID] = @MenuItemID"
```

To get the value into the SQL statement, there is a <DeleteParameters> section, identifying the Name and Type of the property:

```
<DeleteParameters>
   <asp:Parameter Name="MenuItemID" Type="Int32" />
</DeleteParameters>
```

Figure 6-4 shows how the parameters are matched between the SQL statements and the parameter sections.

The commands and associated parameters are used only if that particular command is executed. Binding a GridView control to this SqlDataSource control, but not allowing any updates, would mean that the commands shown in Figure 6-4 would never get used. If you don't need editing for a grid, then you don't need to generate these commands (see Figure 6-3).

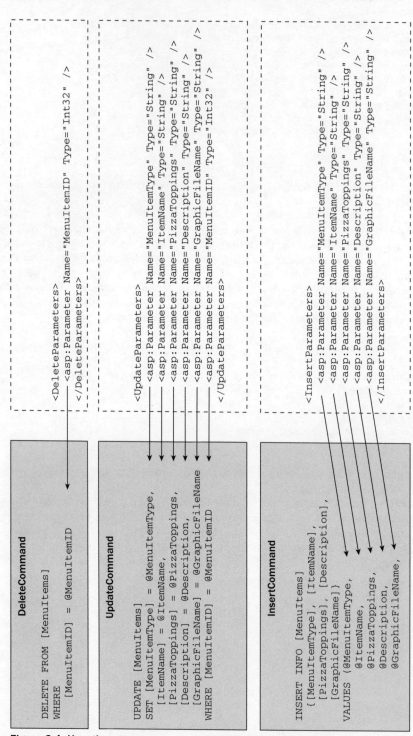

Figure 6-4: How the parameters are mapped to the SQL statements

Let's now add a grid so that you can see the editing in practice.

Editing with the GridView Control

1.   Ensure that the Admin page is in Design view.

2.   From the Data section of the Toolbox, drag a `GridView` onto the page.

3.   On the GridView Tasks, choose the Data Source `SqlDataSource1` from the list (see Figure 6-5).

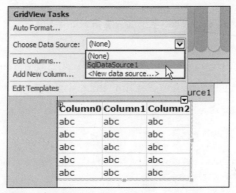

Figure 6-5: Setting the data source for a `GridView` control

4.   Tick the Enable Editing and Enable Deleting selections (see Figure 6-6).

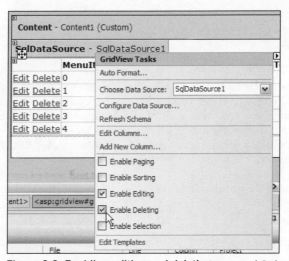

Figure 6-6: Enabling editing and deleting on a `GridView` control

5.   Close the GridView Tasks, and save the file.

6. Right-click anywhere on the page background, and select View in Browser (this page isn't available from the PPQ menu).

7. On the running page, click Edit on the first pizza. Notice how some columns turn from just displaying data into text areas that allow editing, and that the links no longer say "Edit" and "Delete," but rather "Update" and "Cancel" (see Figure 6-7).

	MenuItemID	MenuItemType	ItemName
Update Cancel	1	Pizza	Margherita

Figure 6-7: A `GridView` **row in edit mode**

8. Edit the `PizzaToppings` column, adding "**and garlic**" to the end of the toppings.

9. Click Update to save the changes. See how the row is now read-only.

10. Click Edit again, and change the toppings back to what they were.

11. Close the browser window.

Let's now take a look at what code is generated for the `GridView` and how it works in conjunction with the `SqlDataSource` control.

How It Works

If you switch to Source view, you'll see the code that has been added by configuring the grid to use the data source control. Apart from the `ID` and `runat` properties, three properties are configured on the `GridView` control itself:

```
<asp:GridView ID="GridView1" runat="server"
    AutoGenerateColumns="False" DataKeyNames="MenuItemID"
    DataSourceID="SqlDataSource1">
```

The first of these properties, `AutoGenerateColumns`, indicates whether the grid automatically generates the columns when fetching data. When you configure the data source for a grid, VWD will query the database for the columns, and add these explicitly. So, `AutogenerateColumns` is set to `False`. `DataKeyNames`, which indicates the columns that uniquely identify the row — in this case it is just `MenuItemID`, but it could be a comma-separated list of column names. `DataSourceID` is set to the `ID` property of the `SqlDataSource` control.

As VWD explicitly added the columns, there is a `<columns>` element, which contains the columns to show:

```
<Columns>
```

The first column is a `CommandField`, which details the commands to be shown. The `ShowDeleteButton` is set to `True` to ensure that the Delete button is visible, and `ShowEditButton` is `True` to show the Edit button.

```
<asp:CommandField ShowDeleteButton="True" ShowEditButton="True" />
```

Notice that there is nothing set for the Update and Cancel buttons, which ASP.NET shows when you edit a row. This is because ASP.NET generates these automatically when you edit the row. The `CommandField` is intelligent and changes what it displays depending upon the current state of the row. So, for a row that is being displayed, "Edit" and "Delete" are shown, but for the row you are editing, "Update" and "Cancel" are shown.

After the `CommandField` come the individual fields, each represented by a `BoundField`. We looked at fields in detail in Chapter 4, in the "About the GridView Control" section, although there we were only concerned with viewing data. The important point to note here is the `ReadOnly` property on the first field, for `MenuItemID`. This property is set to `True`, indicating that when you edit a row, this field isn't editable. Instead of becoming a text box like other text entry fields, this field remains a display label.

```
<asp:BoundField DataField="MenuItemID" HeaderText="MenuItemID"
  InsertVisible="False" ReadOnly="True" SortExpression="MenuItemID" />
<asp:BoundField DataField="MenuItemType" HeaderText="MenuItemType"
  SortExpression="MenuItemType" />
<asp:BoundField DataField="ItemName" HeaderText="ItemName"
  SortExpression="ItemName" />
<asp:BoundField DataField="PizzaToppings" HeaderText="PizzaToppings"
  SortExpression="PizzaToppings" />
<asp:BoundField DataField="Description" HeaderText="Description"
  SortExpression="Description" />
<asp:BoundField DataField="GraphicFileName" HeaderText="GraphicFileName"
  SortExpression="GraphicFileName" />
</Columns>
</asp:GridView>
```

At its simplest, that's all there is to editing data with a `GridView` control, but as with much of ASP.NET, you can dig a bit deeper. For example, instead of explicitly adding editing capabilities with the `CommandField`, you can let ASP.NET generate this. The `GridView` control has two properties to do this for you: `AutoGenerateEditButton` (which when set to `True` displays the Edit button) and `AutoGenerateDeleteButton` (which when set to `True` displays the Delete button).

You saw that the `AutoGenerateColumns` property was set to `False`, so that you had define the columns yourself, rather than letting the `GridView` do it for you. The advantage of explicitly defining columns is that you can edit the column headings, set the column order, and control the contents of the various templates. We looked at templates in the "Using Data Display Control Templates" section in Chapter 4, so let's extend that knowledge by looking at the template used for editing.

Try It Out   Using Edit Templates

1. Switch the Admin page to Design view, and select the `GridView` control.

2. From the GridView Tasks, select Edit Columns (see Figure 6-8).

Figure 6-8: How to edit the columns of a `GridView` control

3. In the "Selected fields" select `MenuItemID`, and in the "BoundField properties" set the `Visible` property to `False` (see Figure 6-9).

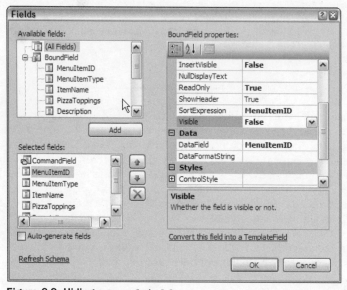

Figure 6-9: Hiding a `BoundField`

4. In the "Selected fields" select `MenuItemType` and click the "Convert this field into a TemplateField" link, at the bottom of the window, on the right.

5. Click the OK button.

6. On the GridView Tasks, select Edit Templates, and from the Display list select `EditItemTemplate` (see Figure 6-10).

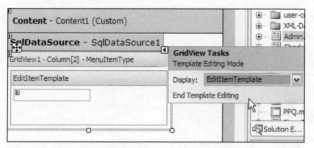

Figure 6-10: Editing the `EditItemTemplate`

7. Select the text box within the template and delete it.

8. From the Standard section of the Toolbox, drag a `DropDownList` into the `EditItemTemplate`.

9. From the DropDownList Tasks, select `Edit DataBindings` (see Figure 6-11).

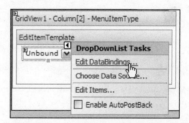

Figure 6-11: Editing the data bindings for a `DropDownList`

10. On the DropDownList1 DataBindings window, ensure that `SelectedValue` in the "Bindable properties" is selected, and pick `MenuItemType` from the "Binding for SelectedValue" (see Figure 6-12).

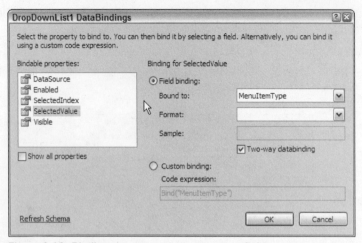

Figure 6-12: Binding the `SelectedValue` to a field

11. Click the OK button to close the window.

12. On the DropDownList Tasks, select Edit Items . . . .

13. On the ListItem Collection Editor, click Add to add a new member. Set the `Text` and `Value` properties to `Pizza`. Click Add again, and for the new member set the `Text` and `Value` properties to `Drink`.

14. Click OK to close the editor.

15. Select End Template Editing from the GridView Tasks.

16. Save the file. Right-click on the file background, and select View in Browser.

17. Select the Margherita pizza, and click the Edit link. Notice how the `MenuItemType` has a drop-down list displayed.

18. From this list, select `Drink` (well, Margherita *is* a drink, too), and click the Update button. Notice that back in view mode, the list isn't shown. Change the type back to `Pizza`, and close the browser.

Let's see how this works.

How It Works

The first thing you did was to hide the `MenuItemID` column by setting its `Visible` property to `False`. Although this is set to read-only, you don't need to see this column, and we deleted it to show that updates work even though you don't have the key field visible.

Next, you converted the `MenuItemType` into a `TemplateColumn`, so instead of a `BoundField`, you have a `TemplateField`:

```
<asp:TemplateField HeaderText="MenuItemType" SortExpression="MenuItemType">
```

The `TemplateField` has the `HeaderText` property set to display text in the header, and the `SortExpression` to the name of the column (we haven't enabled sorting on this grid).

Within the `TemplateField` there are two templates:

❑ The `EditItemTemplate` is used when the row is in Edit mode (that is, when a user clicks the Edit link). When that happens, ASP.NET automatically displays the contents of the `EditItemTemplate`.

❑ The `ItemTemplate` is used when the row is in View mode.

Therefore, the templates contain the controls to be displayed when that template is active.

```
<EditItemTemplate>
```

For the `EditItemTemplate` you added a `DropDownList`, which gives the user a choice of values, so, instead of typing in the text (and possibly getting it wrong), the list limits users to the correct choices.

```
<asp:DropDownList ID="DropDownList1" runat="server"
    SelectedValue='<%# Bind("MenuItemType") %>'>
  <asp:ListItem Selected="True" Value="Pizza">Pizza</asp:ListItem>
  <asp:ListItem>Drink</asp:ListItem>
</asp:DropDownList>
</EditItemTemplate>
```

The list automatically displays the value held in the `MenuItemType` column because you set the data bindings, setting the `SelectedValue` property to the `MenuItemType`. This manifests itself in a data binding expression, which is:

```
<%# Bind("MenuItemType") %>
```

This simply indicates that the value for the property should be bound to the `MenuItemType` column.

The `ItemTemplate` shows fields only when in View mode, so it simply contains a `Label` control. The `Text` property of the label is set to the same binding expression as used by the `DropDownList` — it simply displays the value of the `MenuItemType` field.

```
<ItemTemplate>
  <asp:Label ID="Label1" runat="server"
      Text='<%# Bind("MenuItemType") %>'></asp:Label>
</ItemTemplate>
</asp:TemplateField>
```

Using edit templates is useful for a number of reasons. For a start, it gives you control over exactly what is displayed, allowing you to show content other than just the column. Also, it allows you to add validation, ensuring that the data entered by the user is correct.

One key area to understand is how the data being edited gets back into the database. You saw how the `SqlDataSource` control has commands that define the SQL statements to be run for inserts, updates, and deletes. There are also parameters that define the names and data types of the columns, and it is these parameters that are significant because they match up to the fields used. So, a BoundField with a DataField property of ItemName will match to a parameter named ItemName—the BoundField is two-way, so it both displays data from the SqlDataSource, and sends the value back when editing. The same applies to the MenuItemType, where a BoundField wasn't used, but a TemplateField was used instead. Within the TemplateField, though, the Bind statement has the name of the column. Because Bind provides two-way binding, we have the same functionality as with a BoundField.

Adding New Rows

One of disadvantages of the GridView is that it doesn't support adding rows. There are Edit and Delete buttons, but no Add button. You can modify the CommandField to show a new link by setting the ShowInsertButton property to True, but the GridView itself doesn't support the idea of new rows.

In fact, you might also think that using the Grid for editing isn't the best solution, especially if you have fields that contain large amounts of text—the description field for example, is displayed in a short text field, so not all of it can be seen.

One way around these problems is to use the DetailsView control, so let's modify the page to use a DetailsView for both adding rows and editing. There are a lot of steps in this exercise, but it's really very simple.

Try It Out   **Using the DetailsView Control**

1. Close the running browser, and in Design view, select the GridView. For the CommandField, set the ShowDeleteButton and ShowEditButton properties to False, and the ShowSelectButton to True.

2. Drag a SqlDataSource control onto the page, and drop it underneath the GridView.

3. From the SqlDataSource Tasks, select Configure Data Source . . . .

4. Select PPQ_DataConnectionString1 for the data connection, and click the Next button.

5. To configure the data source, select the MenuItems table, and select the * item from the Fields.

6. Click Next and then Finish to close the configuration.

7. Select the GridView and open the GridView Tasks. In Choose Data Source, select SqlDataSource2, and you will see a warning dialog asking if you wish to refresh the fields (see Figure 6-13). Select Yes.

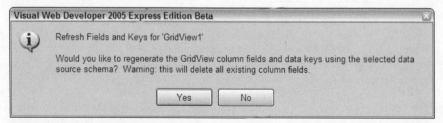

Figure 6-13: Refreshing keys and fields

8. On the GridView Tasks, tick the Enable Selection option.

9. Select the first data source, SqlDataSource1, and from SqlDataSource Tasks, select Configure Data Source . . . .

10. Click Next (because the data connection is OK), and, on the configuration page, click the WHERE . . . button.

11. On the Add WHERE Clause window (see Figure 6-14), set the Column to MenuItemID, the Operator to =, and the Source to Control. In the Parameter properties area, select GridView1, and click the Add button.

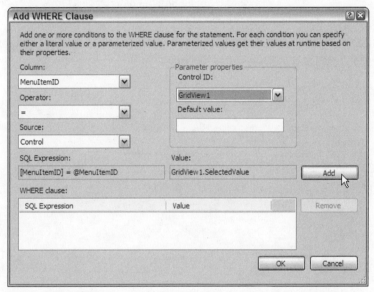

Figure 6-14: Adding a WHERE clause to a SqlDataSource control

12. Click the OK button to return to the SqlDataSource Configuration Wizard. Click Next and then Finish.

13. Drag a DetailsView control onto the form, dropping it underneath SqlDataSource2.

14. On the DetailsViewTasks, select SqlDataSource1 from the Choose Data Source list.

15. Tick the Enable Inserting, Enable Editing, and Enable Deleting options.

16. On the DetailsViewTasks, click Edit Fields . . . .

17. Select MenuItemType from the Selected fields, and click "Convert this field into a TemplateField".

18. Click OK to close the field editor.

19. Click the Edit Templates link, and from the Template Editing Mode, select EditItemTemplate.

20. Select the text box in the template and delete it.

21. From the Standard section of the Toolbox, drag a DropDownList into the EditItemTemplate.

22. From the DropDownList Tasks, select Edit DataBindings (see Figure 6-15).

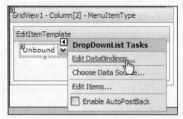

Figure 6-15: Editing the data bindings for a `DropDownList`

23. On the DropDownList1 DataBindings window, ensure that `SelectedValue` from the "Bindable properties" is selected, and pick `MenuItemType` from the "Binding for SelectedValue" (see Figure 6-16).

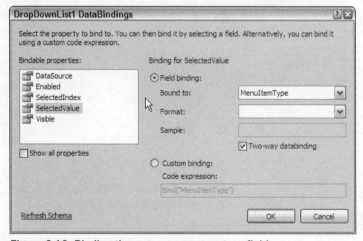

Figure 6-16: Binding the `SelectedValue` **to a field**

24. Click the OK button to close the window.

25. On the DropDownList Tasks, select Edit Items . . . .

26. On the ListItem Collection Editor, click Add to add a new member. Set the `Text` and `Value` properties to `Pizza`. Click Add again, and for the new member, set the `Text` and `Value` properties to `Drink`.

27. Click OK to close the editor.

28. Repeat steps 20 to 27 for the `InsertItemTemplate`, deleting the existing text box, and adding and configuring a `DropDownList` control.

29. Select End Template Editing from the GridView Tasks.

30. Save the file. Right-click on the file background, and select View in Browser.

31. Click the Select link on the `Margherita` item.

32. On the `DetailsView` click the Edit button, change the `MenuItemType` to `Drink`, and click the Update button. Notice that the `GridView` hasn't changed.

33. Click the New button, and enter the following for the new, empty item:

❑ `MenuItemType`—`Drink`

❑ `ItemName`—`Margarita`

❑ `Pizza Toppings`—Leave empty

❑ `Description`—`Tequila, Cointreau, Lime juice`

❑ `GraphicFileName`—Leave empty

34. Click the Insert link to insert the new item. Notice that the new item doesn't appear in the `GridView`.

35. Close the browser window.

36. Select `SqlDataSource1`, and select the Events in the properties window (the button that looks like a fork of lightning).

37. Double-click next to the `Updated` property, to have the event procedure created for you.

38. Between the `Protected Sub` and `End Sub`, add the following:

```
GridView1.DataBind()
```

39. From the list at the top of the code page, select `SqlDataSource1`, and from the list on the right, select `Inserted` (see Figure 6-17).

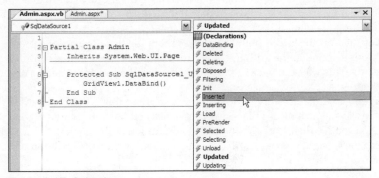

Figure 6-17: Selecting `Inserted`

40. Between the `Protected Sub` and `End Sub`, add the following:

```
GridView1.DataBind()
```

41. From the list at the top of the code page select `SqlDataSource1`. From the list on the right, select `Deleted` (see Figure 6-17).

42. Between the `Protected Sub` and `End Sub`, add the following:

```
GridView1.DataBind()
```

43. Save both files, and view the page in the browser (you'll need to be on the `Admin.aspx` page to do this).

44. Select the `Margherita` pizza, and edit it, changing the item type from `Drink` to `Pizza`. Click the Update link in the `DetailsView`, and notice that the grid updates this time.

45. Click the New link, and add a new item, using the following:

- ❏ `MenuItemType` — `Pizza`
- ❏ `ItemName` — `Pepperoni Special`
- ❏ `Pizza Toppings` — `Sliced meat`
- ❏ `Description` — `Several inches of pepperoni.`
- ❏ `GraphicFileName` — Leave empty

46. Click the Insert button to insert the new item, and notice that the new item shows up on the grid.

47. Select this new item, and click the Delete link.

There's a lot here, so let's see how all of this works.

How It Works

In this exercise, you used the `GridView` for selection of rows, and you used a second `SqlDataSource` control for this. The reason is that you already had a `SqlDataSource` control configured for updates (`SqlDataSource1`), and rather than change that to remove the modify commands and parameters, it made sense to use it for the `DetailsView`, which does require updates. You modified this to add a `WHERE` clause, setting the `MenuItemID` column to match the `SelectedValue` of `GridView1`. This works because the key field for the grid is `MenuItemID`, as set in the `DataKeyFields` property. This means that whenever a row is selected in the grid, the query for the second data source control is rerun, using the newly selected ID. This way, the `DetailsView` will be refreshed with the details of the selected row.

The `DetailsView` is similar in working to the `GridView`, and this is deliberate. Many of the controls work in similar ways, which means that once you've learned how one works, it's easy to learn how the others work. You can see this clearly by the initial declaration of the `DetailsView`, which has properties `AutoGenerateRows`, `DataKeyNames`, and `DataSourceID`, which work in the same way as the `GridView` control.

```
<asp:DetailsView ID="DetailsView1" runat="server"
    AutoGenerateRows="False" DataKeyNames="MenuItemID"
    DataSourceID="SqlDataSource1" Height="50px" Width="125px">
```

The `DetailsView` uses a `<Fields>` element to identify the fields to show, and these, too, should be familiar.

```
<Fields>
```

The first field is a `BoundField` for the `MenuItemID`, with the `ReadOnly` property set to `True`, so that it cannot be edited.

```
<asp:BoundField DataField="MenuItemID" HeaderText="MenuItemID"
    InsertVisible="False" ReadOnly="True" SortExpression="MenuItemID" />
```

Next is a `TemplateField`, for the `MenuItemType`.

```
<asp:TemplateField HeaderText="MenuItemType" SortExpression="MenuItemType">
```

The `TemplateField` contains three templates: one for editing, one for inserting, and one for displaying. Having separate templates allows you to have different functionality — for example, you might not want to allow editing of the `MenuItemType` once it has been set, so you could have a different template. For our template, the content of the `EditItemTemplate` and the `InsertItem` template is the same — a `DropDownList` whose `SelectedValue` property is bound to `MenuItemType`. The `ItemTemplate` is a `Label` control, which simply displays the item type when the `DetailsView` is not being edited or inserting data.

```
<EditItemTemplate>
  <asp:DropDownList ID="DropDownList1" runat="server"
      SelectedValue='<%# Bind("MenuItemType") %>'>
    <asp:ListItem>Pizza</asp:ListItem>
    <asp:ListItem>Drink</asp:ListItem>
  </asp:DropDownList>
</EditItemTemplate>
<InsertItemTemplate>
  <asp:DropDownList ID="DropDownList2" runat="server"
      SelectedValue='<%# Bind("MenuItemType") %>'>
    <asp:ListItem Selected="True">Pizza</asp:ListItem>
    <asp:ListItem>Drink</asp:ListItem>
  </asp:DropDownList>
</InsertItemTemplate>
<ItemTemplate>
  <asp:Label ID="Label1" runat="server"
      Text='<%# Bind("MenuItemType") %>'></asp:Label>
</ItemTemplate>
</asp:TemplateField>
```

The next four fields are all `BoundField` controls. So, display data in View mode, and show a text box when in Edit or Insert mode.

```
<asp:BoundField DataField="ItemName" HeaderText="ItemName"
    SortExpression="ItemName" />
<asp:BoundField DataField="PizzaToppings" HeaderText="PizzaToppings"
    SortExpression="PizzaToppings" />
<asp:BoundField DataField="Description" HeaderText="Description"
    SortExpression="Description" />
<asp:BoundField DataField="GraphicFileName" HeaderText="GraphicFileName"
    SortExpression="GraphicFileName" />
```

The final field is a `CommandField`, where the Delete, Edit, and Insert buttons are visible.

```
<asp:CommandField ShowDeleteButton="True" ShowEditButton="True"
    ShowInsertButton="True" />
</Fields>
</asp:DetailsView>
```

You can see that the `DetailsView` control behaves in a similar way to the `GridView`, with columns and commands that react in different modes. Clicking the Update button places the control in update mode, so the `EditItemTemplate` is shown for `TemplateField` controls, and for `BoundField` controls a text box is shown. Clicking Insert displays the `InsertItemTemplate` for `TemplateField` controls, and a text box for `BoundField` controls. Actually, saving the data runs the appropriate SQL command to update the database.

The first time you ran the page, you could edit data in the `DetailsView`, but the changes weren't reflected in the `GridView`. This is because the grid and data source control don't know that the data has changed. To get around this, you have to resort to code and you used three events for this: the `Deleted`, `Inserted`, and `Updated` events (we've wrapped the code to make it clearer to read, but in your code, the event procedure declaration will be on a single line).

```
Protected Sub SqlDataSource1_Deleted(ByVal sender As Object,
    ByVal e As System.Web.UI.WebControls.SqlDataSourceStatusEventArgs)
    Handles SqlDataSource1.Deleted
  GridView1.DataBind()
End Sub

Protected Sub SqlDataSource1_Inserted(ByVal sender As Object,
    ByVal e As System.Web.UI.WebControls.SqlDataSourceStatusEventArgs)
    Handles SqlDataSource1.Inserted
  GridView1.DataBind()
End Sub

Protected Sub SqlDataSource1_Updated(ByVal sender As Object,
    ByVal e As System.Web.UI.WebControls.SqlDataSourceStatusEventArgs)
    Handles SqlDataSource1.Updated
  GridView1.DataBind()
End Sub
```

The data source control raises these events after it has sent the changes back to the database, and in the event procedure for these, the grid is simply re-bound to the data using the `DataBind` method. This tells the data source to fetch a new copy of the data.

There is also another control, the `FormView`, which works like the `DetailsView` control to provide display and editing of a single row. The difference is that the `DetailsView` automatically displays the row in a table, with the field names on the left, and the fields on the right. The `FormView` has no automatic display — you have to provide the layout yourself. We're not going to cover it here, but it works in the same way, and allows you to lay out the fields however you want, rather than sticking to the table design of the `DetailsView`.

Summary

In this chapter, we have looked at how to edit data from the database, using three controls. The `SqlDataSource` control provides the link between the database and the display of data, and has properties allowing you to set different SQL commands for different types of changes—inserts, deletes, and updates.

The `GridView` not only displays data, but also allows editing, simply by setting a few properties—`AutoGenerateEditButton` and `AutoGenerateDeleteButton`. These add a link to the grid allowing editing—no code is required.

The `DetailsView` provides the same features, but a different view of the data, showing only a single row at a time. This is much more useful for editing data because it shows the data in a formlike way, which is much more intuitive.

The one trouble with this page is that anyone can access it and update the details. In Chapter 9, we will look at how to protect this page from users, allowing access to it only when one is logged into the site. For now though, let's continue our exploration of editing data and look at the ordering process, seeing how users can order menu items online.

Placing an Order

You saw in the Chapters 4 and 5 how to display data (as you created the pizza menu pages using data source controls and grids), and in Chapter 6 you saw how to use the `GridView` and `DetailsView` controls to edit data. In this chapter, you will be reusing some of those techniques from Chapters 4 and 5 as we build a page to allow customers to order pizzas.

There are several stages to the order process, starting with an order page, which allows customers to add pizzas and drinks to a shopping cart. Once customers have selected their order items, they can then proceed to the checkout, where the delivery address and credit card details need to be collected. Finally, you create the order in the database, and the trusty delivery boy hops on his skateboard to head out with lots of cheesy goodness.

The checkout and creation of the order in the database is discussed in Chapter 8, so in this chapter, you will:

- ❑ Learn how to create custom classes
- ❑ See how to use the `Session` object to store the shopping cart
- ❑ Learn about the `ObjectDataSource` control

There is much more code in this chapter than the previous one, but don't worry because we'll explain it all carefully. You don't necessarily have to understand all of the code at this stage—after all, the book is primarily focused on getting you used to using VWD and ASP.NET. Knowing what it does and how it is structured is more important at this stage in your learning, and once you feel comfortable with ASP.NET and data handling, you can revisit the code later on. We felt it was more important to have a real-life situation that included code, rather than a gratuitous example that wasn't practical. Even if you don't understand all of the code yet, you'll gain an understanding of the techniques involved, and the things you need to think about in the future.

The Order Process

Before building the order pages, you must work out the process of ordering items. This will give you an indication of exactly what you will need. Following are the things you will need:

❏   An order page, where you can select the menu items.

❏   A shopping cart, to store the selected menu items.

❏   A page to collect the delivery details and credit card payment. We'll be looking at this in Chapter 8, but it's still part of the overall order process.

Each of these pages needs some thought, with the process of ordering and storing data worked out in advance. For example, you must decide whether to have an order page that is separate from the menu page. Keeping them the same would mean that you can simply add a button alongside the menu item size — this would add the item to the shopping cart. Alternatively, you could have a text area allowing the user to enter the number of items to be added. This makes the page a little harder to code, and changes the look — rather than a great-looking menu page, it would now have a text box on it.

For this sample, the menu page has been duplicated as the order page and a simple button added to allow ordering of a single item. The button can be clicked many times if more than one of an item is required. The reason for having two pages is simply so that you can keep the two parts distinct as you are working through the book — the menu page is the page built in Chapters 4 and 5 and doesn't change. The ordering page is the one built in this chapter — they are essentially the same, with only small changes to the design, plus some code. In real life, there would probably be only a single page. Figure 7-1 shows how you can add a button and link to add the item to the shopping cart.

Figure 7-1: The "Add item to order" button

Once you've decided on the way orders will be performed, you can decide where to store them before the order is confirmed — the shopping cart. There are places to store shopping carts:

❏   *In a database* — As the user adds items to the cart, the items could be added to a table in the database. When the order is confirmed, the entries could be copied into the OrderItems table. One problem with this approach is that if the user leaves the site without confirming the order, then the shopping cart table will have unused data in it, which will need to be removed.

❏   *In the Profile* — The Profile is a feature of ASP.NET 2.0 that allows storage of data against a user. We won't be using the Profile in this book, but one problem with using the Profile for storing the shopping cart is that the Profile is meant for long-lived data — data that persists across user sessions. Some sites allow shopping carts to keep their data for when you come back to the site, but for the PPQ site that doesn't really make sense.

❑ *In the* Session — The Session contains data about the active session. It starts when you first access the site and ends when you exit the site (plus a timeout value). Any data stored in the session will be held only while you are browsing the site.

For the PPQ site, the Session will be used for the storage of the shopping cart, but there are still the decisions of what it will store, and how it will store the data. The cart obviously needs details of the item (the name, the price, the quantity, and so on), so one option is to use a DataTable — this is one of the data handling objects and is used by DataSets for storing tabular data. This would seem ideal for storing the cart items, since the DataTable automatically handles rows and columns, but the cart could be so much more. For example, it would be good if the cart could automatically give us a total price of the items, including delivery and sales tax. The DataTable wouldn't accomplish this because it is designed to store rows of the same information — multiple order items in this case. What the cart needs are properties for the total, sales tax, delivery charge, plus a collection of items. To give this flexibility, you will use custom classes for the shopping cart.

Finally, you must decide on the payment. You'll need to collect the delivery address, as well as take the credit card details and show all of the items in the cart, including the totals. Then, once the user confirms the order, the items in the cart can be used to create an order in the Orders and OrderItems tables in the database.

Understanding Classes

Before you start coding, you must have an understanding of classes, and some of the terms used when dealing with them. Let's start with the basics of what a class is — it is simply a template for an object to wrap some functionality. Classes are held within Class Files — a separate file in the App_Code folder underneath the Web site, and you will be creating this in an exercise soon. Think of a class as a cookie cutter; it's not a cookie but defines what the cookie will look like.

You've already seen classes in action, even if you didn't realize it. All the ASP.NET server controls are created as classes, which provide the functionality required for that control. The grid controls, for example, can fetch data from a data source and format it for display — all done within the class.

So, what does a "class being a template" mean? Well classes are used as the basis for objects. An *object* (or *class instance*, as it is sometimes called) is the running version of a class — it's the cookie that is cut from the cookie cutter. You create an object by using the New statement in Visual Basic, as you saw when building the ShowMenu.aspx page in the Chapter 5:

```
Dim da As New SqlDataAdapter(sGetMenuItems, con)
```

This creates a new SqlDataAdapter instance. The SqlDataAdapter class defines the functionality of what the object can do once the object is created.

You implement the functionality of a class in one of three ways:

❑ *Properties* — These define the behavior of the object. For example, the following line of code sets the CommandText of the SelectCommand to the value contained within the variable sGetSizesAndPrices:

```
da.SelectCommand.CommandText = sGetSizesAndPrices
```

❏   *Methods*—These define the actions the object can perform. For example, the following line of code uses the `Fill` method to fill the DataSet (`ds`) with data from a database:

```
da.Fill(ds, "MenuItems")
```

❏   *Events*—These allow the object to inform the code using the object that something has happened. For example, in Chapter 5, step 15 in the section, "Creating Nested Data Displays Declaratively," shows how the `RowDataBound` event of the `GridView` is used. The `GridView` raises this event whenever a row of data is bound from the underlying database. The grid is telling you that something is happening, and you use the event procedure to run your own code. The "Object-Oriented and Event-Driven Architecture" section at the beginning of Chapter 4 briefly describes this process.

For the custom classes in PPQ, there will not be any events, but there will be properties and methods, as well as a way of declaring how new objects can be created. So, let's build the shopping cart classes.

Creating the Shopping Cart

The shopping cart itself will be pure code—it's just a storage mechanism. Later you'll see how to display the cart, but to start, you need to create the classes, and these live in a special directory called `App_Code`. This directory contains just code files, and ASP.NET will automatically compile them, so all you have to do is create your file—ASP.NET takes care of everything else.

The Shopping Cart Classes

The shopping cart consists of two classes: one for the items within the cart and one for the cart itself. The cart itself has a class so that it can store the delivery charge, and calculate the subtotal and total.

You can use a single file for this, because you don't have to create a file for each class—the classes can share the same physical file. The two classes will be called `CartItem` and `ShoppingCart`. The `ShoppingCart` will have a collection of `CartItem` objects to store the items being ordered.

There is a lot of code in these classes, and it would mean a lot of typing, so this exercise will show the basics of what classes contain and how you lay them out. To save you typing in all of the code, you can find the entire class in the `ShoppingCart.vb.txt` file in the page-content directory, allowing you to copy and paste as much as you like. The code in the template file is also commented, making it easy to understand.

Try It Out	Creating the Shopping Cart Classes

1.   In the Solution Explorer in VWD, select the solution directory (`C:\Websites\PPQ`) and right-click the mouse. From the Add ASP.NET Folder menu item, select App_Code to create the directory (see Figure 7-2).

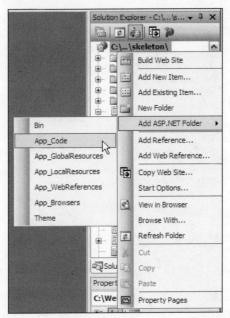

Figure 7-2: Creating the `App_Code` directory

2. Click on the newly added `App_Code` directory, and select the Add New Item . . . menu item. From the Add New Item window, select Class, and change the Name to `ShoppingCart.vb` (see Figure 7-3).

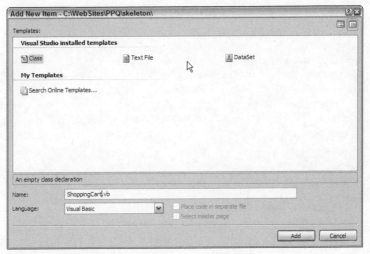

Figure 7-3: Adding a new class

3. The new class will look like Figure 7-4.

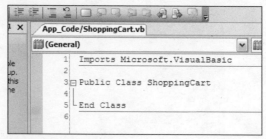

Figure 7-4: An empty class

4. Below the existing `Imports` statement, add the following:

```
Imports System.Collections.Generic

Public Class CartItem
End Class
```

5. Within the class, underneath the `Public Class CartItem` declaration, add the following:

```
Private _menuItemID As Integer
Private _itemName As String
Private _itemSize As String
Private _quantity As Integer
Private _itemPrice As Decimal
```

6. Underneath that, add the following:

```
Public Sub New()
End Sub

Public Sub New(ByVal MenuItemID As Integer, ByVal ItemName As String, _
            ByVal ItemSize As String, ByVal Quantity As Integer, _
            ByVal ItemPrice As Decimal)

    _menuItemID = MenuItemID
    _itemName = ItemName
    _itemSize = ItemSize
    _quantity = Quantity
    _itemPrice = ItemPrice

End Sub
```

7. Next, add properties for the menu ID and item name:

```
Public Property MenuItemID() As Integer
  Get
    Return _menuItemID
  End Get
  Set(ByVal value As Integer)
    _menuItemID = value
```

```
      End Set
   End Property

   Public Property ItemName() As String
      Get
         Return _itemName
      End Get
      Set(ByVal value As String)
         _itemName = value
      End Set
   End Property
```

8. To save more typing, copy the remaining properties from the template ShoppingCart.vb.txt file. You will need the following properties: ItemSize, Quantity, ItemPrice, and LineValue.

9. Now to edit the ShoppingCart. Move the cursor to the end of the class file, to the class declaration that was visible when you created the file:

```
Public Class ShoppingCart
End Class
```

10. Within that class, add the following:

```
   Private _salesTaxPercent As Decimal
   Private _items As List(Of CartItem)

   Public Sub New()

      If _items Is Nothing Then
         _items = New List(Of CartItem)
      End If

      _salesTaxPercent = _
         Convert.ToDecimal(ConfigurationManager.AppSettings("SalesTax"))
   End Sub

   Public ReadOnly Property Items() As List(Of CartItem)
      Get
         Return _items
      End Get
   End Property

   Public ReadOnly Property SubTotal() As Decimal
      Get
         Dim tot As Decimal
         For Each item As CartItem In _items
            tot += item.LineValue
         Next
         Return tot
      End Get
   End Property
```

11. To save more typing, copy the remaining properties from the template `ShoppingCart.vb.txt` file. You will need the following properties: `DeliveryCharge`, `SalesTaxpercent`, `SalesTax`, and `Total`.

12. Now you can add the methods that allow the cart items to be modified.

```
Public Sub Insert(ByVal MenuItemID As Integer, ByVal ItemSize As String, _
                ByVal itemName As String, ByVal ItemPrice As Decimal, _
                ByVal Quantity As Integer)

    Dim idx As Integer = ItemIndex(MenuItemID, ItemSize)

    If idx = -1 Then
        ' create a new cart item
        Dim NewItem As New CartItem()

        NewItem.MenuItemID = MenuItemID
        NewItem.ItemSize = ItemSize
        NewItem.ItemName = itemName
        NewItem.Quantity = Quantity
        NewItem.ItemPrice = ItemPrice

        _items.Add(NewItem)
    Else
        _items(idx).Quantity += 1
    End If

End Sub

Public Sub Update(ByVal MenuItemID As Integer, ByVal ItemSize As String, _
                ByVal Quantity As Integer)

    Dim idx As Integer = ItemIndex(MenuItemID, ItemSize)

    If idx <> -1 Then
        _items(idx).Quantity = Quantity
    End If

End Sub

Public Sub Delete(ByVal MenuItemID As Integer, ByVal ItemSize As String)

    Dim idx As Integer = ItemIndex(MenuItemID, ItemSize)

    If idx <> -1 Then
        _items.RemoveAt(idx)
    End If

End Sub

Private Function ItemIndex(ByVal MenuItemID As Integer, _
                    ByVal ItemSize As String) As Integer

    Dim index As Integer

    For Each item As CartItem In _items
```

```
        If item.MenuItemID = MenuItemID AndAlso item.ItemSize = ItemSize Then
          Return index
      End If
      index += 1
  Next

  Return -1

End Function
```

13. Save the file. You're not going to be able to use this yet, because we need to create more code and pages, but let's see how the code works.

How It Works

The first thing we did was to add an `Imports` statement:

```
Imports System.Collections.Generic
```

This tells the compiler where to find some of the classes our new class will use. We'll explain what those are later, but all of the classes are divided into *namespaces*, which is a way to logically separate the classes, making them easy to find. For example, all of the classes relating to SQL Server are in the `System.Data .SqlClient` namespace. Learning about namespaces and the classes within them is useful when you start to use code because there are a large number of supplied classes that can make your life as a programmer much easier.

At the start of the chapter, we mentioned that classes are templates that provide properties, methods, and events, and that's exactly what this code does. It defines a class with properties and methods — there are no events in this one, because they aren't needed. You define a class with the `Class` statement:

```
Public Class CartItem
End Class
```

The `Public Class` and `End Class` keywords define the start and end of the class, while `CartItem` is the name given to the class. This class will store a single item within the shopping cart.

Within the class, we defined some variables:

```
Private _menuItemID As Integer
Private _itemName As String
Private _itemSize As String
Private _quantity As Integer
Private _itemPrice As Decimal
```

These are used to hold the values of a cart item. Following are the parts of these variable declarations:

❑ `Private`, which means that the variable cannot be seen outside of the class, and we'll explain why this is a good thing when we look at the declaration of the properties.

❑ Variable name (for example, `_menuItemID`).

❑ `As Data Type` (for example, `As Integer`).

All variables have a data type, and following are the ones we are using:

❏   `Integer`, which holds whole numbers.

❏   `String`, which holds text.

❏   `Decimal`, which holds decimal values, such as prices.

There are other data types, such as `DateTime` for date and time values, but we don't need these for this class.

Once the variables are declared, the constructors are defined. Constructors are run when the class is created, so remember when we talked about creating an *object* (or a *class instance,* as it is sometimes called), like this:

```
Dim da As New SqlDataAdapter(sGetMenuItems, con)
```

When the `New` keyword is used, the constructor of the class is run. The constructors are called `New`, and the first is declared like this:

```
Public Sub New()
End Sub
```

There is no code within the constructor, but having it there allows you to create the class like this:

```
Dim MyCartItem As New CartItem()
```

Also required is a way to create a cart item with the details of the item, the name, price, and so on. To do that, you create another constructor, with the same name, but different parameters:

```
Public Sub New(ByVal MenuItemID As Integer, ByVal ItemName As String, _
               ByVal ItemSize As String, ByVal Quantity As Integer, _
               ByVal ItemPrice As Decimal)

    _menuItemID = MenuItemID
    _itemName = ItemName
    _itemSize = ItemSize
    _quantity = Quantity
    _itemPrice = ItemPrice

End Sub
```

The parameters are variable declarations within the parenthesis and define how you can create the class. So, with this constructor, you can also create the class like this:

```
Dim MyCartItem As New CartItem(1, "Three Cheeses", "Large", 1, 10.95)
```

This allows you to define the values that the cart item has when you create the item. Within the constructor, the parameters are assigned to the variables declared at the top of the class. Those variables were `Private` and so couldn't be seen outside of the class. So, next we defined properties, and the syntax is as follows:

```
Public Property PropertyName As DataType
  Get
    ' this is the code that returns a value, run when a value is read
  End Get
  Set(ByVal value As DataType)
    ' this is the code that sets a value, run when the value is assigned
  End Set
End Property
```

Our first property is:

```
Public Property MenuItemID() As Integer
  Get
    Return _menuItemID
  End Get
  Set(ByVal value As Integer)
    _menuItemID = value
  End Set
End Property
```

MenuItemID is the name of the property, and it stores an Integer value—a whole number. The Get part returns the variable declared at the top of the class, while the Set part, sets the value of that variable. To make this a little clearer, let's take a look at what happens when classes are created, and properties read from and written to, starting with creating the class object:

```
Dim MyCartItem As New CartItem(1, "Three Cheeses", "Large", 1, 10.95)
```

Figure 7-5 shows what happens when the class object is created. The constructor is run and the values passed into the constructor are placed into the variables.

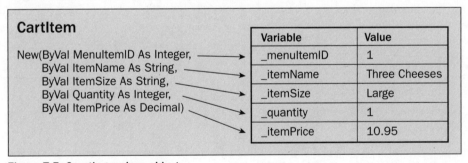

Figure 7-5: Creating a class object

To access a property, you place the property name after the class object name. For example, to read the ItemName property into a new variable you would use the following code:

```
Dim MyItemName As String
MyItemName = MyCartItem.ItemName
```

As Figure 7-6 shows, this calls the property Get and returns the value of the variable.

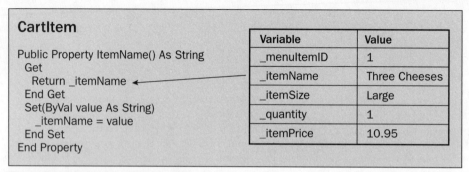

Figure 7-6: Reading a property value

The value of the variable _itemName is returned, so MyItemName would contain Three Cheeses. To set the value of a property you use the following:

```
MyCartItem.ItemName = "Hawaiian"
```

Figure 7-7 shows what happens when a property is written to. The Set part of the Property runs, which assigns the value passed in to the variable _itemName.

CartItem

Public Property ItemName() As String
  Get
    Return _itemName
  End Get
  Set(ByVal value As String)
    _itemName = value
  End Set
End Property

Variable	Value
_menuItemID	1
_itemName	Hawaiian
_itemSize	Large
_quantity	1
_itemPrice	10.95

Figure 7-7: Writing a property value

The reason for using properties is that it is a feature of *object-oriented programming* (which is what you are doing, even if you didn't realize it), and it's called *abstraction*. What abstraction does is hide the inner workings of the class from those programs that use the class, which don't need to know how it works, just that it does. For example, you set the value of a property like this:

```
MyCartItem.ItemName = "Hawaiian"
```

You don't need to know how the MyCartItem object actually stores the contents of the property, just that it does.

All of the properties of the `CartItem` class follow the same syntax, and that's all that the `CartItem` consists of, the constructors and the properties.

Let's now look at the `ShoppingCart` class, the definition of which is similar to the `CartItem` class:

```
Public Class ShoppingCart
End Class
```

This class needs to store the items, so you need some form of storage for multiple copies of the `CartItem` class. For this we use a `List`, but a special one — a generic `List`. There are different types of lists — some that allow storing of any type of data, and some that can be restricted to store only a certain data type. A generic list is one of the latter, and when you declare the list, you determine what data it can hold. This helps to alleviate any potential coding errors, reduces the amount of code you have to write, and makes the code faster than if you used a normal list.

Using a generic list is why we added the `Imports` statement at the top of the file, referencing the `System.Collections.Generic` namespace because that's where the generic `List` resides. You don't really need to know about this `List` in detail, except that it is useful for storing collections of custom classes. The syntax for creating a list of this type is:

```
Private VariableName As List(Of DataType)
```

The `DataType` defines the type of object that will be stored, which in this case is a `CartItem` object. So, our variable is declared as follows:

```
Private _items As List(Of CartItem)
```

This line only declares the variable and what it contains but doesn't initialize it. The next line is another variable declaration:

```
Private _salesTaxPercent As Decimal
```

This will be used to store the percentage of sales tax, which is stored in the Web configuration file.

Neither of the previous two variables has values so we add a constructor to the class to do that:

```
Public Sub New()

  If _items Is Nothing Then
    _items = New List(Of CartItem)
  End If

  _salesTaxPercent = _
    Convert.ToDecimal(ConfigurationManager.AppSettings("SalesTax"))
End Sub
```

Within the constructor a new `List` object is created but only if it already hasn't been created. When the class is first created, the `_items` variable will be `Nothing`, a special value indicating that the object variable doesn't contain anything. Therefore, if the variable is `Nothing`, we need to create a new `List` object.

The `salesTaxPercent` variable is set to the value stored in the Web configuration file and shows an important point, one of storing configuration details. The order must include sales tax, but including an explicit figure in code means that the code must be changed if the sales tax ever changes. To avoid this problem, the information is stored in the Web configuration file, `web.config`, which contains a section called `<appSettings/>`, used for application settings:

```
<configuration>
  <appSettings>
    <add key="SalesTax" value="0.08" />
  </appSettings>
```

To add a setting, you use the `add` element, with the `key` providing a unique identifier, and `value` providing the value of the setting. If the sales tax ever changes, all that's required is a simple change to this configuration file — you don't have to change any code.

Within the property, the configuration value can be read using the `AppSettings` property of the `ConfigurationManager` class. You use the key to identity a value from the `<appSettings />` section:

```
ConfigurationManager.AppSettings("SalesTax")
```

The value returned from this line of code needs converting to a `Decimal` type, so we use the `ToDecimal` method of the `Convert` class.

The sales tax value is read in the class constructor because the constructor happens only once, when the class is instantiated.

Since the `_items` variable is private, it needs to be exposed to programs using the shopping cart, so a property is created:

```
Public ReadOnly Property Items() As List(Of CartItem)
  Get
    Return _items
  End Get
End Property
```

This shows a different form of creating properties, ones that are read-only. The declaration has the addition of a `ReadOnly` keyword in it, and the body of the property includes only the `Get` section, which simply returns the list of items. You can also create write-only properties by using the `WriteOnly` keyword and including only the `Set` section.

Next, there is a property for the subtotal of the items in the cart, which is also read-only since you can never directly set the value of the subtotal.

```
Public ReadOnly Property SubTotal() As Decimal
  Get
    Dim tot As Decimal
    For Each item As CartItem In _items
      tot += item.LineValue
    Next
    Return tot
  End Get
End Property
```

The subtotal is calculated by adding up the line value of each item in the cart — this is exposed through the LineValue property of the CartItem. So, the SubTotal property simply loops through each item, adding to a total, which is then returned. This code shows that properties do not simply have to return the value of a variable; they can also have more complex code. One good thing about having the subtotal in a property such as this is that it will always be correct. If we had stored the subtotal as a separate variable, then every time there was a change to the items in the cart, we would have to update the subtotal. This way the total is always calculated based upon the items within the cart.

Other properties that the cart has (and that you copied from the template code) are for the percentage of sales tax, the amount of sales tax, and the total. The percentage of sales tax simply returns the variable that was set in the class constructor — this way the value is read from the Web configuration file once, and the variable used every time the property is read.

```
Public ReadOnly Property SalesTaxPercent() As Decimal
    Get
        Return _salesTaxPercent.
    End Get
End Property
```

The next property is for the sales tax:

```
Public ReadOnly Property SalesTax() As Decimal
    Get
        Return (SubTotal + DeliveryCharge) * SalesTaxPercent
    End Get
End Property
```

The sales tax is calculated from the subtotal, the delivery charge, and the percentage sales tax, so this property simply returns the calculated amount. Notice that the values used for the calculation are themselves properties. The same technique is used for the order Total:

```
Public ReadOnly Property Total() As Decimal
    Get
        Return SubTotal + DeliveryCharge + SalesTax
    End Get
End Property
```

With the properties defined, we then moved on to the methods — the actions that the shopping cart can perform. The first method allows you to insert an item into the cart, and takes the same parameters as a CartItem object constructor:

```
Public Sub Insert(ByVal MenuItemID As Integer, ByVal ItemSize As String, _
                ByVal itemName As String, ByVal ItemPrice As Decimal, _
                ByVal Quantity As Integer)
```

The first thing the Insert method does is to find the index of the item in the cart, by calling the ItemIndex method (which we'll look at shortly). Remember that the items are stored in a List object, and we don't want to add the same item more that once, so we look up the index to see if it already exists:

```
Dim idx As Integer = ItemIndex(MenuItemID, ItemSize)
```

If the index is -1, then it doesn't already exist, so a new CartItem is created and the properties are used to set the values for the item. We could have passed these values into the constructor, but this shows another way of creating objects and setting property values.

```
If idx = -1 Then
   ' create a new cart item
   Dim NewItem As New CartItem()

   NewItem.MenuItemID = MenuItemID
   NewItem.ItemSize = ItemSize
   NewItem.ItemName = itemName
   NewItem.Quantity = Quantity
   NewItem.ItemPrice = ItemPrice
```

Once the new item is set, it is added to the _items list.

```
_items.Add(NewItem)
```

If the index returned from ItemIndex is a value other than -1, then the item already exists in the cart, so there's no point adding it again. In this situation, we can simply update the Quantity, adding 1 to it.

```
Else
   _items(idx).Quantity += 1
End If

End Sub
```

The Update method is even easier because only the Quantity can be updated.

```
Public Sub Update(ByVal MenuItemID As Integer, ByVal ItemSize As String, _
                  ByVal Quantity As Integer)
```

First, the index of the item is fetched, and if the item exists, the index will not be -1, so the Quantity is updated.

```
Dim idx As Integer = ItemIndex(MenuItemID, ItemSize)

If idx <> -1 Then
   _items(idx).Quantity = Quantity
End If

End Sub
```

The method to delete items follows a similar form. First, the index is returned, and if the item exists, the RemoveAt method of the _items list is called to remove the item.

```
Public Sub Delete(ByVal MenuItemID As Integer, ByVal ItemSize As String)

   Dim idx As Integer = ItemIndex(MenuItemID, ItemSize)

   If idx <> -1 Then
      _items.RemoveAt(idx)
```

```
      End If

  End Sub
```

The final method is one used only by the other methods, which is why the `Private` keyword is used, which means the method cannot be used outside of the class. Private methods are a great way to break functionality into small units without making them visible to users of the class. This method accepts two parameters: the ID of the item and the size. These uniquely identify an item in the list.

```
  Private Function ItemIndex(ByVal MenuItemID As Integer, _
                             ByVal ItemSize As String) As Integer

    Dim index As Integer
```

To find the index number, we loop through the items in the list, comparing the ID and size to those passed in as parameters. If a match is found, then the position in the list is returned.

```
  For Each item As CartItem In _items
     If item.MenuItemID = MenuItemID AndAlso item.ItemSize = ItemSize Then
        Return index
     End If
     index += 1
  Next
```

If no match is found, then −1 is returned.

```
    Return -1

  End Function
```

There's a lot of code here, but what it means is that we have a class called `ShoppingCart` with the following properties:

❏ `Items` — A collection of `CartItem` objects

❏ `SubTotal` — The total of the `CartItem` objects

❏ `DeliveryCharge` — The fee charged for delivery (which will be user-selectable)

❏ `SalesTaxPercent` — The percentage of sales tax

❏ `SalesTax` — The amount added to the order for sales tax

❏ `Total` — The total cost of the order

The methods are:

❏ `Insert` — To insert a new item

❏ `Update` — To update the quantity of an existing item

❏ `Delete` — To delete an item

At this stage, we simply have a way of storing the items for a shopping cart but don't have anywhere to store it, and for that we need a data layer.

The Shopping Cart Data Layer

At the beginning of the chapter, we stated that the storage for the cart was going to be the `Session`. The `Session` is an *intrinsic object* (that is, it is provided automatically by ASP.NET and can be used to store information for the duration of a user's session on a site or after a specific time period). The timeout defaults to 20 minutes, so as long as you stay active on a site, the session remains active. If you request a page and leave the browser for 20 minutes, then the session times out, and all data stored in the session is lost. For some shopping carts this would be a problem, but for PPQ the timeout is acceptable — ordering pizzas is a quick business.

To store something in the session, you use the following code:

```
Session("MyKey") = "MyValue"
```

This stores the string `MyValue` in the session, using `MyKey` as the key. To read the value you use:

```
Dim MyString As String
MyString = Session("MyKey")
```

The session can store objects as well as strings, so we'll use it to store the shopping cart.

The ObjectDataSource Control

At the moment, our shopping cart exists as just a class. It doesn't actually store the data anywhere, so we need some more classes to store the cart in the session. Why do we need more classes? Well, we are going to use the `ObjectDataSource` control on our pages to provide the interface between the controls that will display the data and the storage of the data. The `ObjectDataSource` control works in much the same way as a `SqlDataSource` control, except that instead of dealing with a database it deals with a class. It has the same idea of commands to read and update data that we saw in Chapter 6, but they point to methods of a class, rather than SQL statements.

The properties of the `ObjectDataSource` control we will use are:

❑   `TypeName` — The name of the class providing the data

❑   `DeleteMethod` — The method called when an item is to be deleted

❑   `InsertMethod` — The method called when an item is to be inserted

❑   `SelectMethod` — The method called to read the items

❑   `UpdateMethod` — The method called to update an item

In all other respects, the `ObjectDataSource` control provides the same features as the `SqlDataSource` control.

The Data Layer Classes

The data layer will consist of a single class, called `StoredShoppingCart`, with six public methods:

- ❑ `Read` — To return the shopping cart
- ❑ `Update` — To update the delivery charge
- ❑ `ReadItems` — To read the items in the cart
- ❑ `DeleteItem` — To delete an item from the cart
- ❑ `InsertItem` — To insert a new item into the cart
- ❑ `UpdateItems` — To update an item in the cart

These will be linked to two `ObjectDataSource` controls: one for the cart itself (totals, etc.), and one for the cart items, as shown in Figure 7-8.

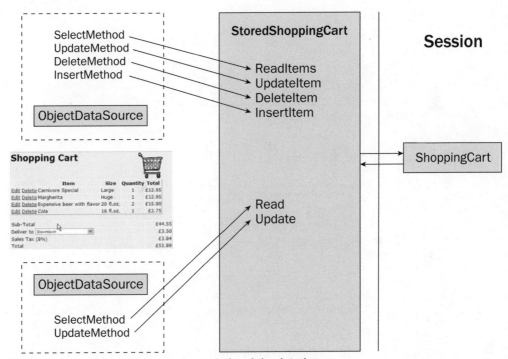

Figure 7-8: The`ObjectDataSource` **control and the data layer**

Here you can see that the methods of the `ObjectDataSource` control map to the methods in the `StoredShoppongCart` object, which interacts with the `ShoppingCart` object stored in the session.

The `StoredShoppingCart` class is much simpler than the `ShoppingCart` and `CartItem` classes, so let's go ahead and build it.

Try It Out   The Shopping Cart Data Layer

1. In VWD, click on the `App_Code` directory, and select the Add New Item . . . menu item. From the Add New Item window select Class, and change the Name to **StoredShoppingCart.vb** (see Figure 7-9).

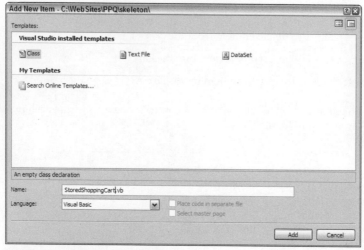

Figure 7-9: Adding a new class

2. The new class will look like Figure 7-10.

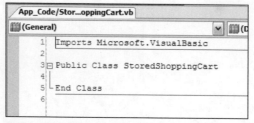

Figure 7-10: The new `StoredShoppingCart` class

3. Below the existing `Imports` statement, add the following:

```
Imports System.Collections.Generic

Public Class StoredShoppingCart
End Class
```

4. Within the class, underneath the `Public Class StoredShoppingCart` declaration, add the following methods for the shopping cart:

```
Public Shared Function Read() As ShoppingCart

  Return FetchCart()

End Function

Public Shared Function Update(ByVal DeliveryCharge As Decimal) As Integer

  Dim cart As ShoppingCart = FetchCart()

  cart.DeliveryCharge = DeliveryCharge

End Function
```

5. Next, add the following methods for the items:

```
Public Shared Function ReadItems() As List(Of CartItem)

  Dim cart As ShoppingCart = StoredShoppingCart.FetchCart()

  Return cart.Items

End Function

Public Shared Function UpdateItem(ByVal MenuItemID As Integer, _
      ByVal ItemSize As String, ByVal Quantity As Integer) As Integer

  Dim cart As ShoppingCart = StoredShoppingCart.FetchCart()

  cart.Update(MenuItemID, ItemSize, Quantity)

End Function

Public Shared Function DeleteItem(ByVal MenuItemID As Integer, _
      ByVal ItemSize As String) As Integer

  Dim cart As ShoppingCart = StoredShoppingCart.FetchCart()

  cart.Delete(MenuItemID, ItemSize)

End Function

Public Shared Function InsertItem(ByVal MenuItemID As Integer, _
      ByVal ItemName As String, ByVal ItemSize As String, _
      ByVal Quantity As Integer, ByVal ItemPrice As Decimal) As Integer

  Dim cart As ShoppingCart = StoredShoppingCart.FetchCart()

  cart.Insert(MenuItemID, ItemSize, ItemName, ItemPrice, Quantity)

End Function
```

6. Finally, add the `private` method to fetch the cart from the session:

```
Private Shared Function FetchCart() As ShoppingCart

  Dim cart As ShoppingCart = _
              DirectCast(HttpContext.Current.Session("Cart"), ShoppingCart)

  If cart Is Nothing Then
    cart = New ShoppingCart()
    HttpContext.Current.Session("Cart") = cart
  End If

  Return cart

End Function
```

7. Save the file.

How It Works

Like the `ShoppingCart` class, the first thing we did was to add a reference to the `System.Collections`
`.Generic` namespace, so that ASP.NET knows where to find the generic `List` class:

```
Imports System.Collections.Generic
```

Then there were two methods for the shopping cart. The first, `Read`, simply returns the stored cart,
which it fetches by calling `FetchCart`, a private method we'll examine shortly.

```
Public Shared Function Read() As ShoppingCart

  Return FetchCart()

End Function
```

One important thing to note is the use of the keyword `Shared` in the method declaration. `Shared` means
that you don't have to create an instance of a class. Normally, a class must be created with the `New`
keyword, such as the following:

```
Dim NewItem As New CartItem()
```

This creates a new class instance, with properties and methods, and private variables. Some classes,
however, are only wrappers for methods — they don't have any properties or private variables, and each
method stands alone, not relying on anything else in the class. The `StoredShoppingCart` class is one of
those and exists only because you can't have methods outside of a class. If the methods weren't shared,
to use them you would have to use the following code:

```
Dim ssc As New StoredShoppingCart()
Dim cart As ShoppingCart = ssc.Read()
```

With a `Shared` method, however, you don't have to instantiate the class. So, you can have the following:

```
Dim cart As ShoppingCart = StoredShoppingCart.StoredShoppingCart.Read()
```

In this code, instead of using a class instance variable `ssc`, we simply use the class name. Using `Shared` methods reduces the overhead that ASP.NET has when managing variables, so not only does it make the code shorter and easier to read, but it also helps with performance.

The second method of the `StoredShoppingCart` class, `Update`, fetches the cart, and updates the delivery charge. This will be used on the checkout page where the user will select the delivery area.

```
Public Shared Function Update(ByVal DeliveryCharge As Decimal) As Integer

    Dim cart As ShoppingCart = FetchCart()

    cart.DeliveryCharge = DeliveryCharge

End Function
```

Next are the methods for the items, starting with `ReadItems`:

```
Public Shared Function ReadItems() As List(Of CartItem)

    Dim cart As ShoppingCart = StoredShoppingCart.FetchCart()

    Return cart.Items

End Function
```

This fetches the cart and returns the `Items` collection. This will be used to display a list of the items in the cart.

Then there are the methods to update, delete, and insert items in the cart. These simply fetch the cart and call the appropriate method on the cart itself. For example, the `UpdateItem` method calls the `Update` method on the cart.

```
Public Shared Function UpdateItem(ByVal MenuItemID As Integer, _
        ByVal ItemSize As String, ByVal Quantity As Integer) As Integer

    Dim cart As ShoppingCart = StoredShoppingCart.FetchCart()

    cart.Update(MenuItemID, ItemSize, Quantity)

End Function

Public Shared Function DeleteItem(ByVal MenuItemID As Integer, _
        ByVal ItemSize As String) As Integer

    Dim cart As ShoppingCart = StoredShoppingCart.FetchCart()

    cart.Delete(MenuItemID, ItemSize)

End Function

Public Shared Function InsertItem(ByVal MenuItemID As Integer, _
        ByVal ItemName As String, ByVal ItemSize As String, _
```

```
            ByVal Quantity As Integer, ByVal ItemPrice As Decimal) As Integer

        Dim cart As ShoppingCart = StoredShoppingCart.FetchCart()

        cart.Insert(MenuItemID, ItemSize, ItemName, ItemPrice, Quantity)

    End Function
```

These methods show that the StoredShoppingCart class is just a wrapper around the actual cart; it knows where the cart is stored and has equivalent methods to the cart.

The FetchCart method is only used internally by the StoredShoppingCart class, and it returns a ShoppingCart object—the cart stored in the session.

```
        Private Shared Function FetchCart() As ShoppingCart
```

Fetching the cart from the session is the first thing this method does:

```
        Dim cart As ShoppingCart = _
                    DirectCast(HttpContext.Current.Session("Cart"), ShoppingCart)
```

This requires a little explanation. Earlier in the chapter, we showed how to store items in, and fetch them from, the session, and this is just an extension of that. The first thing to know is that the Session object is part of the ASP.NET page, and this is a class, so we don't automatically have access to the Session object. For that reason, we have to access it indirectly—don't worry about what the HttpContext .Current means; it's just how we access the Session object from within a class.

The second thing to consider is that, when fetching items from the Session object, these items are returned as an Object type (Object is a distinct type, just like String and Integer). We know that the cart isn't an Object, but a ShoppingCart class, so we have to cast the type. *Casting* is a way of telling ASP.NET that an object of one type should be treated as a different type, and we use DirectCast for that, the syntax of which is as follows:

```
    DirectCast(object, DataType)
```

This converts the object into the DataType. So, our code is converting an object into a ShoppingCart. Another way of casting, or converting types, is to use CType, the syntax of which is:

```
    CType(object, DataType)
```

The difference between CType and DirectCast is that DirectCast will raise an exception if the object is not of the correct DataType. We know that we've stored a ShoppingCart object into the Session, so either conversion method could be used, but DirectCast was picked for an added degree of protection. If something did go wrong with the Session storage, then the error would occur during the conversion, and not later on in the code. At this stage, we have a variable called cart, which contains the cart from the session. However, if this is the first time this code has been run, the cart will not have been placed into the session, so the cart variable might be Nothing (remember, Nothing tells us that the variable doesn't contain anything). If cart is Nothing, then we need to create a new cart object and place it into the session:

```
    If cart Is Nothing Then
      cart = New ShoppingCart()
      HttpContext.Current.Session("Cart") = cart
    End If

    Return cart

  End Function
```

The reason we used the FetchCart method is because it contains code that is needed in all of the other methods — they need to fetch the cart from the session. But because the cart might not exist and might have to be created, all of this code would be needed in every method. Instead of repeating the code, it is better to create a separate method with the repeated code and just call that method from the others.

The reason for creating the StoredShoppingCart class is that it keeps the storage of the cart separate from the cart itself. This means that the internals of the cart could be completely changed without affecting the rest of the application, since the application uses the StoredShoppingCart to access it. As long as the public methods remain the same, the application will still work. Likewise, the storage of the cart could be change without affecting the cart class itself. For example, if we wanted to store the cart in a database instead of the session, then only the StoredShoppingCart class would need to be changed.

Now that the guts of the cart have been done, let's look at how to use this code by creating an order page.

Creating the Order Page

The order page is created as a separate page purely to keep it separate from the book perspective. The order page is actually based upon the menu page, and in reality there would probably be only one page on the real Web site, but we've made it a different page so that you can keep the two pages separate.

The difference to the look of the page is small, adding a link and image, which when clicked adds the item to the shopping cart. Let's build this page.

Try It Out   **Creating the Order Page**

1. Open Order.aspx — this is the order page completed in Chapter 5, but without any code.

2. Currently the ItemTemplate of the Repeater contains the following:

```
<span style="color: Firebrick">
  <%# Eval("ItemSize") %>: <%#Eval("ItemPrice", "${0:F2}")%>  </span>
```

3. This just displays the item size and price, and we need to have a button that adds the item to the shopping cart. Change the code within the ItemTemplate to the following:

```
<span style="color: Firebrick;">
  <asp:LinkButton ID="OrderItem" runat="server" ToolTip="Add item to order"
                  style="text-decoration:none;"
                  CommandName='<%# Eval("ItemSize") %>'
                  CommandArgument='<%# Eval("ItemPrice") %>'>
    <asp:Image ID="Image1" runat="server"
```

```
                   ImageUrl="~/images/cartIcon.gif"
                   AlternateText="Add item to order button" />
     <%# Eval("ItemSize") %>: <%#Eval("ItemPrice", "${0:F2}")%>  
   </asp:LinkButton>
</span>
```

4. Save the file.

5. Switch to Design view and double-click anywhere on the gray background, which will open the code-behind file and create an empty `Page_Load` event for you.

6. Open `Order.aspx.vb.txt` from the page-content directory, and copy all of the code into the `Page_Load` event in `Order.aspx.vb`.

7. Next, you need to create an event for the `ItemDataBound` event of the DataList, so switch to `Order.aspx` in Design view. Select the `DataList` and view the events by clicking the events icon (see Figure 7-11) in the Properties area.

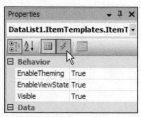

Figure 7-11: Viewing the events for a control

8. Double-click into the space next to the `ItemDataBound` event to have the empty event procedure created for you.

9. Within the event procedure, add the following code:

```
If e.Item.ItemType = ListItemType.Item OrElse _
    e.Item.ItemType = ListItemType.AlternatingItem Then

  Dim rpt As Repeater = DirectCast(e.Item.FindControl("Repeater1"), Repeater)

  Dim ItemID As HiddenField = New HiddenField
  Dim ItemName As HiddenField = New HiddenField

  ItemID.ID = "ItemID"
  ItemName.ID = "ItemName"

  ItemID.Value = e.Item.DataItem("MenuItemID")
  ItemName.Value = e.Item.DataItem("ItemName")

  rpt.Controls.Add(ItemID)
  rpt.Controls.Add(ItemName)
End If
```

10. Next, you need to create an event handler for the `ItemCommand` of the `Repeater`, so switch back to `Order.aspx` in Design view. Select the `DataList`, and from the DataList Tasks select Edit Templates (see Figure 7-12).

Figure 7-12: Editing the DataList templates

11. Select the `Repeater` and, from the Properties area, click the events icon (the one that looks like a lightning bolt, as seen in Figure 7-11).

12. Double-click in the blank area to the right of the `ItemCommand` event. This will switch to the code-behind file and create an empty event procedure for you.

13. Within the event procedure, add the following code:

```
Dim rpt As Repeater = DirectCast(source, Repeater)

Dim IDControl As HiddenField = _
                DirectCast(rpt.FindControl("ItemID"), HiddenField)
Dim NameControl As HiddenField = _
                DirectCast(rpt.FindControl("ItemName"), HiddenField)

Dim ItemID As Integer = Convert.ToInt32(IDControl.Value)
Dim ItemName As String = NameControl.Value
Dim ItemSize As String = e.CommandName.ToString()
Dim ItemPrice As Decimal = Convert.ToDecimal(e.CommandArgument)

StoredShoppingCart.InsertItem(ItemID, ItemName, ItemSize, 1, ItemPrice)

Label1.Text = String.Format("{0} ({1}) added to the shopping cart", _
                        ItemName, ItemSize)
```

14. Save both files, run the application, and pick Select Pizza from the Order menu. Notice how the size and price are clickable, as is the shopping cart item (see Figure 7-13).

Figure 7-13: Adding an item to the shopping cart

You can click this link, or the same link on any of the items, and at the top of the page you will see a label telling you that the selected item has been added to the cart. We haven't built the page that displays the cart yet, but the item has definitely been added. Let's see how this code works.

How It Works

We'll start by looking at the changes to the `ItemTemplate` of the `Repeater`. Within the span (which hasn't changed), we first create a `LinkButton`:

```
<span style="color: Firebrick;">
  <asp:LinkButton ID="OrderItem" runat="server" ToolTip="Add item to order"
                  style="text-decoration:none;"
                  CommandName='<%# Eval("ItemSize") %>'
                  CommandArgument='<%# Eval("ItemPrice") %>'>
```

A `LinkButton` is a control that acts like a button but that looks like a link. We've used one here because it looks nicer than a normal button. The `ToolTip` is the text shown when you hover the cursor over the button, and the `style` sets how the text looks — in this case, the text has no decoration, so appears normally (the default is to have the text underlined, like a hyperlink). The `CommandName` property is set to the size of the item displayed (the `ItemSize` column from the database), and the `CommandArgument` property is set to the price of the item (the `ItemPrice` from the database). These values are set using the same `Eval` method of data binding as shown in earlier chapters. The `CommandName` and `CommandArgument` properties are used to pass the size and price of the item to the event procedure when the button is clicked — you'll see how that's used a little later.

Next, we include an image, a small shopping cart icon, just to make the page look a little nicer.

```
<asp:Image ID="Image1" runat="server"
           ImageUrl="~/images/cartIcon.gif"
           AlternateText="Add item to order button" />
```

Next, there is the display of the item size and price, and this is the same display as used in the menu page.

```
<%# Eval("ItemSize") %>: <%#Eval("ItemPrice", "${0:F2}")%>  
```

Finally the `LinkButton` and span elements are closed.

```
    </asp:LinkButton>
  </span>
```

An important point to note here is that the `LinkButton` encloses the image and the text for the size and price, which means that these controls become part of the link. This technique allows users to click either the image or the text to add the item to the cart.

Now, onto the code, and we will ignore the `Page_Load` event because that contains exactly the same code as for the menu page, and you looked at that in Chapter 5. Before we dive into the code added to the page though, we need some theory first. Remember that this page is using master-detail type data binding, with the pizza and drink types being the master, and the sizes and prices being the details. We want to allow the user to click one of the detail items, at which point the item will be added to the cart. Since we are clicking a detail item, we can easily get access to the size and price, but the ID and Name of the pizza or drink is more problematic because they are contained within the master record, rather than the child record. This means that we have to find some way of making the ID and Name available, and the way we do it is by adding the ID and Name as HiddenControls within the repeater. But we do this within code. (There are ways to get around code if using different data bound controls, but those different controls don't provide the features that we need.)

So, let's now look at the code for the ItemDataBound event of the DataList. Remember that the DataList displays the item types—the pizzas and drinks, and the ItemDataBound event will be raised by ASP.NET every time a pizza or drink is bound. It will also be raised when other rows are bound, such as the header and footer rows. So, the first thing our code does is to check to see which type of row is being bound. This is easy because one of the parameters to this event is of type DataListItemEventArgs:

```
Protected Sub DataList1_ItemDataBound(ByVal sender As Object, _
        ByVal e As System.Web.UI.WebControls.DataListItemEventArgs) _
        Handles DataList1.ItemDataBound
```

The parameter e contains information about the item being bound and has an Item property, which represents the row being bound. The Item property has a property of its own, ItemType, which defines the template type being bound, and we want to run our code only for items or alternating items—that's each and every other row.

```
If e.Item.ItemType = ListItemType.Item OrElse _
        e.Item.ItemType = ListItemType.AlternatingItem Then
```

For rows and alternating rows, we want to find the Repeater contained within the template because this will show the item sizes and prices. When using templates, controls aren't directly accessible, because ASP.NET generates them dynamically, so we use the FindControl method to find the Repeater. We know the repeater is within the row of the DataList, and that row is represented by e.Item. FindControl returns a variable of type Object, so we use DirectCast to convert it to a Repeater.

```
Dim rpt As Repeater = DirectCast(e.Item.FindControl("Repeater1"), Repeater)
```

Next, we create two HiddenField controls, one for the ID of the item, and one for the Name, and the ID properties of these are set to ItemID and ItemName, respectively. Different names are used because the ID of a control has to be unique.

```
Dim ItemID As HiddenField = New HiddenField
Dim ItemName As HiddenField = New HiddenField
ItemID.ID = "ItemID"
ItemName.ID = "ItemName"
```

Now, we need to set the Value property of these HiddenField controls to the ID and name of the menu item. Once again, we use e.Item, which represents the row being bound, this time using the DataItem property. The DataItem property gives us access to the underlying data—the data from the database—so we can look up the values by using the column names—MenuItemID and ItemName.

```
ItemID.Value = e.Item.DataItem("MenuItemID")
ItemName.Value = e.Item.DataItem("ItemName")
```

Finally, we add these two new `HiddenField` controls to the `Repeater`, which has a collection called `Controls`. This is a collection of all child controls, so we just add our new controls to this collection. This means that when the repeater is displayed, it will contain two additional values — the ID and Name of the menu item. But because they are `HiddenField` controls, they won't actually be seen by the user.

```
        rpt.Controls.Add(ItemID)
        rpt.Controls.Add(ItemName)
    End If
End Sub
```

All of the previous code is the code that runs during the creation of the page. So, the only code left is used to add the item to the cart. For this, we are using the `ItemCommand` of the `Repeater`, which the `Repeater` raises when a button is clicked within it. Similarly to the `ItemDataBound` event of the `DataList`, the `ItemCommand` has parameters. The first, `source`, is the source of the command, which is the `Repeater`, and the second, `e`, contains details of the command.

```
Protected Sub Repeater1_ItemCommand(ByVal source As Object, _
        ByVal e As System.Web.UI.WebControls.RepeaterCommandEventArgs)
```

Like the `ItemDataBound` event of the `DataList`, we need access to the `Repeater`, but since the `Repeater` raises the event, we can use the `source` parameter. We still need to convert it to a `Repeater` type though, because the parameter is an `Object` type.

```
    Dim rpt As Repeater = DirectCast(source, Repeater)
```

Next, we need to get the values for the ID and Name of the item. Remember that we stored these in `HiddenField` controls, so we use the same `FindControl` technique to find these controls, and `DirectCast` to convert them to the correct type.

```
    Dim IDControl As HiddenField = _
                    DirectCast(rpt.FindControl("ItemID"), HiddenField)
    Dim NameControl As HiddenField = _
                    DirectCast(rpt.FindControl("ItemName"), HiddenField)
```

Once we have the `HiddenField` controls, we can extract the values. The `Value` property of the `HiddenField` is a string type, so for the `ItemID`, this is converted to an `Integer` (`Int32` is the .NET Framework type that represents an Integer — there isn't a `ToInteger` method on the `Convert` class). The `ItemName` is a string type, so no conversion is needed.

```
    Dim ItemID As Integer = Convert.ToInt32(IDControl.Value)
    Dim ItemName As String = NameControl.Value
```

Now that we have the ID and Name of the item, we need the size and price. Remember how these were set using data binding, using the `CommandName` property to store the size, and `CommandArgument` to store the price. Both of these properties are available through the `e` parameter passed into the event procedure, and both are `Object` types. So, the `ItemSize` is set by converting the `CommandName` to a string using the `ToString` method of the property, and the `ItemPrice` is set by using the `ToDecimal` method of the `Convert` class.

```
    Dim ItemSize As String = e.CommandName.ToString()
    Dim ItemPrice As Decimal = Convert.ToDecimal(e.CommandArgument)
```

We now have all of the information we need to add the item to the shopping cart, so we can use the `StoredShoppingCart` class created earlier. We use the `InsertItem` method, passing in the ID and Name of the item, and the size and price. The 1 represents the quantity—this is part of the `Insert` method because it adds flexibility—you could for example, have a text entry area allowing users to enter the number of items they would like. We've decided to make it simpler by just adding a single item to the cart when the user clicks on the item.

```
StoredShoppingCart.InsertItem(ItemID, ItemName, ItemSize, 1, ItemPrice)
```

Finally, we display a note to the users, telling them that their items have been added to the cart.

```
Label1.Text = String.Format("{0} ({1}) added to the shopping cart", _
                            ItemName, ItemSize)
End Sub
```

The `Format` method of the `String` object is useful for building strings that contain variables. It's quite simple—the first argument is the fixed string, but it contains placeholders enclosed in curly braces. The placeholders are simply a number and indicate the area to be replaced by a parameter. For example, in the previous code, the `{0}` placeholder would be replaced by the value of the `ItemName` variable, and `{1}` would be replaced by the `ItemSize` value. So, if `ItemName` was `Hawaiian`, and `ItemSize` was `Large`, the string would be:

```
Hawaiian (Large) added to the shopping cart
```

That's all there is to creating the order page and adding items to the cart. You can see that the ordering system is quite simple, around 20 lines of code. The shopping cart and storage are longer but are still relatively simple.

There are two stages left in the ordering process. First, we need a page to show the shopping cart, so users can see what they've ordered so far, and second, we need a checkout page, where the delivery address and payment can be collected. The checkout page will be covered in Chapter 8, so let's start with the shopping cart page.

The Shopping Cart Page

The cart page is going to be extremely simple because we're actually going to put some of the functionality into a user control. We do this because we want to show a grid of cart items in two places: on the "Shopping Cart" page and on the "Checkout" page. Placing the cart grid into a user control allows us to reuse the same functionality without any extra work. This is another key object oriented concept—code reuse. Reusing code and components allows you to not only save time but also to reduce potential errors, because once a component has been tested, you don't have to worry about errors in it.

Let's create this.

Try It Out   **The Shopping Cart User Control**

1. In the Solution Explorer, select the user-controls directory, and from the right-mouse menu select Add New Item.

2. From the Add New Item dialog, pick Web User Control (see Figure 7-14), and change the name to `Cart.ascx`. It doesn't matter if you place the code in a separate file because there will be no code.

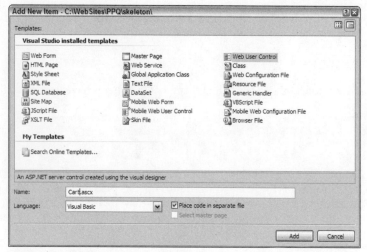

Figure 7-14: Adding a Web user control

3. When the control is created, switch to Design view.

4. From the Data section of the Toolbox, drag an `ObjectDataSource` control onto the page.

5. From the ObjectDataSource Tasks, select Configure Data Source (see Figure 7-15).

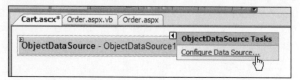

Figure 7-15: Configuring an `ObjectDataSource`

6. On the first screen of the Configure Data Source Wizard, select the `StoredShoppingCart` class from the list (see Figure 7-16) and click the Next button.

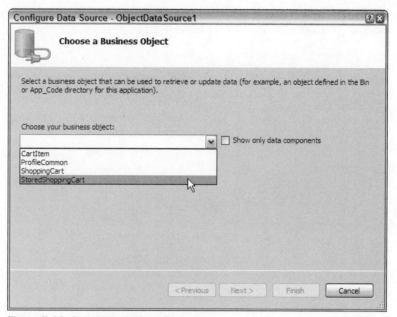

Figure 7-16: Selecting the business object

7. Next, you need to set the methods that will fetch and change data (see Figure 7-17).

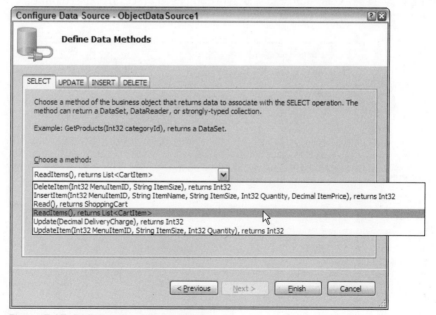

Figure 7-17: Defining the data methods

8. To define the data methods, you need to match the method on the tabs on the window with the methods in the class, as shown in the following table:

Tab	Class Method
SELECT	`ReadItems()`, `returns List<CartItem>`
UPDATE	`UpdateItem(Int32 MenuItemID, StringItemSize, Int32 Quantity), returns Int32`
INSERT	`InsertItem(Int32 MenuItemID, String ItemName, String ItemSize, Int32 Quantity, Decimal ItemPrice), returns Int32`
DELETE	`DeleteItem(Int32 MenuItemID, StringItemSize), returns Int32`

Don't worry about the odd looking format of the methods, as the wizard always shows these in C# format.

9. When you've matched the methods, click the Finish button.

10. From the Data section of the Toolbox, drag a `GridView` onto the page, dropping it underneath the `ObjectDataSource` control.

11. From the GridView Tasks, select `ObjectDataSource1` (see Figure 7-18) from the list alongside the Choose Data Source option. The `GridView` control will be refreshed showing the columns from the `Items` collection of the cart. We don't need to see all of the columns, so from the GridView Tasks, select Edit Columns (see Figure 7-19).

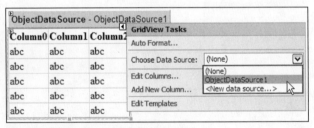

Figure 7-18: Setting the Data Source

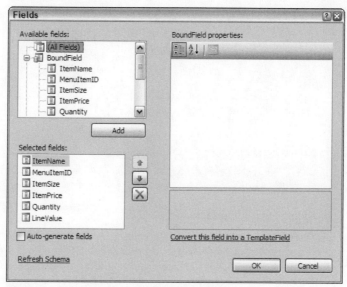

Figure 7-19: Editing the fields of a GridView

12. In the Selected fields area, select `MenuItemID`, and in the BoundField properties area, scroll down to find the `Visible` property. Set the value to `False`.

13. In the Selected fields area, select `ItemName` and set the `ReadOnly` property to `False`. Repeat this action for the `ItemSize`, `ItemPrice`, and `LineValue` fields.

14. From the Available fields list, select `CommandField`, and click the Add button. This will add a `CommandField` to the Selected fields list. Select that field and click the up arrow until the `CommandField` is at the top of the list.

15. With the `CommandField` still selected, in the `BoundField` properties, move to the behavior section. Set the `InsertVisible` property to `False`, the `ShowDelete` property to `True`, and the `ShowEdit` property to `True`.

16. Click OK to close the field editor.

17. On the GridView Tasks select Edit Templates, and pick the `EmptyDataTemplate` (see Figure 7-20).

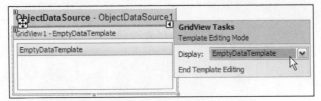

Figure 7-20: The `EmptyDataTemplate`

18. In the `EmptyDataTemplate`, enter the following text:

```
You have not ordered any items yet.<br />
Please visit the order pages to add items to the cart.
```

19. Click the End Template Editing Link.

20. With the GridView still selected, move to the properties area and find the `DataKeyNames` property (the Data section). Click into the empty area on the right, and then click the button that appears (the one with ... on it). On the Data Fields Collection Editor, select `MenuItemID` and click the button with the right arrow on it, to move the field to the right-hand list. Do the same for the `ItemSize` field (see Figure 7-21), and click OK to close the editor.

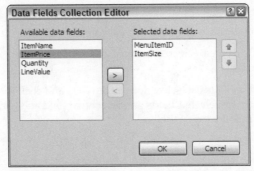

Figure 7-21: Editing the `DataKeyFields` **property**

21. Save and close the user control.

Let's see how this works.

How It Works

The cart user control relies upon the `ObjectDataSource` control. We created this in Design view, but it's worth looking at in Source view to see what the Configuration Wizard has done. The `ObjectDataSource` control is similar to the `SqlDataSource` control, except that instead of dealing with databases, it deals with classes. Both controls have methods for handling data: the `SelectMethod` to read items, the `InsertMethod` insert items, the `DeleteMethod` to delete items, and the `UpdateMethod` to update items. But instead of SQL commands, the `ObjectDataSource` simply sets these to the methods in the underlying class. To find that class, the `TypeName` property is used, in this case being set to `StoredShoppingCart`.

```
<asp:ObjectDataSource ID="CartItemsData" runat="server"
  TypeName="StoredShoppingCart"
  DeleteMethod="DeleteItem" InsertMethod="InsertItem"
  SelectMethod="ReadItems" UpdateMethod="UpdateItem" >
```

When you selected the class methods for the SELECT, UPDATE, INSERT, and DELETE methods (see Figure 7-17), the wizard automatically queried the methods and created parameters for the ObjectDataSource control based upon the parameters of the method. So, the DeleteMethod has MenuItemID and ItemSize defined.

```
<DeleteParameters>
  <asp:Parameter Name="MenuItemID" Type="Int32" />
  <asp:Parameter Name="ItemSize" Type="String" />
</DeleteParameters>
<UpdateParameters>
  <asp:Parameter Name="MenuItemID" Type="Int32" />
  <asp:Parameter Name="ItemSize" Type="String" />
  <asp:Parameter Name="Quantity" Type="Int32" />
</UpdateParameters>
<InsertParameters>
  <asp:Parameter Name="MenuItemID" Type="Int32" />
  <asp:Parameter Name="ItemSize" Type="String" />
  <asp:Parameter Name="ItemName" Type="String" />
  <asp:Parameter Name="Quantity" Type="Int32" />
  <asp:Parameter Name="ItemPrice" Type="Decimal" />
</InsertParameters>
</asp:ObjectDataSource>
```

We explained how the parameters of a grid worked with updates, inserts, and deletes in Chapter 6 when looking at the SqlDataSource control, and the ObjectDataSource control works in the same way. Figure 7-22 shows that the parameters in the UpdateParameters section of the control map through to the parameters of the UpdateItems method in the StoredShoppingCart class. The DeleteParameters and InsertParmaters work in the same way, with each <asp:Parameter> object mapping to a parameter of the class method. The insert functionality isn't used in the grid because we manually add items to the cart, but we've included it here just so you can see that the technique is the same as we discussed in Chapter 6.

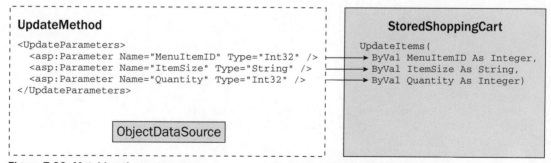

Figure 7-22: Matching the ObjectDataSource parameters to class method parameters

The GridView control uses the same techniques as seen in previous chapters, but this time is bound to the ObjectDataSource control. The DataKeyNames has been set to the fields that uniquely identify a row within the items — this is the ID of the item, and the size. The ID alone isn't sufficient because you might order one large pizza and one small, so the size is also included. The `AutoGenerateColumns` property is `false` so that the grid doesn't automatically generate the columns for display.

```
<asp:GridView ID="CartView" runat="server" EnableViewState="false"
  DataKeyNames="MenuItemID,ItemSize"
  DataSourceID="CartItemsData" AutoGenerateColumns="False">
```

The `EmptyDataTemplate` is displayed when there is no data — when there are no items in the cart.

```
<EmptyDataTemplate>
  You have not ordered any items yet.<br />
  Please visit the order pages to add items to the cart.
</EmptyDataTemplate>
```

The `Columns` define the columns (fields) to be shown. The first of these is a `CommandField`, which shows the commands that can be used on each row. The `ShowDeleteButton` and `ShowEditButton` properties are set to `True`, so that each row will allow deletion and editing.

```
<Columns>
    <asp:CommandField ShowDeleteButton="True" ShowEditButton="True" />
```

Next come the actual fields to be displayed. A `BoundField` is used for each of these. For the fields that don't allow editing (all but the quantity), the `ReadOnly` property is set to `True`, which means that when the Edit button is selected, only the `Quantity` field will show a text area.

```
    <asp:BoundField DataField="MenuItemID" Visible="False" />
    <asp:BoundField DataField="ItemName" HeaderText="Item" ReadOnly="True" />
    <asp:BoundField DataField="ItemSize" HeaderText="Size" ReadOnly="True" />
```

For the money fields (`ItemPrice` and `LineValue`) the `DataFormatString` is set to `{0:c}`, which displays the number in the currency format as set by the Regional Settings from the control panel.

```
    <asp:BoundField DataField="ItemPrice" HeaderText="Price"
      DataFormatString="{0:C}" ReadOnly="True"
      ItemStyle-HorizontalAlign="Right" />
    <asp:BoundField DataField="Quantity" HeaderText="Quantity"
      ItemStyle-HorizontalAlign="Center" />
    <asp:BoundField DataField="LineValue" HeaderText="Total"
      DataFormatString="{0:C}" ReadOnly="True"
      ItemStyle-HorizontalAlign="Right" />
  </Columns>
</asp:GridView>
```

That's all there is to the cart — an `ObjectDataControl` to interact with the `StoredShoppingCart` class, and a `GridView` to display the items. Let's build a new page that uses the user control just created so we can actually see the cart items.

Try It Out   The Shopping Cart Page

1. In the Solution Explorer, select the top-level directory and add a New Web form, called `ShowCart.ascx`, making sure that you select the `PPQ.master` master page.

2. When the form is created, switch to Design view, and from the Solution Explorer select `Cart.ascx` in the user-controls directory. Drag the `Cart.ascx` user control from the Solution Explorer, and drop it in the `Content` control, where you'll see the contents of the user control (see Figure 7-23).

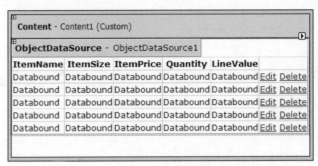

Figure 7-23: The `Cart` **user control on the form**

3. From the Toolbox, drag a `Hyperlink` control and drop it underneath the user control. If the `Hyperlink` appears to the right of the user control, just move the cursor and press Return.

4. Select the new `Hyperlink`, and change the `NavigateURL` to `~/Checkout.aspx`, and the `Text` property to `Proceed to the checkout`. We'll be building the checkout page in Chapter 8.

5. Save the file and run the application.

6. Navigate to the Order page, and order some items, clicking the Add item to order button. For one of the items, make sure that you add it to the cart twice.

7. Navigate to the Cart page to see the cart with those items in it (see Figure 7-24).

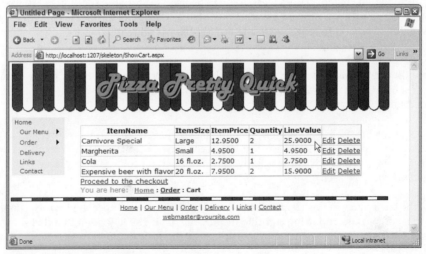

Figure 7-24: The shopping cart in action

8. Click the Edit button, and edit the Quantity of one of the items (see Figure 7-25). Press Update to save the changes.

ItemName	ItemSize	ItemPrice	Quantity	LineValue	
Carnivore Special	Large	12.9500	2 ▪	25.9000	Update Cancel
Margherita	Small	4.9500	1	4.9500	Edit Delete
Cola	16 fl.oz.	2.7500	1	2.7500	Edit Delete
Expensive beer with flavor	20 fl.oz.	7.9500	2	15.9000	Edit Delete

Figure 7-25: Editing a cart item

9.   Use the Delete button to delete one of the items from the cart.

How It Works

The working of this is all to do with the user control, and the `ObjectDataSource` and `GridView` controls within it. The `ObjectDataSource` control interacts with the `StoredShoppingCart` class to provide read and write functionality of the cart data. The `GridView` provides the interface for displaying and editing that data. What's so good about this is that you haven't had to learn anything new about the `GridView` to use custom classes — the grid interacts with the `ObjectDataSource` control, which isn't very different from the `SqlDataSource` control. This means you have to learn only one set of techniques and makes using new objects easier.

Summary

We've covered a lot of ground in this chapter, and although we haven't explained all the ins and outs of the Visual Basic .NET language, much of the code is simple. We started the chapter by taking a look at the order process, and the idea of thinking about the requirements — what is needed for ordering items and where they would be stored during the order.

Having decided that custom classes were going to be used to store the shopping cart, we then looked at how you create classes. We showed the creation of two classes (one for the cart and one for the cart items), and how you add properties and methods to them. Following that was another class, to provide the storage for the cart using the `Session` object.

We then built a page that added items into the shopping cart. This was similar to the menu page, but instead of showing just the size and price of the item, a link was added so that, when clicked, the item was added to the cart.

Next was the creation of a user control, containing an `ObjectDataSource` control and a `GridView` control, so that the display of the cart items could be seen. The `ObjectDataSource` control interacts with the classes to both read and write data to the cart. This use control was then placed on a Web form so that the items could be seen.

Many of the techniques in this chapter follow similar principles to those in previous chapters: using a control to fetch the data and using a grid to display the data. The key point that this shows is that many of the ASP.NET controls have similar properties, or methods of working, which means that you have less to learn.

In Chapter 8, we'll take the order process one step further by building the checkout page, where we'll let customers enter payment and delivery details.

The Checkout Process

In Chapter 7, we looked at the process of ordering items, which involved the creation of custom classes to store the order and the order items. These were stored in the Session object and bound to a GridView by way of an ObjectDataSource control. We left the chapter with the shopping cart page, showing all items in the cart. Now we need to take the next step and build the checkout process.

In this chapter, we will build a single page that walks the user through the checkout, so we will be covering the following:

❑   The Wizard control, and how you can use it for multistep operations

❑   How to make the checkout page react to user selections, by viewing and hiding sections

❑   How to use transactions so that database changes remain consistent

At the end of this chapter, we will have a page that steps the user through the purchase process.

Paying for the Order

The order process requires three key pieces of information:

❑   The name and address of the user

❑   How they would like to pay

❑   Confirmation of the order

We could have all of these on the page at once, but the page would probably look a little cluttered, so we'll use the Wizard control instead. This introduces the notion of steps, where each step is a template into which we can place controls. The Wizard manages the navigation between the steps, so we don't have to worry about that ourselves. As we step through the Wizard, ASP.NET shows and hides the templates so that only the correct controls are shown.

Once the user confirms the order, we will need to add the order details into the database, which means creating an order and then copying the order items from the shopping cart into the order items table. Once this is done the shopping cart can be cleared, so that the old items don't remain around.

We're going to split the checkout process into several steps, one step for each of the steps in the process.

Try It Out   Using the Wizard Control

1. Create a new Web Form called `Checkout.aspx`. Don't forget to place the code in a separate file and use the `PPQ.master` master page.

2. Switch the page to Design view, and drag a `Wizard` control onto the Content area. Set the `Width` property of the `Wizard` to `100%`.

3. From the Wizard Tasks, select Add/Remove WizardSteps. . . (see Figure 8-1).

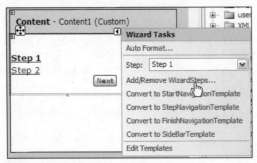

Figure 8-1: Add/Remove Wizard Steps

4. On the WizardStep Collection Editor, select `Step 1` and change the `Title` property to `Delivery Address`, and the `StepType` property to `Start`.

5. Select `Step 2` and change the `Title` property to `Payment`.

6. Click the Add button to add a new `WizardStep`, and for the new step set the `Title` property to `Shopping Cart` and the `StepType` property to `Finish`.

7. Click the Add button to add a new `WizardStep`, and for the new step set the `Title` property to `Order Complete` and the `StepType` property to `Complete`.

8. Click OK to close the editor window.

9. From the Wizard Tasks select AutoFormat, and on the Auto Format window select the `Simple` scheme and click OK. Your `Wizard` control should look like Figure 8-2.

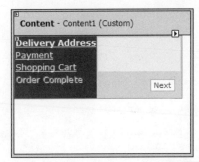

Figure 8-2: The formatted Wizard control

10. Save the file and View the page in the browser. Step through the wizard, using both the links and the buttons provided. Notice how the buttons change depending on your current step.

Let's see how this works.

How It Works

All you've done in this exercise is to use one control, but you can see that it provides quite a bit of functionality. What you did was configure the steps through the Wizard Tasks interface, so let's have a look at the code and see what it created, starting with the definition of the control and the styling:

```
<asp:Wizard ID="Wizard1" runat="server"
  BackColor="#E6E2D8" BorderColor="#999999"
  BorderStyle="Solid" BorderWidth="1px" Font-Names="Verdana" Font-Size="0.8em">
  <StepStyle BackColor="#F7F6F3"
    BorderColor="#E6E2D8" BorderStyle="Solid" BorderWidth="2px" />
  <SideBarStyle BackColor="#1C5E55" Font-Size="0.9em" VerticalAlign="Top" />
  <NavigationButtonStyle BackColor="White"
    BorderColor="#C5BBAF" BorderStyle="Solid"
    BorderWidth="1px" Font-Names="Verdana" Font-Size="0.8em"
      ForeColor="#1C5E55" />
  <SideBarButtonStyle ForeColor="White" />
  <HeaderStyle BackColor="#666666"
    BorderColor="#E6E2D8" BorderStyle="Solid" BorderWidth="2px"
    Font-Bold="True" Font-Size="0.9em" ForeColor="White"
    HorizontalAlign="Center" />
```

Here you can see what the AutoFormat has done by setting colors and styles. You can see that there are separate styles for the steps, the sidebar, the buttons in the sidebar, the header, and for the navigation buttons, which gives you a great deal of flexibility in how the `Wizard` looks. You can even remove the sidebar and just rely on the buttons, as well as configuring steps to disallow backward movement. Some of the styles shown here may actually appear after the `WizardSteps` in the code, but that's OK — where they appear doesn't matter. We've moved them together here so that it's easier to read.

For the steps, you can see that there are four `WizardStep` controls within the `WizardSteps` section.

```
<WizardSteps>
   <asp:WizardStep runat="server" Title="Delivery Address" StepType="Start">
   </asp:WizardStep>
   <asp:WizardStep runat="server" Title="Payment">
   </asp:WizardStep>
   <asp:WizardStep runat="server" Title="Shopping Cart" StepType="Finish">
   </asp:WizardStep>
   <asp:WizardStep runat="server" StepType="Complete" Title="Complete">
   </asp:WizardStep>
</WizardSteps>
</asp:Wizard>
```

Each of the `WizardStep` controls has a `Title` property, which is shown in the sidebar. The `StepType` property defines the functionality of the step, and the values are described in Table 8-1.

Table 8-1: The StepType Values

Type	Description
Auto	This is the default value for `StepType` and means that the type of step is decided by the order in which it is declared. For example, if the step is the first declared then it automatically becomes a Start step.
Complete	The step is the last one to appear, and no navigation buttons are shown.
Finish	The step is the final data collection step, and the Finish and Previous buttons are shown.
Start	The step is the first one to appear, and a Next button is shown but a Previous button is not.
Step	The step is any step between the Start and the Finish step, and the Previous and Next buttons are shown.

You set the `StepType` property of the first step, the `Delivery Address`, to be `Start`, since that is the first step, which means that only the Next button is displayed — you can't go backward from the first step. `Payment` doesn't have a specific `StepType`, so it defaults to `Auto`, which means no specific functionality is associated with the step, but that Previous and Next buttons are shown. The `Shopping Cart` step had the `StepType` set to `Finish`, which means that it is the last step where data is collected, and a Previous button is shown, but the Next button isn't — instead a Finish button is shown, letting the user know that this is the last step. The `Complete` step had a `StepType` of `Complete`, and there are no buttons shown. This is because the navigation process has finished, and this step will be used to display a message to let the user know the order is on its way.

Collecting the Delivery Address

Now that the `Wizard` and steps have been set, it's time to start filling in those steps. The first part of this process is to collect the delivery address. In Chapter 9, you'll see how we can have users join a membership to the PPQ restaurant, so instead of filling in their details, it will remember who they are. You'll still be using the controls you created in this chapter, so let's go ahead and create them.

Try It Out   **Collecting the Delivery Address**

1. On the `Checkout.aspx` page, select the `Delivery Address` step. You can do this either by clicking the link or by selecting the `Step` from the Wizard Tasks.

2. Click into the area to the right of the steps and above the Next button. From the main Layout menu, select Insert Table. On the Insert Table window (see Figure 8-3), select the Custom option, and change the Rows to 4 and the Columns to 2. Tick the `Width` and `Height` properties, making sure that the value for both is set to `100%`. Set the `Align` property to `left`, and from the Attributes area, tick `Border` and set the value to 0.

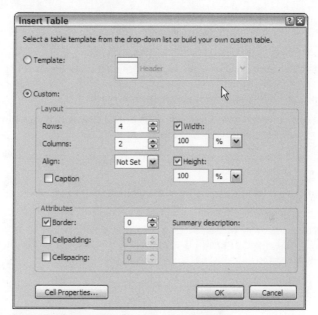

Figure 8-3: Inserting a table onto a form

3. Click the Cell Properties button, and on the Cell Properties window set the `Vertical align` property to `top` (see Figure 8-4).

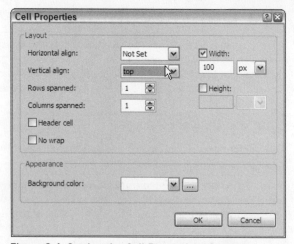

Figure 8-4: Setting the Cell Properties of a table

4. You now have a two-column, four-row table. Into the first cell on row 1, type **Name**, and drag a `TextBox` control into the second cell on row 1. Set the `ID` property of the `TextBox` to `txtName`.

5. In the first cell on row 2, type **Address**, and drag a `TextBox` control into the second cell on row 2. Set the `ID` property of the `TextBox` to `txtAddress`, the `TextMode` property to `MultiLine`, the `Rows` property to `5`, and the `Columns` property to `30`.

6. In the first cell of row 3, type **Zip Code**, and drag a `TextBox` control into the second cell on row 3. Set the `ID` property of the `TextBox` to `txtZipCode`.

7. In the first cell of row 4, type **Area**. Into cell 2, place an `ObjectDataSource` control, from the Data area of the Toolbox.

8. Select Configure Data Source . . . from the ObjectDataSource Tasks, and for the business object, select `StoredShoppingCart`.

9. For the `SELECT` method, pick `Read` (see Figure 8-5), and for the `UPDATE` method pick `Update` (see Figure 8-6). Leave `INSERT` and `DELETE` empty. Click the Finish button to close the data source configuration.

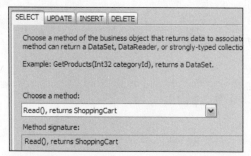

Figure 8-5: Setting the `SELECT` method for the `ObjectDataSource` control

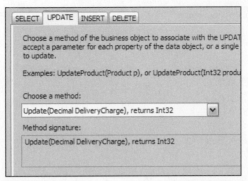

Figure 8-6: Setting the `UPDATE` **method for the** `ObjectDataSource`
control

10. With the `ObjectDataSource` selected, view the events (the lightning icon in the properties area), and find the `Updating` event. Double-click into the area to the right of it to open the code window. Between the `Protected Sub` and `End Sub`, add the following:

```
Dim ddl As DropDownList = _
    DirectCast(FormView1.FindControl("DropDownList1"), DropDownList)

e.InputParameters.Add("DeliveryCharge", ddl.SelectedValue)
```

11. Back in `Checkout.aspx`, underneath the `ObjectDataSource`, place a `FormView`, also from the Data section of the Toolbox. Don't select the data source because this creates lots of controls, and we don't need them all—we'll set the data source manually a little later. Set the `DefaultMode` property of the `FormView` to `Edit`.

12. On the FormView Tasks, select EditItemTemplate from the Display list.

13. From the Data section of the Toolbox, drag an `XmlDataSource` control, and drop it into the `EditItemTemplate`. From the XmlSource Tasks, select Configure Data Source . . .. On the configuration window, click the XML-Data button alongside the Data file, and pick `delivery-costs.xml` from the `XML-Data` folder. Click OK to close the window.

14. Underneath the `XmlDataSource`, type **Deliver to**, and alongside that place a `DropDownList`. From the DropDownList Tasks select Choose DataSource . . ., and pick `XmlDataSource1` from the data source list. Enter **name** for the display field and **delivery-cost** for the value field (see Figure 8-7). Click OK to close the window.

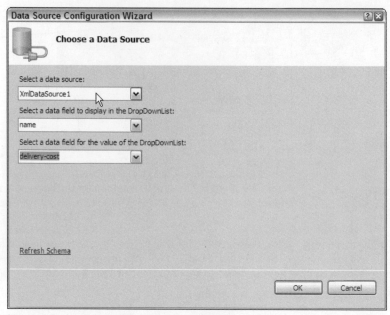

Figure 8-7: Configuring the delivery costs list

15. Select Edit DataBindings . . . from the DropDownList Tasks. Ensure that `SelectedValue` is highlighted on the "Bindable properties" list, and that the "Custom binding" option is selected. Into the "Code expression" text box, enter the following:

```
Bind("DeliveryCharge")
```

16. Click OK to close the bindings window.

17. On the DropDownList Tasks, tick the Enable AutoPostBack option.

18. With `DropDownList1` selected, view the events, and double-click into the area next to the `SelectedIndexChanged` event.

19. In the event procedure, add the following:

```
FormView1.UpdateItem(False)
```

20. Save the file and view the page in the browser (see Figure 8-8). Navigate on and off the delivery address step, noting how the controls appear only in the first step. You won't see any effect from changing the area list, apart from the page refreshing, but you'll see where it is used later.

Figure 8-8: The completed first step

How It Works

The first part of this exercise was simple, as you added a table. Using the Insert Table window, you created a four-row, two-column table and set some properties for it. Using the Insert Table window means that you don't have to know what these properties are in HTML, nor even what HTML is used for a table — it makes creating Web pages easier. Within the table cells for the first three rows, you added text and `TextBox` controls to collection the name and address:

```
<asp:WizardStep runat="server" Title="Delivery Address" StepType="Start" >
  <table border="0" style="width: 100%; height: 100%">
    <tr>
      <td style="width: 100px" valign="top">
        Name</td>
      <td style="width: 100px" valign="top">
        <asp:TextBox ID="txtName" runat="server"></asp:TextBox>
      </td>
    </tr>
    <tr>
      <td style="width: 100px" valign="top">
        Address</td>
      <td style="width: 100px" valign="top">
        <asp:TextBox ID="txtAddress" runat="server"
          Columns="30" Rows="5" TextMode="MultiLine"></asp:TextBox>
      </td>
    </tr>
    <tr>
      <td style="width: 100px" valign="top">
        Zip Code</td>
      <td style="width: 100px" valign="top">
        <asp:TextBox ID="txtZipCode" runat="server"></asp:TextBox>
      </td>
    </tr>
```

The first cell of the final table row just contains the text description of the row, but the second cell is more complex because you added two lots of data bound controls:

```
<tr>
  <td style="width: 100px" valign="top">
    Area</td>
  <td style="width: 100px" valign="top">
```

The first of these is an `ObjectDataSource` control, which is bound to the `StoredShoppingCart` class. This uses a technique similar to that used in Chapter 7, when we bound the items of the shopping cart. Here we set the `TypeName` to `StoredShoppingCart` — this is the class that handles the cart for us, with the `SelectMethod` set to `Read` (which returns the cart) and the `UpdateMethod` set to `Update` (which updates the cart). The only updateable field is the `DeliveryCharge`, so the `UpdateParameters` reflect that.

```
<asp:ObjectDataSource ID="ObjectDataSource1" runat="server"
   SelectMethod="Read" TypeName="StoredShoppingCart"
   UpdateMethod="Update">
   <UpdateParameters>
     <asp:Parameter Name="DeliveryCharge" Type="Decimal" />
   </UpdateParameters>
</asp:ObjectDataSource>
```

Next you added a `FormView` control. In Chapter 6 you looked at the `DetailsView`, and the `FormView` is similar, the main difference being that the `FormView` doesn't automatically display anything; you have to supply the controls. You set the `DataSourceID` property of the `FormView` to `ObjectDataSource1`, so it will be bound to the shopping cart. The `DefaultMode` property is `Edit` so that the `FormView` is always in Edit mode, which allows us to update the underlying data (the shopping cart) without explicitly clicking Edit and Update buttons.

```
<asp:FormView ID="FormView1" runat="server"
   DataSourceID="ObjectDataSource1" DefaultMode="Edit">
```

Since we are permanently in edit mode, we need only the `EditItemTemplate`:

```
<EditItemTemplate>
```

Within the template, you placed an `XmlDataSource`, fetching the data from the `delivery-costs.xml` file.

```
<asp:XmlDataSource ID="XmlDataSource1" runat="server"
   DataFile="~/XML-Data/delivery-costs.xml">
</asp:XmlDataSource>
```

Next you added a `DropDownList`, binding it to the `XmlDataSource` and setting the `AutoPostBack` property to `True`, so that simply selecting a value causes the page to be refreshed. Nothing visibly changes from that refresh, but an event procedure is raised (the `SelectedIndexChanged` event, as set by the `OnSelectedIndexChanged` property — we'll be coming to that shortly).

The `DataTextField` defines the value that is seen on the form, while the `DataValue` field is used to store the value. The `SelectedValue` property is bound to the `DeliveryCharge` property of the `FormView`, which itself is bound to the shopping cart. Since you used the `Bind` statement, the binding is two-way, meaning that any changes to the selection will be pushed back to the shopping cart.

```
              <asp:DropDownList ID="DropDownList1" runat="server"
                DataSourceID="XmlDataSource1" AutoPostBack="True"
                DataTextField="name" DataValueField="delivery-cost"
                OnSelectedIndexChanged="DropDownList1_SelectedIndexChanged"
                SelectedValue='<%# Bind("DeliveryCharge") %>' >
              </asp:DropDownList>
            </EditItemTemplate>
          </asp:FormView>
        </td>
      </tr>
    </table>
  </asp:WizardStep>
```

For the event procedure, you add a single line of code, calling the UpdateItem on FormView1 — this tells the FormView to push the changes back to the data source and update the data. The parameter False indicates that no validation should be performed.

```
Protected Sub DropDownList1_SelectedIndexChanged(ByVal sender As Object,
  ByVal e As System.EventArgs)

    FormView1.UpdateItem(False)


    End Sub
```

That's the first step complete, so let's move on to the next.

Collecting the Payment Details

For the next part in the process, we have to ask how the customer is going to pay for the order. There are two options here: cash on delivery or by credit card (because, you know, on those late night beer and pizza nights, you never have enough cash). This step will introduce a little code, because you don't need to see the credit card data entry area if cash is being used.

Try It Out   Collecting the Payment Details

1. Back on the Checkout.aspx page, select the Payment step, and into the empty area above the Previous and Next buttons, place a RadioButtonList control.

2. Click the Edit Items . . . link, and from the ListItem Collection Editor window. Click the Add button. For the new ListItem, set the Selected property to True, the Text property to Cash On Delivery, and the Value property to COD. Click the Add button to add another ListItem, and set the Text property to Credit Card, and the Value property to CC. Click OK to close the ListItem Collection Editor.

3. Set the AutoPostBack property of the RadioButtonList to True, and view the events (the lightning icon). Double-click next to the SelectedIndexChanged event to open the code window. Between the Protected Sub and End Sub, add the following code:

```
Dim rbl As RadioButtonList = DirectCast(source, RadioButtonList)
Dim ccp As Panel = DirectCast(Wizard1.FindControl("CreditCardPayment"), Panel)

If rbl.SelectedValue = "CC" Then
```

```
        ccp.Visible = True
    Else
        ccp.Visible = False
    End If
```

4. Back on the `Checkout.aspx` page, drag a `Panel` control from the Toolbox, and drop it under-
    neath the `RadioButtonList`, set the `ID` property to `CreditCardPayment`, and set the `Width`
    property to `100%` and the `Visible` property to `False`.

5. Click into the Panel and type **Card Type:**.

6. Drag a `DropDownList` from the Toolbox and drop it next to the `Card Type` text, and from the
    DropDownList Tasks select Edit Items. From the ListItem Collection Editor, click Add to add a
    new `ListItem`. Set the `Text` and `Value` properties to `MasterCard`. Add another `ListItem`,
    and set the `Text` and `Value` properties to `Visa`. Click OK to close the ListItem Collection Editor
    window. Set the `ID` property of the `DropDownList` to `lstCardType`.

7. Underneath the card type `DropDownList`, type **Card Number:**. Next to that, place a `TextBox`
    control, and set its `ID` property to `txtCardNumber`.

8. Underneath the card number, type **Expires:**, and place a `TextBox` control there, setting its `ID`
    property to `txtExpiresMonth`, and its `Columns` property to `2`. Type a **/** character after the
    `TextBox`, and after the **/** character add another `TextBox` control. Set its `ID` property to
    `txtExpiresYear` and its `Columns` property to `4`. Your finished payment step should now look
    like Figure 8-9.

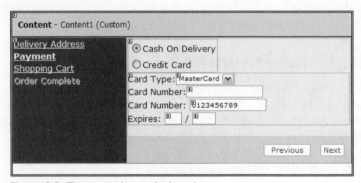

Figure 8-9: The second step designed

9. Save the page and run it. Select the `Payment` step and notice that the cash option is selected,
    and the details of the credit card aren't shown. Select `Credit Card` and see how the details now
    appear.

How It Works

The placement of the controls you added to the page follows the same rules as the previous step, with
them being placed into the `Wizard Step`. The first control was the list:

```
<asp:RadioButtonList ID="RadioButtonList1" runat="server" AutoPostBack="True">
  <asp:ListItem Selected="True" Value="COD">Cash on Delivery</asp:ListItem>
  <asp:ListItem Value="CC">Credit Card</asp:ListItem>
</asp:RadioButtonList>
```

Here the list contains two items, for selecting cash or credit card. You set the `AutoPostBack` property to `True`, which means that when the selection changes, the page is posted back to the Web server. When you created the event procedure by double-clicking next to the `SelectedIndexChanged` event, the following was created:

```
Protected Sub RadioButtonList1_SelectedIndexChanged(ByVal sender As Object,
    ByVal e As System.EventArgs) Handles RadioButtonList1.SelectedIndexChanged
End Sub
```

This is the event procedure and will be used to run code when the radio button selection changes, which is what the `SelectedIndexChanged` event means. Each `ListItem` has an index number (created automatically by ASP.NET), and when the selected item changes, so does its index number, and this event is raised when that index number changes.

Within the event procedure, the first line of code is as follows:

```
Dim rbl As RadioButtonList = DirectCast(source, RadioButtonList)
```

This defines a variable as a `RadioButtonList` and takes its value from the `source` argument of the event procedure, which identifies the control that raised the event. However, the `source` argument is passed into this event procedure by ASP.NET as an `object` type, so you used `DirectCast` to convert it to a `RadioButtonList`.

The next line declares a `Panel` object, which is used to reference the panel containing the credit card details. You use the `FindControl` method of the `Wizard` control to find the panel (called `CreditCardPayment`), and use the `DirectCast` statement to convert this to a `Panel` type (`FindControl` returns an `object` type).

```
Dim ccp As Panel = DirectCast(Wizard1.FindControl("CreditCardPayment"), Panel)
```

Next, you test the `SelectedValue` of the `RadioButtonList` to see if it is `CC`. If it is, then the user has selected credit card option, so you set the `Visible` property of the `Panel` to `True`. This shows the panel containing the credit card details. If the `SelectedValue` is not `CC`, then the user has selected the cash option, so the panel is hidden by setting the `Visible` property to `False`.

```
If rbl.SelectedValue = "CC" Then
    ccp.Visible = True
Else
    ccp.Visible = False
End If
```

This code makes the page react to the user, showing and hiding controls depending upon what the user does. It's a common, and very useful, technique.

Once you finished the code, the `Panel` and credit card details were added.

```
<asp:Panel ID="CreditCardPayment" runat="server"
  Height="50px" Width="100%" Visible="false">
  Card Type:
  <asp:DropDownList ID="lstCardType" runat="server">
    <asp:ListItem>MasterCard</asp:ListItem>
    <asp:ListItem>Visa</asp:ListItem>
```

```
</asp:DropDownList>
<br />
Card Number:
<asp:TextBox ID="txtCardNumber" runat="server"></asp:TextBox>
<br />
Expires:
<asp:textbox id="txtExpiresMonth" runat="server" columns="2" />
/
<asp:textbox id="txtExpiresYear" runat="server"  columns="4" />
</asp:Panel>
```

These details are simply placeholders to show you a part of the process. In reality, you'd use these credit card details to pay for the order once the Finish button is clicked by interacting with a credit card processing company. How you do this depends upon the company selected, so we won't be covering that here.

Confirming the Order

Confirming the order requires two sets of information:

❑   The shopping cart needs to be shown, so that the customer can see what has been ordered.

❑   The totals (including delivery charge and sales tax) need to be shown.

The cart items is easy, because you created a user control for that in Chapter 7, so you only need to add data binding for the totals.

Try It Out   **Confirming the Order**

1.   Select the `Shopping Cart` step. From the Solution Explorer, open the `user-controls` folder and drag `Cart.ascx` onto the page, dropping it into the empty area on above the Previous and Finish buttons (see Figure 8-10).

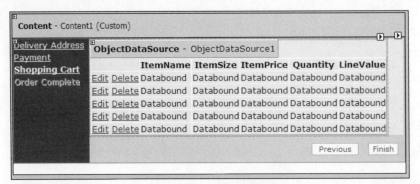

Figure 8-10: The `Shopping Cart` **user control in the** `Wizard`

2.   From the Data section of the Toolbox, drag an `ObjectDataSource` control onto the page, dropping it to the right of the `Shopping Cart` user control.

3. From the ObjectDataSource Tasks, select Configure Data Source . . .. On the Choose a Business Object of the data source configuration, select StoredShoppingCart from the list, and click the Next button.

4. For the SELECT method, pick Read (see Figure 8-11). Leave the Update, Insert, and Delete methods empty, and click Finish to close the data source configuration.

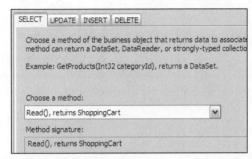

Figure 8-11: Setting the SELECT method for the ObjectDataSource **control**

5. From the Data section of the Toolbox, drag a DetailsView onto the page, drop it underneath the ObjectDataSource, and set the Width property to 100%. From the DetailsView Tasks select ObjectDataSource2 as the data source, and then select Edit Fields . . ..

6. On the Fields window, move to the selected fields area. Select the SalesTax field, removing it from the list. Modify the other fields so that they are in the following order, and set the properties accordingly:

Control	HeaderTextData	FormatString	ReadOnly	ItemStyle HorizontalAlign
SubTotal	Sub-Total	{0:C}	True	Right
DeliveryCharge	Delivery	{0:C}	True	Right
SalesTaxPercent	Sales Tax	{0:C}	True	Right
Total	Total	{0:C}	True	Right

7. Select SalesTaxPercent and at the bottom right of the window, click the "Convert this field into a TemplateField" link.

8. For each of the fields, move to the Styles section of the properties, and open the ItemStyle. Set the HorizontalAlign property to Right. Click OK to close the Fields window.

9. Select the DetailsView and set its Width property to 100%. Set the DefaultMode property to Edit.

10. From the DetailsView Tasks, select Edit Templates, and from the Display list select the HeaderTemplate for SalesTaxPercent (see Figure 8-12).

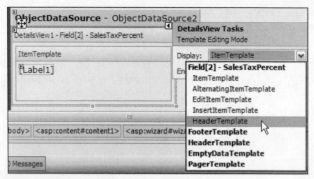

Figure 8-12: Selecting `HeaderTemplate`

11. Switch to Source view, move to the `DetailsView`, and find the `TemplateField` called `SalesTaxPercent`. Remove the `InsertItemTemplate` and `ItemTemplate` completely. Remove the contents of the `EditItemTemplate`, replacing them with:

```
<%# Eval("SalesTax ", "{0:C}") %>
```

12. Create a new `HeaderTemplate`, adding the following code just before the `EditItemTemplate`:

```
<HeaderTemplate>
  Sales Tax (<%#Eval("SalesTaxPercent", "{0:0%}")%>)
</HeaderTemplate>
<EditItemTemplate>
```

13. The `Shopping Cart` step should now look like Figure 8-13 in Design view.

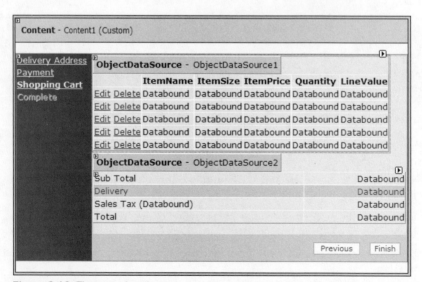

Figure 8-13: The completed `Shopping Cart` **step**

14. Switch to Source view, and find the `Wizard` control, `Wizard1`. Remove the `ActiveStepIndex` property and its associated value.

15. Save the file, and view it in the browser. Select the Delivery Address and change the area to Out of State, and click Next twice to get to the Shopping Cart screen. Notice that the Delivery Charge shows the charge for the Out of State area (see Figure 8-14).

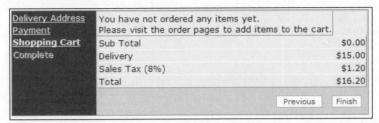

Delivery Address	You have not ordered any items yet.	
Payment	Please visit the order pages to add items to the cart.	
Shopping Cart	Sub Total	$0.00
Complete	Delivery	$15.00
	Sales Tax (8%)	$1.20
	Total	$16.20
		Previous Finish

Figure 8-14: Running the Wizard

16. There are no items in the cart, so no rows show. Add some items to the cart and then navigate back to this step of the wizard (see Figure 8-15).

Delivery Address		ItemName	ItemSize	ItemPrice	Quantity	LineValue
Payment	Edit Delete	Carnivore Special	Large	$12.95	1	$12.95
Shopping Cart	Edit Delete	Hawaiian	Small	$5.95	1	$5.95
Complete	Edit Delete	Cola	16 fl.oz.	$2.75	1	$2.75
	Edit Delete	Expensive beer with flavor	20 fl.oz.	$7.95	2	$15.90
	Sub Total					$37.55
	Delivery					$3.00
	Sales Tax (8%)					$3.24
	Total					$43.79
					Previous	Finish

Figure 8-15: The Wizard **with** Shopping Cart **items**

Let's see how this step works.

How It Works

The first thing you did was drag the Shopping Cart user control onto the page, which does two things to the code. First, it adds a Register directive at the top of the page:

```
<%@ Register Src="user-controls/Cart.ascx" TagName="Cart" TagPrefix="uc1" %>
```

This defines the source (the src attribute) of the user control, plus the name and prefix to be used when the control is placed on the page. You can see this by the code used to include the control:

```
<uc1:Cart ID="Cart1" runat="server" />
```

The next thing you did was to create an ObjectDataSource, bound to the StoredShoppingCart, but using only the SelectMethod because this will be read-only:

```
<asp:ObjectDataSource ID="ObjectDataSource2" runat="server" SelectMethod="Read"
TypeName="StoredShoppingCart">
</asp:ObjectDataSource>
```

Bound to the `ObjectDataSource` is a `DetailsView`:

```
<asp:DetailsView ID="DetailsView1" runat="server" AutoGenerateRows="False"
    DataSourceID="ObjectDataSource2"
    Height="50px" Width="100%" DefaultMode="Edit">
```

The `DefaultMode` is set to `Edit` so that the user doesn't have to click an Edit or Update link.

The first two fields, `SubTotal` and `DeliveryCharge`, are bound to the `SubTotal` and `DeliveryCharge` from the shopping cart. Remember that in the first step, where the address was collected, we had a list for the area, which updated the delivery charge. This is where that delivery charge is displayed.

```
<Fields>
    <asp:BoundField DataField="SubTotal" DataFormatString="{0:C}"
        HeaderText="Sub Total"
        ReadOnly="True" SortExpression="SubTotal">
        <ItemStyle HorizontalAlign="Right" />
    </asp:BoundField>
    <asp:BoundField DataField="DeliveryCharge" HeaderText="Delivery"
        SortExpression="DeliveryCharge" DataFormatString="{0:C}"
        ReadOnly="True">
        <ItemStyle HorizontalAlign="Right" />
    </asp:BoundField>
```

The `DataFormatString` is set to `{0:C}`, which displays the data in the currency format set on the machine. Our test machine is set to US, so it shows a $, but with UK settings you would see Figure 8-16. The `ItemStyle` element allows styling of the item, and here every field is right-aligned, so they line up.

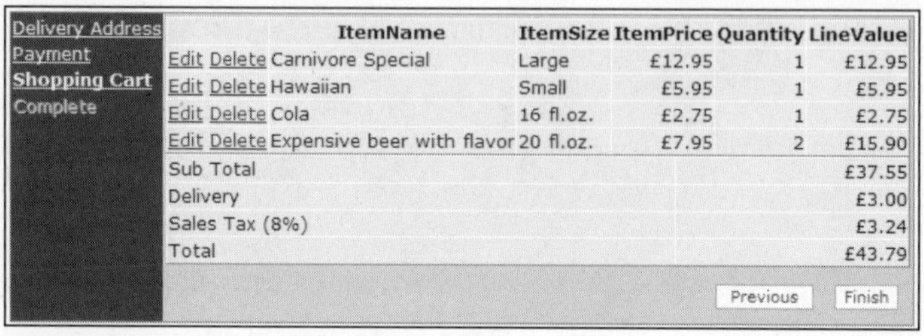

		ItemName	ItemSize	ItemPrice	Quantity	LineValue
Delivery Address	Edit Delete	Carnivore Special	Large	£12.95	1	£12.95
Payment	Edit Delete	Hawaiian	Small	£5.95	1	£5.95
Shopping Cart	Edit Delete	Cola	16 fl.oz.	£2.75	1	£2.75
Complete	Edit Delete	Expensive beer with flavor	20 fl.oz.	£7.95	2	£15.90
	Sub Total					£37.55
	Delivery					£3.00
	Sales Tax (8%)					£3.24
	Total					£43.79
					Previous	Finish

Figure 8-16: The shopping cart with UK settings

The next field is a template field for the sales tax. We didn't use a `BoundField` for this because we need a bit of customization to show the percentage in the header (the first column), and the amount in the second column.

```
<asp:TemplateField HeaderText="Sales Tax"
    SortExpression="SalesTaxPercent">
```

The `HeaderTemplate` shows for the header, and this is a combination of some text and the percentage of the sales tax. You've seen the `Eval` statement before, where only a single parameter was passed into it — the field to be shown. But here we use another form, passing in a second parameter which is the format string. This follows the same style as the `DataFormatString` property of a `BoundField`, but instead of a currency, a percentage is displayed.

```
<HeaderTemplate>
    Sales Tax (<%# Eval("SalesTaxPercent", "{0:0%}") %>)
</HeaderTemplate>
```

For the `EditItemTemplate`, just the sales tax is displayed, and this is a currency — the amount of the tax, rather than the percentage.

```
<EditItemTemplate>
    <%#Eval("SalesTax", "{0:C}")%>
</EditItemTemplate>
<ItemStyle HorizontalAlign="Right" />
</asp:TemplateField>
```

That's all there is to this step. It is simply using an `ObjectDataSource` to display the values from the shopping cart. The items are displayed by the user control, which shows how great user controls are — all of the work to code that has already been done, and we can simply reuse the functionality. It's a great way to create sections of a site that will be used in multiple places.

The `DetailsView` showed the use of `BoundFields` as well as `TemplateFields` and that you can easily customize the display.

The `ActiveStepIndex` property was removed because this affects how the wizard appears when the program is run. It is used at both design and run time, and when run retains the value of the last selected step at design time.

Let's now move on to completing the order.

Completing the Order

To complete the order, the order needs to be added to the `Orders` table in the database, and the items must be added to the `OrderItems` table. This will involve extracting the order and address details and writing them to one table, and then looping through the order items to add those. Let's give this a go.

Try It Out   Completing the Order

1. Switch back to Design view, and select the Order Complete step. Enter the following text into the step area:

    ```
    Thank you for your order.
    ```

2. Underneath the `Wizard`, add two label controls. Copy these from `Checkout.aspx.txt` in the page-content folder — you can paste straight into the area underneath the `Wizard` (see Figure 8-17). These will be used to let the user know whether or not the order was placed successfully.

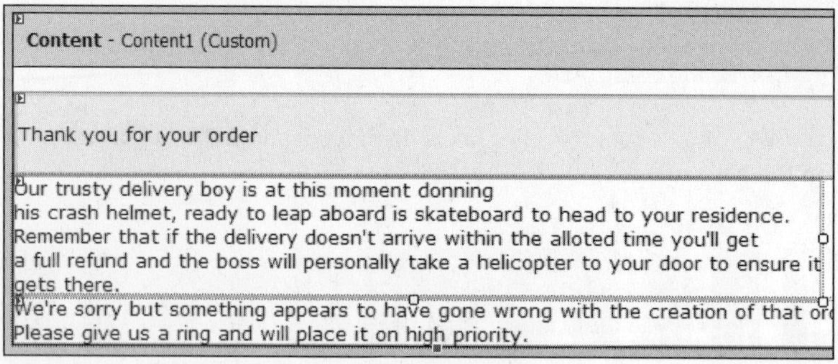

Figure 8-17: The success and failure messages

3. Select the `Wizard` control, `Wizard1`, and in the properties area select the events. Double-click in the area to the right of the `FinishButtonClick` event, which will create the event procedure in the code window.

4. Copy the code from `Checkout.aspx.vb.txt` in the `page-content` folder, and paste it into the event procedure.

5. At the very top of the file, add the following:

```
Imports System.Data
Imports System.Data.SqlClient
```

6. Switch back to `Checkout.aspx`. Switch to Source view, and find the `Wizard` control, `Wizard1`. Remove the `ActiveStepIndex` property and its associated value.

7. Save the files and run the application. Add some items to the cart and step through the checkout process, and you should see the success order. At the moment, there is no method to view the orders, so let's create a page for that.

8. Close the browser window, and add a new Web Form to the application called `ViewOrder.aspx`, remembering to place the code in a separate file, and select the `PPQ.master` master page.

9. Switch to Design view, and from the Database Explorer, expand the tables, and drag the `Orders` table onto the page.

10. When the GridView Tasks appear, tick Enable Paging and Enable Selection.

11. From the Database Explorer, drag the `OrderItems` table onto the page. Select the GridView Tasks, and tick Enable Paging.

12. Select `SqlDataSource2`, and select Configure Data Source . . . from the SqlDataSource Tasks. Click Next on the Choose Your Data Connection page, and on the Configure the Select Statement page click the WHERE . . . button.

13. On the Add WHERE Clause page select `fkOrderID` for the `Column` and `Control` for the `Source`. Then select `GridView1` for the `ControlID`, and click the Add button. Click the OK button to close the window.

14. Back on the configuration window, click Next and then Finish.

15. Save the page and run it. Click Select on an order, and you'll see something like Figure 8-18. We've added two orders, so the top grid has two items.

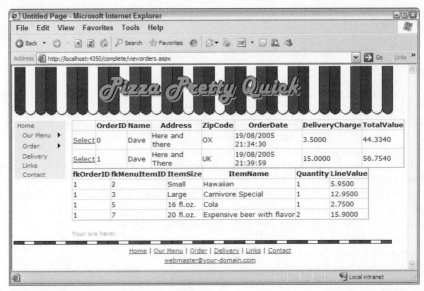

Figure 8-18: The `View Orders` **page**

We've not formatted any of the columns, which is why it looks a little raw, but it's perfectly functional, and lets you see the orders and order items. Let's see how all of this works.

How It Works

The first part of this step was to simply add some text into the step area — this is the text that will be displayed when the step is completed.

We then added two `Label` controls, one for the successful order message and one for the failed order message. The `Visible` property for both is `False`, so that these aren't initially shown — we'll show them from the code.

```
<asp:Label ID="CreateOrderSuccessLabel" runat="server" Visible="False">
  Our trusty delivery boy is at this moment donning <br />
  his crash helmet, ready to leap aboard is skateboard to head to your
residence.<br />
  Remember that if the delivery doesn't arrive within the alloted time you'll
get<br />
  a full refund and the boss will personally take a helicopter to your door to
ensure it<br />
  gets there.
</asp:Label>
<asp:Label ID="CreateOrderErrorLabel" runat="server" Visible="False">
  We're sorry but something appears to have gone wrong with the creation of that
order.<br />
  Please give us a ring and will place it on high priority.
```

```
</asp:Label>
```

Next, we created an event procedure for the `FinishButtonClick` event. This is the event that is run when the Finish button is clicked. Into this, we pasted some prebuilt code — there's a lot of it, but we'll go through it all.

The first line is the event procedure declaration. The second parameter, `e`, can be used to work out what step you are on, and even cancel the navigation to this step — you'll see this in a little while.

```
Protected Sub Wizard1_FinishButtonClick(ByVal sender As Object,
    ByVal e As System.Web.UI.WebControls.WizardNavigationEventArgs)
    Handles Wizard1.FinishButtonClick
```

Next, we have the variable declarations, starting with a `SqlConnection` object, which will be used to connect to the database. After that there is a `SqlTransaction` object, which will be used to ensure that the database remains in a stable state — don't worry about it for now, as we'll explain transactions soon, in the "Understanding Transaction" section later in this chapter. After the transaction is a `SqlCommand` object, which will be used to run the SQL commands. Finally, there is a `ShoppingCart` object, which is set to the value of the current cart — this contains the order details.

```
Dim conn As SqlConnection = Nothing
Dim trans As SqlTransaction = Nothing
Dim cmd As SqlCommand
Dim cart As ShoppingCart = StoredShoppingCart.Read()
```

Next, we check that the `cart` object is valid by testing to see if it is `Nothing`. This is a special test for an object, and if it is `Nothing`, then there is no shopping cart — something has gone wrong in the creation of it. We also test the `Count` property to see if the `Items` collection of the cart has any items — if `0` then no items have been added to the cart. In either of these two cases, we don't want to continue processing the order, we set the `Cancel` property of the parameter `e` to `True`. This tells the `Wizard` that we are canceling the navigation of this step, and not to allow it. The `Return` statement returns from the procedure without processing the order. You can go ahead and try this if you like. Navigate to the Checkout page without adding any items, and notice that even though you click the Finish button, you don't move onto the `Complete` step.

```
If cart Is Nothing OrElse cart.Items.Count = 0 Then
    e.Cancel = True
    Return
End If
```

Next, we have a `Try` statement, which is part of the error handling. Like transactions, we'll explain this fully in the "Understanding Exception Handling" section later in this chapter.

```
Try
```

Within the `Try` block, we define an `Integer` variable, `OrderID`, to hold the Order ID. We'll need this because when we create the order, an ID will be created, and this will be used in the `OrderItems` table in the `fkOrderID` column, which is the foreign key to the `Orders` table (this was covered in Chapter 3).

```
Dim OrderID As Integer
```

Next, we create the connection to the database, using the `SqlConnection` object. The `ConfigurationManager` is a class supplied by ASP.NET that lets us get values from `web.config`—the configuration file. The value we want is in the `<connectionStrings>` section, and stores the details of the database connection. We use this so it is defined only once, in a central location. Once the connection is set, it is opened using the `Open` method.

```
    conn = New SqlConnection(ConfigurationManager.ConnectionStrings
("PPQ_DataConnectionString1").ConnectionString)
    conn.Open()
```

Next, we begin the transaction—again, this is something we'll be coming back to later.

```
    trans = conn.BeginTransaction
```

We now create a `SqlCommand` object, and set the `Connection` and `Transaction` properties to the connection and transaction created earlier.

```
    cmd = New SqlCommand()
    cmd.Connection = conn
    cmd.Transaction = trans
```

We then set the command to be run, and the type of command. The `CommandText` is set to the name of a stored procedure, which is already in the database, and `CommandType` is set to `CommandType.StoredProcedure` to tell ASP.NET that a stored procedure is being used, rather than a plain SQL statement.

```
    cmd.CommandText = "usp_InsertOrder"
    cmd.CommandType = CommandType.StoredProcedure
```

We then define the `Parameters` of the command, adding a parameter for each parameter in the stored procedure.

```
    cmd.Parameters.Add("@Name", Data.SqlDbType.VarChar, 25)
    cmd.Parameters.Add("@Address", Data.SqlDbType.VarChar, 255)
    cmd.Parameters.Add("@ZipCode", Data.SqlDbType.VarChar, 15)
    cmd.Parameters.Add("@OrderDate", Data.SqlDbType.DateTime)
    cmd.Parameters.Add("@DeliveryCharge", Data.SqlDbType.Money)
    cmd.Parameters.Add("@TotalValue", Data.SqlDbType.Money)
    cmd.Parameters.Add("@OrderID", SqlDbType.Int)
    cmd.Parameters("@OrderID").Direction = ParameterDirection.Output
```

`Parameters` is a collection on the `SqlCommand` object, and the `Add` method creates a new parameter in the collection. `Add` takes two or three arguments, depending upon the type of parameter being added. The first argument is always the parameter name, and the second is the data type. For parameters that have a variable length (such as strings), the `VarChar` type is used as the data type, and the third argument is the length—the number of characters. So, for the first line in the previous code, the name of the parameter is @Name, and it is a string of 25 characters. The `DateTime` type is used to store dates and time, `Money` is used to store monetary values, and `Int` is used for whole numbers.

The final line sets the `Direction` property of the `OrderID` parameter to `ParameterDirection.Output`, which tells the command which direction data is going to flow. The `Direction` defaults to `ParameterDirection.Input`, meaning that values flow into the stored procedure, but an `Output` parameter means that the value flows out of the command (from the stored procedure back to our code). This is used because the OrderID is created by the database. It is automatically generated, and since we need it for the foreign key in the OrderItems table, we need a way to get that value. The output parameter means that once the command has been run, the OrderID parameter will hold the ID of the newly inserted order.

Next, we need to set the values of these parameters, using the Value property, so that the values are passed into the stored procedure. The first three are set to the values from the TextBox controls in the first Wizard step, where the name and address were collected.

```
cmd.Parameters("@Name").Value = _
    CType(Wizard1.FindControl("txtName"), TextBox).Text
cmd.Parameters("@Address").Value = _
    CType(Wizard1.FindControl("txtAddress"), TextBox).Text
cmd.Parameters("@ZipCode").Value = _
    CType(Wizard1.FindControl("txtZipCode"), TextBox).Text
```

In case you are wondering, the "_" character, when the last character on a line and preceded by a space, acts as a line-continuation character. This means that you can have a line of code spanning more than one physical line, which sometimes makes the code easier to read.

The next parameter, @OrderDate, is set to the current date and time, using the Now method of the DateTime object. @DeliveryCharge is set to the DeliveryCharge value from the cart, and @TotalValue to the Total value from the cart.

```
cmd.Parameters("@OrderDate").Value = DateTime.Now()
cmd.Parameters("@DeliveryCharge").Value = cart.DeliveryCharge
cmd.Parameters("@TotalValue").Value = cart.Total
```

The parameters have now been set, so the command can be run, using the ExecuteNonQuery method. This tells ASP.NET to run the command but not to expect any data—the output parameters still come back, but no other data (such as a set of rows) is returned.

```
cmd.ExecuteNonQuery()
```

With the command run, the output parameters can be extracted. We take the Value of the @OrderID parameter, and using a conversion routine, convert it to an Integer. (ToInt32 refers to the length of the Integer type, which is 32 bits.)

```
OrderID = Convert.ToInt32(cmd.Parameters("@OrderID").Value)
```

At this stage, the order has been inserted and we have the ID of the order, so we need to insert the order items. The first part of that is to change the name of the stored procedure being used.

```
cmd.CommandText = "usp_InsertOrderItem"
```

We then empty the Parameters collection using the Clear method because it currently contains the parameters for the Orders table.

```
cmd.Parameters.Clear()
```

Now, the parameters for the OrderItems are set, using the same method as used previously.

```
cmd.Parameters.Add("@fkOrderID", Data.SqlDbType.Int)
cmd.Parameters.Add("@MenuItemID", Data.SqlDbType.Int)
cmd.Parameters.Add("@ItemSize", Data.SqlDbType.VarChar, 50)
cmd.Parameters.Add("@ItemName", Data.SqlDbType.VarChar, 50)
cmd.Parameters.Add("@Quantity", Data.SqlDbType.Int)
cmd.Parameters.Add("@LineValue", Data.SqlDbType.Money)
```

The `Value` for the `@fkOrderID` property is set to the `OrderID` variable, as taken from the `@OrderID` output parameter. There may be multiple order items added to the order, but all will have the same `OrderID`, so this is set only once.

```
cmd.Parameters("@fkOrderID").Value = OrderID
```

Now, we need to loop through the items in the shopping cart, and for each item, set the parameter values and run the command. The `For Each` statement allows us to loop through the `Items` collection of the `cart`. Each time through the loop, the `item` variable (a `CartItem` data type) is set to the item in the collection — so each time around, the properties of `item` will be the properties of the order item.

```
For Each item As CartItem In cart.Items
```

The parameter value for each of the parameters comes from the related property of the cart item. Therefore, `@MenuItemID` comes from the `MenuItemID` property, and so on.

```
cmd.Parameters("@MenuItemID").Value = item.MenuItemID
cmd.Parameters("@ItemSize").Value = item.ItemSize
cmd.Parameters("@ItemName").Value = item.ItemName
cmd.Parameters("@Quantity").Value = item.Quantity
cmd.Parameters("@LineValue").Value = item.LineValue
```

Once the parameters have been set, the command can be executed within the loop. Remember that we are inserting multiple rows (one for each cart item), so the command needs to be run multiple types. It's only the parameter values that change, so the parameter definitions are outside of the loop because they need to happen only once.

```
    cmd.ExecuteNonQuery()
Next
```

At this stage, we have inserted both the order and the order items, and there have been no errors (the `Try` statement ensure that, as you'll shortly see). If we know nothing has gone wrong, we can commit the transaction, which tells the database that everything is okay, and we display the success label to let the user know the order has been completed.

```
trans.Commit()
CreateOrderSuccessLabel.Visible = True
```

The next code segment deals with errors. We use the `Catch` statement for this, which is related to the `Try` statement, which was near the top of the code. We'll look at this in more detail later, but for a quick synopsis, if there is an error in code between the `Try` and `Catch` statements, then the code underneath the `Catch` statement runs. This gives us a central place to deal with errors. You can catch different types of errors, but the type we are interested in is a `SqlException`, which would mean that a database problem happened.

```
Catch SqlEx As SqlException
```

Within the Catch block, we check the transaction. If it has a value (that is, it is not Nothing), then we Rollback the transaction. Again more on that later, but a quick definition is that it undoes all database commands since the transaction was started. This keeps the database in a stable state, so that no orders are inserted without order items, and no order items are inserted without an order.

```
If trans IsNot Nothing Then
   trans.Rollback()
End If
```

We now need to generate an error for the user to see, so we simply make the error label visible and return from the procedure.

```
CreateOrderErrorLabel.Visible = True
Return
```

The Finally statement is related to Try and Catch, and is always run after a Try or Catch block. So, you either run the Try code and if everything is OK, then you run the Finally code. Alternatively you run the Try code, and if something goes wrong you run the Catch code, and then the Finally code.

```
Finally
```

Within the finally code we simply Close the connection if it is a valid object (that is, if it has a value other than Nothing).

```
If conn IsNot Nothing Then
   conn.Close()
End If

End Try
```

The very last piece of code to run is to clear the items collected in the cart, since all of the items have been added to the database:

```
cart.Items.Clear()

End Sub
```

That's all the code for creating the order. Although there was quite a lot of code, it falls neatly into blocks. First we create the command and parameters for the order, set the parameter values, and insert the order. Then we set the command and parameters for the order items, and for each order item set the parameter values and run the command, thus inserting each order item. The Try, Catch, and Finally statements allow us to protect out code against errors. Let's have a look at this exception handling in a little more detail.

Understanding Exception Handling

Exception handling is a core piece of programming in ASP.NET and provides a way to protect programs against unexpected occurrences (such as the cleaner unplugging the database server to plug in the vacuum cleaner—don't laugh, we've seen it happen). Exception handling in Visual Basic revolves around blocks of code, code that you want to try and run. If it runs, fine, then that's great. But if something goes wrong, you need to handle that gracefully and show a nice message to the user, rather than some horrible error message that the user won't understand.

Exception handling revolves around three statements: Try, Catch, and Finally. Following is some pseudo-code to show the structure:

```
Try
    ' here we have the code that we want to run

Catch SqlEx As SqlException
    ' this code will be run if a SqlException was raised in the Try block

Catch Ex As Exception
    ' this code will be run if a Exception was raised in the Try block

Finally
    ' this code will always run, either after the Code in the Try block,
    ' or after the code in one of the exception blocks

End Try
```

So, walking through, even though there is no code in the code blocks, we start with the Try statement. This says to Visual Basic, "Right, it's up to you to monitor the code for problems — if something happens, don't just fall over and show an error message, jump to one of the Catch blocks."

If something does go wrong, an exception will be raised, and this can come from a number of places. Any of the supplied classes can raise exceptions, and the exception raised will depend upon which code is being run when the problem occurred.

For example, if you are running a database command then you will get a SqlException. When an exception is raised, Visual Basic checks each Catch statement for a match and stops at the first match. In the previous example, the first Catch block is a match, so only the code for that Catch block will be run. The code for other Catch blocks is ignored, and execution continues in the Finally block, or at the line after the End Try if no Finally block is present. The syntax for the Catch block is:

```
Try variable As ExceptionType
```

The variable will contain the details of the exception, and you can use the Message property to get the error message, or the ToString() method to see all of the details about the error. The ExceptionType is the type of exception and allows you to have different error-handling code for different types of exceptions.

The previous code shows two Catch blocks, one for SqlException and one for Exception. The order in which they are declared is important because the test for the exception type is from top to bottom. This may not seem important, but you have to understand that a SqlException is also an Exception. This is so because Visual Basic is an object-oriented programming language and has a feature called *inheritance*. This means that classes can inherit characteristics from other classes, much like the way we inherit things from our parents (yeah, hay fever, thanks Mom). So, Exception is the base class, defining the characteristics that all other exception types contain. The effect this has on us is that if a database error occurs, and a `SqlException` is raised, the exception could match either `SqlException` or `Exception`. So, you can see that the order of the `Catch` blocks is important. In the previous code, the `SqlException` came before the `Exception`, so it would always be matched first. However, imagine if we had the following:

```
Try
    ' here we have the code that we want to run

Catch Ex As Exception
    ' this code will be run if a Exception was raised in the Try block

Catch SqlEx As SqlException
    ' this code will be run if a SqlException was raised in the Try block

Finally
    ' this code will always run, either after the Code in the Try block,
    ' or after the code in one of the exception blocks

End Try
```

If a `SqlException` was raised in the `Try` block, the first exception tested is `Exception`, and because of inheritance, there is a match. This means that any special code to handle the database error in the `SqlException` `Catch` block would not be run. So, the rule is, if you have multiple `Catch` blocks, always put the one matching `Exception` last.

The other rule for exception handling is that you should catch exceptions only if you can handle the error and recover from it gracefully. If there is nothing you can do, then it's not worth catching the exception.

Understanding Transactions

Transactions are an important part of database consistency and work hand-in-hand with exception handling. Transactions ensure either that all database operations succeed or that none do. The classic example used for this is a money transfer operation, where you debit one account and credit another. Both have to happen or neither should happen. You don't want to have money debited but not go anywhere. You might want to have money credited to another account without it being debited from your account, but you can be sure the bank doesn't want that!

In our application, there are several commands that must be run, first to insert the order and then to insert the order items. Neither makes sense without the other; an order without order items is of no use, and order items without an order would leave us unable to find the order items, there being no order to select.

The process of handling transactions is quite simple. Before the commands are run, you start a transaction, which tells the database to keep track of all database changes you are doing. You then proceed to modify data, in our case inserting records. You then either tell the database to commit those changes if nothing went wrong, or to roll back the changes if something did go wrong. *Rolling back* means that every database change since the transaction started is undone, thus leaving the database in a consistent state, the state it was in before the transaction started.

A transaction is held as a `Transaction` object, and you start a transaction by using the `BeginTransaction` method of the connection. If everything was successful, you use the `Commit` method of the transaction to commit the changes, or you use the `Rollback` method if there were errors. You can combine this with exception handling to great effect, as shown in the following:

```
Try
    Dim trans as Transaction
    trans = conn.BeginTransaction()

    ' here we have the code that we want to run
    ' it will insert rows into the database


    ' everything is OK, so commit the changes
    trans.Commit()

Catch SqlEx As SqlException
    ' this code will be run if a SqlException was raised in the Try block

    ' roll back the changes
    trans.Rollback()

Finally
    ' this code will always run, either after the Code in the Try block,
    ' or after the code in one of the exception blocks

End Try
```

You can see that the transaction is started at the beginning of the `Try` block, and the `Commit` is at the end of the `Try` block, which will be reached only if no exception was raised. If a `SqlException` occurs, control will pass to the `Catch` block, where the transaction is rolled back.

Transactions are often not taught in introductory-style books, but they are extremely important when dealing with multiple database commands. (You don't need them for a single command because these have an implicit transaction.) As you can see, they are extremely simple. They protect you from many database troubles, and even if you don't use them much, at least you know about them and how to use them.

Summary

This chapter brings to close the ordering and checkout process, and here we have looked at the latter — converting the items from the shopping cart into an order in the database. We used a `Wizard` control to provide a step-by-step process for collecting the order details, from the delivery address to the credit card details.

For the delivery address, along with some text boxes, we used an `ObjectDataSource` to bind to the shopping cart and a `FormView` control to display the bound data.

A list allowed the selection of the delivery area, which resulted in the delivery charge updating the cart.

On the final step, we used the user control created in Chapter 7 to display the cart items. The totals were shown using an `ObjectDataSource` and a Details view, but in read-only mode, with a templated column to customize the display of the sales tax.

For the final step, we handled an event that is run when the Finish button is clicked, and we inserted the order and order items into the database. This code used a combination of exception handling and ransactions to ensure that the database remained consistent, and that the user received appropriate messages.

Now it's time to have a look at security and personalization, so see how we can protect the Admin page (created in Chapter 6) and the View Orders page (created in this chapter) from prying eyes.

Security and Deployment

In Chapter 6, we created an administration page, allowing a user to update the menu items, and in Chapter 8, we created the checkout page. We don't want everyone to be able to run the administration page, so we need to lock them out somehow. For the checkout, it would be good to recognize members of the site and give them the option of having their order added to their account, instead of paying by cash or credit card.

The aim is to have a site where users can log in, and have functionality change depending upon whom they are.

In this chapter, we will look at the following:

❑   How security works, and how to configure it

❑   How to add users and roles to a site

❑   How to secure pages

❑   How to change the menu system so that secured pages are not shown on the menu

We will also look at the topic of what to do once you've created your first site, and how you can copy this to a service provider to make the site public. Let's start with the security aspects.

Configuring Security

Security revolves around the two concepts: authentication and authorization. *Authentication* is the process of identifying users of a Web site, and *authorization* is checking that the user is allowed to access the page he or she is trying to access. Each of these requires configuration, the first to determine who the users are and the second to define which pages they are allowed access to.

In ASP.NET, you manage authentication with the Membership service, which allows definition of the members of a site. There are many places to store the membership details, including a text file, a database, or even the Windows user accounts store. We'll be using a database, but won't be storing the users in the PPQ database. Instead, we'll use the database that ASP.NET automatically creates for us.

You can configure authorization either on a user-by-user basis or by *roles*, using the Role Manager service. Roles are a way to make configuration easier because you set the configuration for the role and then you add users to the role. This way, if you add or remove users, you only have to add them to the role, rather than changing the configuration. You'll see this in action as we go through the exercises.

The configuration of the authorization is done in the Web configuration file, `web.config`, where we will define which pages users can access. Let's give this a go, starting with creating the users.

Try It Out   **Configuring Security**

1. In VWD, select the Website menu, and then select the ASP.NET Configuration item. This will launch the Web Site Administration Tool (see Figure 9-1).

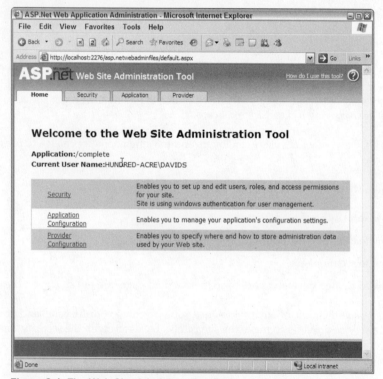

Figure 9-1: The Web Site Administration Tool

2. Select the Security tab, and click the "Use the security Setup Wizard to configure security step by step" link. Step 1 is the welcome step, so click Next.

3. On step 2, select the "From the Internet" option, and click Next.

4. Step 3 tells you that the application is configured to use advanced provider settings, so select Next.

5. Step 4 allows the definition of Roles, so tick the "Enable roles for this Web site" option, and click Next.

6. You now have an option to define the roles. In the New Role Name text box, type **Admin** and click the Add Role button. No more roles are required, so click the Next button.

7. Step 5 allows creation of users, so use the following to create a new user. Make sure that the Active User box is ticked, because that ensures the user is active on the site. When you've entered the details, click the Create User button:

Field	Text to Enter
User Name	Dave
Password	dave@123
Confirm Password	dave@123
E-mail	dave@ppq.org
Security Question	Favorite Pizza
Security Answer	Margerhita

8. When the account is created, click the Continue button, and use the following to add another user:

Field	Text to Enter
User Name	Alex
Password	alex@123
Confirm Password	alex@123
E-mail	alex@ppq.org
Security Question	Favorite Pizza
Security Answer	Three Cheeses

9. When the second user has been created, click the Next button.

10. Step 6 allows you to add new access rules, restricting pages to selected users. This allows security to be added only to folders, but we want individual pages, and we'll do this manually later, so click the Next button.

11. Step 7 is the Complete step and tells you that the wizard has been successful, so click the Finish button, which will return you to the Security tab, now with the number of users and roles shown (see Figure 9-2).

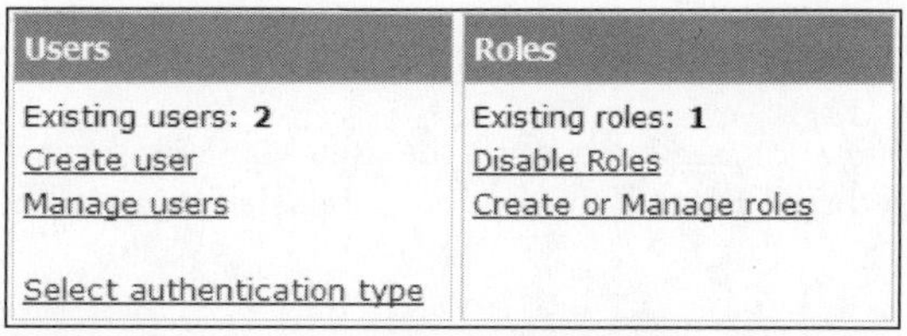

Users	Roles
Existing users: **2**	Existing roles: **1**
Create user	Disable Roles
Manage users	Create or Manage roles
Select authentication type	

Figure 9-2: The user and role configuration options

12. Click the "Create or Manage roles" link, and select the Manage link alongside the Admin role.

13. On the Search for Users page, click the A link to show users whose name begins with "A." Tick the User Is In Role option (see Figure 9-3).

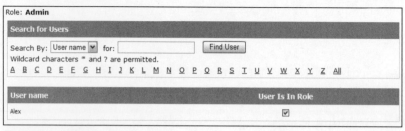

Figure 9-3: Adding a user to a role

14. The users and roles creation is now complete, so close the Web Site Administration Tool.

How It Works

All of this work is done by ASP.NET and the Web Site Configuration Tool, so there is no code to examine. However, you must understand what this tool has done, so we'll start by looking at what additional files the tool has added to the site. In the Solution Explorer, if you select the App_Data folder, and click the Refresh button, you'll see that a new database file base been added, ASPNETDB.MDF (see Figure 9-4).

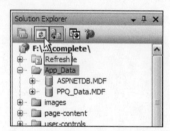

Figure 9-4: The ASP.NET User and Roles File

This is the database that contains the users and roles, as well as details of which users are in which roles. We're not going to look at this database, because you don't really need to know anything about it, just that it works — ASP.NET handles everything to do with this database for us.

You can see the other changes in the Web configuration file, web.config, where the following have been added:

```
<roleManager enabled="true" />
<authentication mode="Forms" />
```

The first of these, roleManager, simply enables the Role Manager service, so that when users log in, they have roles associated with them. If this option is disabled, none of the role-based features will work.

You created two users, Dave and Alex, and Alex was given the Admin role. You'll soon see how we configure the site so that only users in certain roles can access certain pages.

The second addition, authentication, sets the mode of authenticating users. This is set to Forms, which means that a Web form will supply the user credentials (that is, typed by the user on a page). Another common value for this is Windows, which means the user does not have to explicitly enter a user name and password. Instead, the user name used to log in to Windows is used. For a public Web site, you should use Forms authentication.

At this stage, you have only created the users and defined the authentication scheme. Now it's time to configure the authorization.

Try It Out   Securing Pages

1. Run the PPQ application, and when it is displayed in the browser, click the Home link on the menu.

2. In the browser address bar, replace Default.aspx with Admin.aspx (see Figure 9-5) and press Return to view the administration page.

Figure 9-5: Directly navigating to the Admin page

3. Notice that you haven't logged in, but that you can navigate directly to this page, even though it doesn't appear on the menu. Close the browser window.

4. Open web.config, and move to the end of the file.

5. Between the </system.web> and </configuration> elements, add the following:

```
<location path="Admin.aspx">
  <system.web>
    <authorization>
      <allow roles="Admin" />
      <deny users="*" />
    </authorization>
  </system.web>
</location>
```

6. Save the file, and switch to Admin.aspx. From the right mouse menu, select View in Browser, and notice this time that you don't see the admin page, you see an error message (see Figure 9-6).

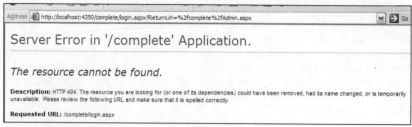

Figure 9-6: Navigating to an unauthorized page

7.   Close the browser window, and return to VWD.

How It Works

The bulk of the work for securing the admin page is done by the Membership service, but that service needs to know what pages users are allowed to access. By default, all users are allowed to access all pages, so you locked down the security by adding a location element. The location element defines a page by using the path attribute, and it is this page that further configuration is applied to:

```
<location path="Admin.aspx">
```

Within the location element, you added a system.web section, which identifies Web site settings (there are other settings, but you don't need to know about them for this example).

```
<system.web>
```

Within the system.web section, you added an authorization section, which details which users you allow access to the Admin.aspx page.

```
<authorization>
```

The first part of the authorization is to allow users who belong to the Admin role, using the allow element (this grants permission to the file). The roles attribute defines the roles to be allowed.

```
<allow roles="Admin" />
```

Next, you must stop all other users accessing the page, so you used the deny element. The users attribute can be a comma-delimited list of users, but you want all users, so the special symbol * is used (this matches any user).

```
<deny users="*" />
```

Finally, all of the open elements were closed:

```
    </authorization>
  </system.web>
</location>
```

So, the process of authorization is to deny all users but then allow selected users or roles. We mentioned earlier that roles are the best way to do this because you only have to configure the security for the role once. For example, the user `Alex` is a member of the `Admin` role, so `Alex` would have access to the `Admin.aspx` page, but `Dave`, who isn't in the `Admin` role, wouldn't be able to access the page. To allow `Dave` access, all you have to do is add him to the role; you don't have to change the configuration.

The syntax of the `allow` and `deny` elements can take several forms (they are both the same, so we'll show only `allow` in the following table:

Configuration	Meaning
`<allow users="?" />`	Allow all anonymous users. An anonymous user is one who hasn't logged in.
`<allow users="*" />`	Allow all users.
`<allow users="Alex, Dave" />`	Allow only the users `Alex` and `Dave`.
`<allow roles="Admin" />`	Allow only users who are in the `Admin` role.

You can see that there is quite a degree in flexibility, and to add to that flexibility, you can configure authorization added at three levels:

- ❑ For the entire Web site, by using an `authorization` element in the main Web configuration file
- ❑ For a folder, by placing a Web configuration file in the folder and setting the `authorization` element
- ❑ For individual files, by using `location` elements

You used the latter, but the other two methods follow the same rules.

What we now need to do is allow users to log in to the site, so that the administrator (or more accurately, users who are in the `Admin` role) can access the admin page. Users can belong to more than one role, but as long as one of those roles is `Admin`, the user will be allowed access to the page.

Try It Out   **Creating the Login Page**

1. In the `web.config` file, change the authentication section so that it looks like the following:

```
<authentication mode="Forms">
  <forms loginUrl="Login.aspx" />
</authentication>
```

2. Save the configuration file and close it.

3. Create a new Web form called `Login.aspx`, remembering to place the code in a separate file, and select the `PPQ.master` master page.

4. Switch the page to Design view, and open the Login section of the Toolbox. Drag a `Login` control, and drop it into the Content area. Select the Auto Format . . . option from the Login Tasks, and select the `Simple` scheme, before clicking OK to format the control (see Figure 9-7).

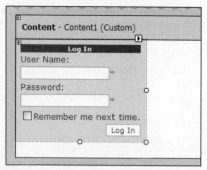

Figure 9-7: The formatted Login **control**

5. Save the file, and switch to Admin.aspx. From the right mouse menu, select View in Browser, and notice that instead of the error message, you now see the login page.

6. For the user, enter **Dave**, and for the password enter **dave@123** and press the Login button. You are returned straight to the login page. Enter **Alex** for the user, and **alex@123** for the password. Press Login and you will see the administration page.

Let's see how this works.

How It Works

The first thing you did was to change the authentication section in web.config. Instead of just defining the mode as Forms, you added a forms element, with the loginUrl attribute set to Login.aspx.

```
<authentication mode="Forms">
  <forms loginUrl="Login.aspx" />
</authentication>
```

The loginUrl defines the login page, and ASP.NET will show this page whenever you try to access a page for which you are unauthorized — it's giving you the opportunity to log in with user credentials that are allowed to access the page.

When you tried to log in as the user Dave, you weren't allowed access to Admin.aspx because Dave isn't a member of the Admin role. Remember, in the earlier exercise you set the authentication, and allowed access only to members of the Admin role. Alex is a member of the Admin role, so when you logged in as Alex, you were allowed access to the page.

You can see how simple security is, because all you have to do is run the Web Site Administration Tool to set the initial configuration, and add users and roles. You then set a few options in the Web configuration file, and ASP.NET handles everything else for you.

Modifying the Menu

One thing that still needs work on the site is usability — you don't want to force the administrators to type in the `Admin.aspx` page name. It would be much simpler if the Admin option appeared on the menu, but this means that all users would be able to see it. Let's see how we can add Admin to the menu but have it visible only to authorized users.

Try It Out   Configuring the Menu

1. Close any browser windows, and return to VWD.

2. Open `Web.sitemap`, and move to the end of the file. Underneath the `Contact` node, add the following:

    ```
    <siteMapNode url="Admin.aspx" title="Admin" description="Edit Pizzas" />
    ```

3. Save the file and close it.

4. Open `PPQ.master`, and switch to Design view.

5. From the Login section of the Toolbox, drag a `LoginStatus` control, and drop it underneath the menu (see Figure 9-8).

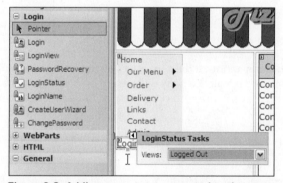

Figure 9-8: Adding a `LoginView` **control to the page**

6. Save the page and run the application. Notice that there is now a Login link under the menu. Click the link, and you are taken to the login page. Log in as `Dave` (the password is `dave@123`), and see how the Login link now says Logout. Also notice that the menu shows the Admin item, even though Dave is not authorized to access the page.

7. Click the Admin link on the menu, and notice how the login page is shown once more.

8. Close the browser window, and return to VWD.

9. From the `page-content` folder, open `Web.Config.txt`, and copy the contents (the `siteMap` section).

10. Open `Web.config`, and underneath the `</authentication>` element, paste the code you copied from `Web.Config.txt`.

11. Save the file and run the application. Notice that the Admin item is now not shown on the menu.

12. Login as `Dave` (using `dave@123`), and you see that the Admin item still isn't shown. Log out, and log in as `Alex` (using `alex@123`), and notice that the Admin item appears.

Let's see how this works.

How It Works

The first thing you did was to add a new `siteMapNode` to the menus structure. This adds the Admin item to the bottom of the menu.

```
<siteMapNode url="Admin.aspx" title="Admin" description="Edit Pizzas" />
```

You then added a `LoginView` control to the master page, and this is a clever control. When you are not logged into the site, the `LoginView` control shows a `Login` link. When you click this link, you are redirected to the login page (the login page you defined earlier in the chapter) with the `loginUrl` attribute on the `login` element in the `authentication` section. Once you have logged in, the `LoginView` control shows a `Logout` link, which, when clicked, will log you out of the site.

You then ran the application and used the `LoginView` to log into, and out of, the site, but noticed that the Admin link was shown no matter who you logged in as. This is because, by default, the menu system doesn't apply any security. To correct that, you modified the Web configuration file, and a `sitemap` element:

```
<siteMap defaultProvider="AspXmlSiteMapProvider" enabled="true">
  <providers>
  <clear/>
  <add name="AspXmlSiteMapProvider" type="System.Web.XmlSiteMapProvider,
System.Web, Version=2.0.3600.0, Culture=neutral, PublicKeyToken=b03f5f7f11d50a3a"
    siteMapFile="web.sitemap" securityTrimmingEnabled="true"/>
  </providers>
</siteMap>
```

You don't need to know what all of this means, except for the `securityTrimmingEnabled` attribute, which is the key to the menu security. When `securityTrimmingEnabled` is set to `True`, the menu system will check the authorization for each page before displaying it. When logged in as `Dave`, the menu system checks each page before showing it, and `Dave` isn't authorized to access the Admin page, so it isn't shown on the menu. `Alex` is authorized, so the page is shown on the menu.

Once again this shows the power of the security system in ASP.NET, and how you can easily add power to your Web sites with very little effort. Let's now see how we can use the security system from code, to help the checkout page.

Try It Out — Modifying the Checkout Page

1. Open Checkout.aspx, and double-click anywhere on the page, outside of the Content control. This will open the code file, and create the Page_Load event.

2. Into the event procedure, add the following code:

```
If Not Page.IsPostBack Then
  If User.Identity.IsAuthenticated Then
    Dim rbl As RadioButtonList = _
        DirectCast(Wizard1.FindControl("RadioButtonList1"), RadioButtonList)
    rbl.Items.Add(New ListItem("Charge my account", "Account"))
  End If
End If
```

3. Save the file and run the application.

4. Navigate to the checkout page, and step into the Payment step. Notice how the payment options list shows only two items.

5. Log in to the site. Repeat step 4, and notice how there are now three items on the payment options list.

Let's see how this works.

How It Works

You added code to the Page_Load event, which will run whenever the page is loaded. The first line checks to see if the IsPostBack property of the Page is set. If it is, then a button or link on the page has been clicked, and it isn't the first time the page is loaded. If the IsPostBack is not set, then it is the first time the page has loaded, so further code is to be run.

```
If Not Page.IsPostBack Then
```

You then use the Membership service from code, starting with the User class, which identifies the current user. The User class has an Identity property, which gives further details about the user, and one of those further details is the IsAuthenticated property. If this is set, then the user is authenticated (that is, logged into the site).

```
If User.Identity.IsAuthenticated Then
```

Next, you obtained a reference to the RadioButtonList control that shows the payment method.

```
Dim rbl As RadioButtonList = _
    DirectCast(Wizard1.FindControl("RadioButtonList1"), RadioButtonList)
```

You then add a new ListItem to the RadioButtonList, with a Text value of Charge my account, and a Value of Account.

```
    rbl.Items.Add(New ListItem("Charge my account", "Account"))
  End If
End If
```

That's all there is to the code. When the page first loads, you check to see if the user is logged in. ASP.NET provides a `User` object, which has a property called `Identity`, and this identifies the user. A property of the Identity object, `IsAuthenticated`, tells us whether or not the user has been authenticated (that is, if they have logged in). If the user is logged in, you add another option to the list, which you could then use in the final stage of the payment to charge the user's account.

That's the end of modifying the pages, so let's now look at how you can transfer this site to a Web server.

Publishing a Site

When using VWD, you have a built-in way to run the Web pages. But for live Web sites, you need a public Web server, and these are managed either by your company or by a service provider. To make your site available, you need to copy it to the target Web server, and there is a utility provided within VWD to help you with it.

This utility is available from the Copy Web Site . . . option from the Website menu, which shows the Copy Web page (see Figure 9-9)

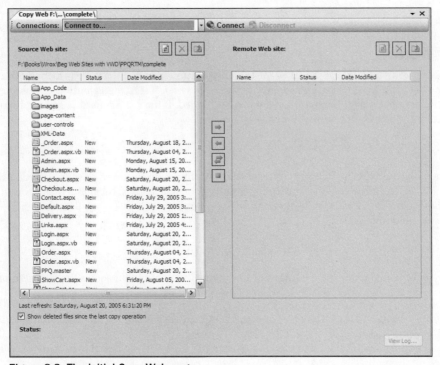

Figure 9-9: The initial Copy Web page

To pick the target site, select the "Connect to . . ." option, which shows the Open Web Site window. You have the option of copying to a folder, a Web server (Local IIS), an FTP Site, or a Web site using HTTP (Remote Site). Figure 9-10 shows connecting to an FTP site.

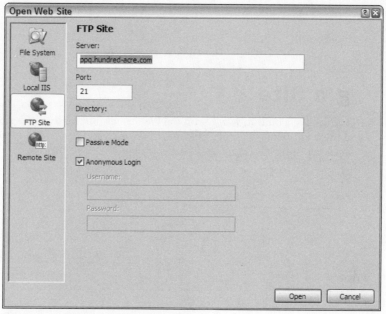

Figure 9-10: The Open Web Site page

Once connected, you can see the files from the local site on the left, with the files from the remote site on the right, and you have options to copy between the two sites. For example, Figure 9-11 shows uploading files to a remote Web site using the FTP option.

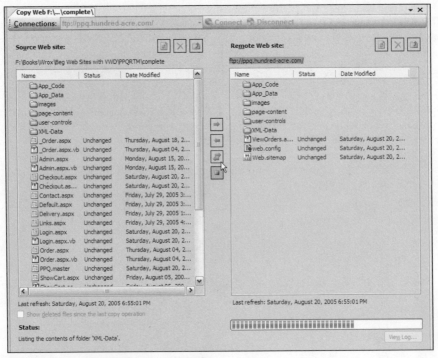

Figure 9-11: Uploading files to a Web site

The Copy Web feature allows copying both ways, so if you've mistakenly deleted some files from the local site, you can always fetch them from the remote site.

Summary

This chapter has covered two major topics: security and deployment.

For security, we looked at how you can use the Web Site Configuration Tool to set up security, add users, and set the roles for the users (that is, authentication). We then discussed how to secure Web pages so that only authorized users can access them, both directly and from a menu. This allows you to create pages that only selected users can see, and this aspect, although not covered here, can be extended to parts of a page, so that a page will show different content depending upon the user.

You saw that the security system is extremely simple to set up, with only a few configuration options required to protect a site. Not only can you use the security controls to interact with the Membership service but you can also use code. This brings added flexibility and becomes more useful as you add more code to your sites.

Finally, we briefly looked at how you can deploy your Web site to a remote location, using the Copy Web tool. This allows you to use a variety of methods to copy sites to public Web servers. There are other ways to deploy applications, but these aren't built into the tool. The deployment offered in VWD allows for a variety of protocols and covers the basics of what you'll need to deploy to a remote location.

In all, we've covered a lot of ground in this book, but we have really only scratched the surface of what ASP.NET can achieve. You've seen how to use databases, how to structure sites using master pages and navigation, how to view and update data in grids, how to create custom classes, and how to implement security. These cover the basics of what you need to construct Web sites and give you good grounding from which to continue your exploration of ASP.NET.

We hope that you've enjoyed this book and that you continue to explore both ASP.NET and Visual Web Developer as a means to creating Web sites.

Index